XY&Z

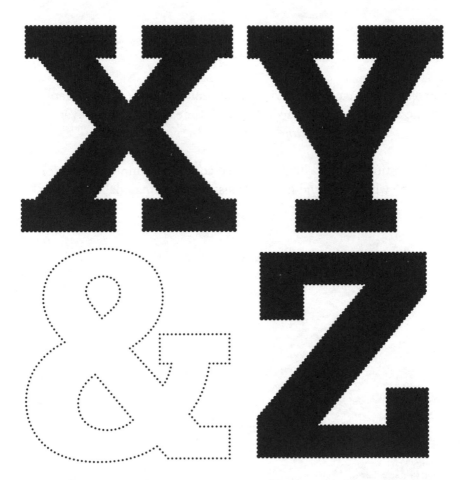

THE REAL STORY OF HOW ENIGMA WAS BROKEN

DERMOT TURING

The
History
Press

La collaboration avec le Service britannique n'a pas cessé pendant
toute la guerre et de la façon la plus intime qui se puisse rêver.
Gustave Bertrand, report of 1 December 1949

[Collaboration with the British Service continued uninterrupted for
the whole war, and in the closest manner imaginable.]

First published 2018

The History Press
The Mill, Brimscombe Port
Stroud, Gloucestershire, GL5 2QG
www.thehistorypress.co.uk

© Dermot Turing, 2018

The right of Dermot Turing to be identified as the Author
of this work has been asserted in accordance with the
Copyright, Designs and Patents Act 1988.

British Library Cataloguing in Publication Data.
A catalogue record for this book is available from the British Library.

ISBN 978 0 7509 8782 0

Typesetting and origination by The History Press
Printed and bound in Great Britain by TJ International Ltd

CONTENTS

LIST OF MAPS

FOREWORD

By H.E. Prof Dr Arkady Rzegocki, Ambassador of the Republic of Poland to the United Kingdom

On 23 March 2018 I was pleased to be the guest of honour at Bletchley Park, where H.R.H. the Duke of Kent ceremonially opened a new permanent exhibition called *The Bombe Breakthrough*, which explains how messages encrypted on the Enigma cipher machine were broken using novel machine techniques. The exhibition describes not only the work done at Bletchley Park itself, but also the foundations laid in Poland before the start of World War Two. The Polish Embassy contributed a full-scale replica of the Polish *bomba* machine, illustrating that the development of machines for code-breaking began in Poland.

The fact that the Enigma code was broken is now well known in both Britain and Poland, but what people know is surprisingly different in the two countries. In Britain, the story is about the achievements of Bletchley Park, centred on the work of Alan Turing, and how the decryption of Enigma messages helped the Allies to victory and shortened World War Two by as much as two years. In Poland, however, the story is about the triumph of mathematicians, especially Marian Rejewski, Jerzy Różyicki and Henryk Zygalski, who achieved the crucial breakthroughs from 1932 onwards, beating their allies to the goal of solving Enigma, and selflessly handing over their secret knowledge to Britain and France. It is the story of a relay race, with the baton changing hands at crucial moments. When America entered the war, the Enigma secrets were once again passed on.

All the countries involved have much to be proud of, and the Enigma story deserves to be told from all the viewpoints. This book will help ensure that the achievements of the Polish code-breakers are better understood in Britain. But there is a wider significance than balancing the narrative. At the heart of the success against Enigma, and its contribution to the outcome of World War Two, was international cooperation in the field of intelligence. Poland, France and Britain (and, later, the United States) were partners in an intelligence-sharing network, contributing knowledge from various sources towards a common goal. The spirit underlying the Enigma relay race remains relevant, with intelligence cooperation continuing to be a matter of vital importance in the face of more modern threats to security. It is in that spirit the Polish Embassy has supported the exhibition about Enigma code-breaking at Bletchley Park.

Meanwhile, the dramatic story of the Polish code-breakers and their colleagues, and what became of them, is set out here. I hope you enjoy this fascinating book written by Sir Dermot Turing, the nephew of Alan Turing. Sir Dermot has, for a number of years now, cooperated closely with the Polish Embassy, historians and academics to tell the true story behind these crucial events, that shaped our modern history. I am very grateful that this story has been told from both sides. It is key to a better understanding of our common history.

Arkady Rzegocki
The Embassy of the Republic of Poland
47 Portland Place
London W1B 1JH

DRAMATIS PERSONAE

Polish

The Assault on Enigma

Antoni Palluth
alias Antoine Balande,
Jean Lenoir, Czarny
Wiktor Michałowski
*alias*Victor Michel
} The first assailants

Maksymilian Ciężki
alias Mathew, Maximilien Muller, Maciej
Gwido Langer
alias Wicher, Luc, Louis Lange
} The leaders

Marian Rejewski
alias Pierre Ranaud
Jerzy Różycki[†]
alias Julien Rouget
Henryk Zygalski
alias Henri Sergant
} The victors

The Other Exiles

Kazimierz Gaca
alias Jean Jacquin
Sylwester Palluth
alias Sylvestre Callis
} German specialists

Henryk Paszkowski
alias Henri Materon, Casanova
} Polish and French specialist

Stanisław Szachno
alias Auguste Charneaux
Tadeusz Suszczewski
alias Dubois
} Russian specialists

Edward Fokczyński
alias Edouard Fonk
Janina Paszkowska
alias Comtesse Makarewicz
⎱ cipher clerks

Piotr Smoleński[†]
alias Pierre Smolny
Jan Graliński[†]
alias Jean Ralewski
Ryszard Krajewski
alias Orkan
⎱ with the team until early 1942

The Wider Picture

Jan Kowalewski ⎱ code-breaker of the Russo-Polish War

Jan Żychoń
alias Janio
⎱ Bydgoszcz Station chief, later head of Polish Intelligence in London

Czesław Kuraś ⎱ Russian specialist in London

Mieczysław Słowikowski
alias Rygor, Dr Skowroński
⎱ head of Ekspozytura AFR

† Perished in the *Lamoricière* shipwreck

The French

The Service de Renseignements

Rodolphe Lemoine
alias Rudolf Stallmann,
Baron von König, Rex
⎱ the go-between

Gustave Bertrand
alias Bolek, Bertie, M. Barsac,
Georges Baudin, Michel Gaudefroy
⎱ the magician

Louis Rivet ⎱ the leader

Henri Braquenié
alias Poacher
⎱ the code-breaker

Paul Paillole ⎱ associate of Rivet

Honoré Louis ⎱ associate of Bertrand

The British

GC&CS

Alastair Denniston } head of GC&CS until February 1942

Dilly Knox
alias Erm } Enigma assailants
Alan Turing

MI6

Stuart Menzies
alias C } Deputy, later head, of MI6

Wilfred Dunderdale } MI6's liaison with the White Russians,
alias Biffy, Dolinoff, Wilski, Bill } the French and the Poles

'World War Two's greatest spy'

Hans-Thilo Schmidt } the German spy
alias Asche, H.E.

Pronunciation

Despite the grumbles of English speakers, Polish is largely phonetic, and strings of consonants are not so daunting once the principles are mastered. The emphasis is almost always placed on the penultimate syllable.

c	ts, as in hats, unless followed by i, when it is softened as in chip
ch	soft ch, as in Bach
ć, cz	hard ch, as in chop
dz	j or ge, as in judge
ę	en, as in penguin
j	y, as in yes
ł	w, as in how
ń	as ñ in the Spanish mañana, or ni in onion
ó	oo, as in hood
ś, sz	soft sh, as in shot; s followed by i is also softened
w	v, as in van
rz, ż	soft z, like the 's' in pleasure; z followed by i is also softened

11

TIMELINE

	France (X)	Britain (Y)	Poland (Z)	Germany
1918				
23 February				Patent filed for Enigma cipher machine
11 November	Armistice Day – cessation of hostilities in World War I			
			Independence Day	
1919				
28 June			Treaty of Versailles fixes Western border	
1 November		Government Code & Cypher School founded		
1920				
April			Russo-Polish War begins	
14–20 August			Battle of Warsaw	
1921				
21 February	Franco-Polish defence treaty			
18 March			Treaty of Riga fixes eastern border	

	France (X)	Britain (Y)	Poland (Z)	Germany
1926				
Mid year		Commercial Enigma machine acquired for study	Commercial Enigma machine acquired for study	First naval Enigma messages observed
1929				
15 January			Langer head of radio intelligence; Cryptology course at Poznań begins	
25 April	Bertrand joins Section du Chiffre			
1930				
31 May				Wehrmacht model Enigma machine in service, with plugboard
1 November	Section D of Service de Renseignements (radio intelligence) created			
1931				
1 November	Rex meets Asche			
7–11 November	Bertrand transfers first haul of documents to Langer			
1932				
December			Rejewski's break	
1933				
30 January				Hitler becomes Chancellor
1934				
26 January			Germano-Polish non-aggression pact	

	France (X)	Britain (Y)	Poland (Z)	Germany
1936				
1 February				Enigma rotor order changed monthly
7 March				Rhineland reoccupied
1 October				Enigma rotor order changed daily, cross-pluggings altered
1937				
24 April		Knox breaks Spanish Enigma		
22 October	Menzies meets Rivet			
1 November				New Enigma reflector in use
1938				
September	Scarlet Pimpernels begin			
15 September				Enigma 'indicator' becomes message-specific
25–30 September	Munich Agreement on Czechoslovakia			
15 December				Two new Enigma rotors in service
1939				
1 January				Cross-pluggings increased to between 7 and 10
9–10 January	X-Y-Z conference in Paris			

	France (X)	Britain (Y)	Poland (Z)	Germany
10 February		Denniston reports that a sufficient supply of professors is available		
31 March	France and Britain 'guarantee' support to Poland			
26–27 July	X-Y-Z conference at Pyry			
23 August				Molotov–Ribbentrop pact
1 September			Invasion of Poland by Germany	
4 September		Turing arrives at Bletchley Park		
17 September			Invasion of Poland by USSR	
September–October			First evacuation of Polish code-breakers to Paris	
1940				
20 January	PC Bruno established			
18 March		Prototype Bombe installed at Bletchley Park		
1 May				Double encipherment of indicator ceases
10 May	Invasion of France by Germany			
10 June	Second evacuation of Polish code-breakers, to Algeria			

	France (X)	Britain (Y)	Poland (Z)	Germany
25 June	Franco-German armistice			
10 July		Battle of Britain begins		
October	PC Cadix established			
1941				
22 June				Germany attacks Russia
11 December				Germany declares war on USA after Pearl Harbor
1942				
9 January	*Lamoricière* sunk			
8 November	Operation TORCH begins; Third evacuation of Polish code-breakers, to Côte d'Azur			
11 November	Occupation of Zone Libre			
1943				
27 February	Rex arrested			
January–July	Polish code-breakers arrested/ imprisoned			
September		Rejewski, Zygalski and others at Felden		Langer and Ciężki at Schloss Eisenberg, Palluth and others at Sachsenhausen

	France (X)	Britain (Y)	Poland (Z)	Germany
1944				
5 January	Bertrand arrested			
7 March				Langer and Ciężki interrogated
6 June	Invasion of France by Britain and America			
August–September			Warsaw Uprising	
1945				
30 April	End of World War Two in Europe			
10 May				Langer and Ciężki liberated to Scotland

INTRODUCTION

The most significant problem for British military and naval intelligence at the beginning of World War Two, was to understand German communications that had been encrypted on the Enigma cipher machine. During the course of the Great War, code-breaking had given the British an edge, notably in the war at sea, but also on the diplomatic front, accelerating the arrival of the point at which the United States became involved in that conflict. Twenty years on, the use of mechanisation to conceal secret communications threatened to deprive the Allies of this most valuable source of information about the Nazis' plans.

Nowadays, we know that the British were not daunted by the problem. They had set up a secret establishment, somewhere between London and Birmingham, specifically dedicated to unravelling the modern encipherment techniques being deployed by Germany (and others). Early in the war, a solution to the Enigma machine was found. German Air Force signals could be read from mid 1940, and signals from their navy could be read from 1941. Thereafter, with some ups and downs, a steady stream of decrypted signals began to flow towards the British authorities. In time, the stream became a flood, enabling the Allies to obtain a full appreciation of German military and naval plans in many theatres and enhancing their commanders' ability to take wise and well-informed battlefield decisions. The success of Bletchley Park is now rooted in the public imagination as an example of triumph in adversity, a showcase of brains excelling over brawn, the cradle of a world-changing technology. Bletchley Park has much to be proud of.

Yet, somewhere in this story, something got lost. In truth, Britain's code-breakers had made no progress against the military version of the Enigma machine before 1940. How were they able to bring about such a rapid and effective transformation of their fortune?

The missing piece is the contribution of the Polish code-breakers, who had been working on the problem for over ten years before the war and who shared their knowledge in a crucial meeting near Warsaw just six weeks before the outbreak of hostilities. In the estimation of those who were there at the time, what the British learned at that meeting advanced their research programme by a year. And what a year it was. Imagine a counterfactual history in which the British had not been able to decipher Enigma messages during the Battle of Britain, the naval war in the Mediterranean, the early years of the Battle of the Atlantic, or the campaign in the Western Desert. Such a scenario is frightening, as it would be a history that depicts not just a longer, drawn-out war but potentially one with a quite different outcome. In this light, the Polish contribution to the reading of Enigma-coded communications deserves to be better understood.

The July 1939 meeting near Warsaw is itself a major mystery: why did the Poles suddenly hand over all their priceless secrets? Again, there is a missing piece. That meeting was the culmination of a relationship built slowly over many years, not by the British, but by the French. Without the French, the Polish code-breakers would not have been as rapid with their breakthroughs and their efforts might even have been thwarted. Without the French, the British attack on Enigma at Bletchley Park could have been stillborn or significantly delayed. The contribution of the French, like that of the Poles, ought to be better known. The Enigma endeavour was, then, an international collaboration by three countries. For the greater security of the joint enterprise, the code-breakers labelled themselves X, Y and Z for the French, English and Polish centres respectively.

To tell the story of X, Y and Z was the original mission of this book. But this book is not principally about code-breaking techniques or international politics. As I uncovered more of the story, the Polish code-breakers themselves, and their French counterparts, began to take charge of the narrative. This book is, therefore, about those people, and its purpose is to re-establish them in the record where they belong.

Bringing the X-Y-Z story to life has had its own subplots. One, almost worthy of a book in its own right, is the tale of the source material. World War Two had some unexpected results: French records were captured by the Germans and, when Berlin was occupied by the USSR, ended up in Moscow. Much of this material was returned (with Soviet annotations) to France in 1994 and 2000. Many Polish records were dispersed with exiled citizens, ending up in London in various collections. Some remain in Moscow and some are actually where you might expect, in Warsaw. German records were captured by the Americans and the British, finding their way to the US and UK national archives. Some original parts of the record have disappeared, leaving the researcher to rely on shadows of original telegrams, surviving in the form of intercepted, decrypted and translated copies, which turn up in unexpected places. A bizarre example is the large collection of Polish telegrams, in German, in the Foreign Office TICOM archive in Berlin, comprising documents seized in Germany by the British 'Target Intelligence Committee' at the end of World War Two: these, the fruits of success of the German signals intelligence service, which monitored and decoded the Poles' radio communications, were thrown into a lake in 1945, dredged out by the British, kept in the UK for decades, and returned to Berlin in the 1990s. The Polish-language originals have long disappeared.

Most of the material relating to X, Y and Z has been declassified. Perhaps the most significant new collection is the archive of an individual who plays a critical part in this story and whose perilous career was spent in France, working for that country's various intelligence systems. Gustave Bertrand's archives were made available in mid 2016 after declassification by the Direction Générale de la Sécurité Extérieure in France. This collection comprises a long report by Bertrand, together with over 200 supporting files, almost all containing original documentation. Alas, the first ninety-nine supporting files (of a total of 304) are missing, but those which remain bring a wealth of colour and light to the events in the years before the disbandment of Bertrand's Franco-Polish code-breaking operation in 1942.

Looking at documents is part of the process of discovery; equally important is hearing from those involved. The families of the code-breakers have embraced my project with great enthusiasm, and I have been overwhelmed by the welcome, support and information given by the families of Maksymilian Ciężki, Antoni Palluth, Marian Rejewski, Wiktor Michałowski and Henryk Zygalski. Anna Zygalska-Cannon gave me privileged access to her archive of letters and Henryk's amazing collection of photographs; she deserves my very special thanks. Especially important to me was the long interview given to me by Jerzy Palluth in January 2017. A man of great courage and intellect – an intellect well spiced with energy and wit – his own life story is every bit as fascinating as that of his code-breaker father. It was a blow to learn of Jerzy's death only a few weeks after we spoke, not least because his parting words to me were 'When you next come, I can tell you all about how we resisted the communists during the Cold War.' I am privileged to have heard at least the first part of his story, and profoundly grateful.

Many others have helped bring this book into being. Katie Beard, Anna Biała, Sébastien Chevereau, Barbara Ciężka, Tony Comer, Prof. Nicolas Courtois, Dorian Dallongeville, Anne Debal-Morche, Georgina Donaldson, John Gallehawk, Dr Marek Grajek, Dr Magdalena Jaroszewska, Prof. Jerzy Jaworski, Dr Zdzisław Kapera, Herbert Karbach, Dr Iwona Korga, Katarzyna Krause, Michal Kubasiewicz, Dariusz Łaska, Stephen Liscoe, Beata Majchrowska, Eva Maresch, Aleksander Markiewicz, Jerry McCarthy, Piotr Michałowski, Prof. David Munro, Lauren Newby, Steve Ovens, Jerzy Palluth, Laura Perehinec, Geoffrey Pidgeon, Halina Piechocka-Lipca, Alicja Rakowska, Katie Read, Ginny Reid, Guy Revell, Jeremy Reynolds, Jeremy Russell, Dr Arkady Rzegocki, Sir John Scarlett, Agnieszka Skolimowska, Eric van Slander, Michael Smith, Anna Stefanicka, Rene Stein, Prof. Michael Stephens, Dr Andrzej Suchcitz, Dr Janina Sylwestrzak, Dr Olga Topol, General Włodzimierz Usarek, Alicja Whiteside, Nicolas Wuest-Famôse and Anna Zygalska-Cannon will all know what contributions they have made and I pay them sincere tribute. My family has also borne with admirable restraint the consequences arising from the process of my writing another book. I have had unfailing help and support from the staffs of the National Archives at Kew; the archive of the

Polish Institute and Sikorski Museum in London; the Józef Piłsudski Institute in London (and its sister organisation in New York); the Service Historique de la Défense in Vincennes; the National Archives and Research Administration at College Park, MD; the Center for Cryptologic History at Fort Meade, MD; and the Politisches Archiv of the Auswärtiges Amt in Berlin. I also drew extensively on the commendable blog of Christos Triantafyllopoulos (Christos military and intelligence corner) which not only has valuable and well-researched commentary, but also useful links to source material.

I cannot sufficiently explain how much I have depended on the inestimable assistance of Dr Janka Skrzypek, who has been at my side as research colleague and translator since the first days. For anyone to try to tell this story without drawing on the Polish-language resources would destroy it at the outset: Janka's participation in the project has enabled me to draw on that essential material. She has provided me with translations of over a hundred documents, some very long, and researched and sifted through many thousands of others to help focus our efforts. She spent several days on my behalf in the Centralne Archiwum Wojskowe (Polish Military Archive) in Rembertów as well as helping me in the Sikorski and Piłsudski Institutes in London. The work has been puzzling, time-consuming, and often tedious, though I hope with some flashes of interest and enjoyment at times. I am extremely grateful to Janka for all the help, guidance and support she has provided over the last two years: without her this book would not have been credible; indeed it would not have been possible.

Finally, a note on style, place names, pronunciations and so forth. Place names have changed since the 1930s and the convention followed here (except where there is an English name, such as Warsaw) is to use the contemporary name with, where necessary, the current name shown in brackets the first time the place is mentioned (for example: Lwów (Lviv)). Pronunciation of Polish names can be troublesome for English speakers, but unless you are reading aloud the correct pronunciation probably doesn't matter, while worrying about it can get in the way of the narrative. Some phonetic guidance is given in the Dramatis Personae. Spellings in quoted passages appear as they do in the original, except where the passage has been translated, in which case the spelling of names has been corrected. The intrusive word *sic* has thus been avoided except to clarify a couple of endnotes. Translations were done by me where the source text was in French or German and by Janka Skrzypek where it was in Polish. Errors of all descriptions are, however, mine. I hope there are few enough of them to make this story enjoyable and much better known.

Dermot Turing
St Albans, UK
April 2018

1

NULLE PART

Quant à l'action, qui va commencer, elle se passe en Pologne, c'est-à-
dire Nulle Part.
[As for the action about to begin, it takes place in Poland, that is,
No Place.]

Alfred Jarry, *Ubu Roi* (1896)

November 1918 was a good month for Maksymilian Ciężki. Revolution
and disorder had broken out everywhere across the German
Empire. The bumptious Kaiser had abdicated and sneaked off to the
Netherlands. And the leaders of the Imperial Army had been made to
sign an Armistice in a railway carriage somewhere in France. A soldier in the Imperial Army ought, perhaps, not to have been gleeful
at these developments, but Maksymilian Ciężki was not an ordinary
German soldier.

In the eastern provinces of the Empire most of the population were
not German, did not want to speak German, and certainly did not want
to be ruled by Germans. Since the previous year, some of them had
been making plans, and Ciężki was among them. Maksymilian Ciężki
was a member of the Boy Scouts before he was called up to serve
on the Western Front, but being in the Boy Scouts in the so-called
Grand Duchy of Posen didn't mean tying knots, making camp-fires
and helping old ladies across the road. The 'Scouts' were a front for
the paramilitary wing of the Polish independence movement – the
POWZP, or Polish Military Organisation of the Prussian Partition. The
'Partition' – the very idea that Poland was divided amongst its imperial
neighbours – was offensive to all Poles.

BALTIC SEA

● Wilno

● Bydgoszcz

● Poznań

● Warsaw

RUSSIAN
EMPIRE

GERMAN
EMPIRE

Lwów
●

AUSTRIAN
EMPIRE

PARTITION OF POLAND BEFORE WORLD WAR I

Poland after 1922

Kingdom of Poland (incorporated into Russia)

German Empire

Russian Empire

For Ciężki it might have been a good thing that he had been invalided home in February 1918. Either at Rheims or Soissons a mine blew up and half-buried him. Some sort of filth in the air got into his lungs and started an infection. Anyhow, it meant that he could spend some more time with the 'Scouts', organising, recruiting and stockpiling weapons; and once he'd recovered, he was spared the front, instead being sent off for training in wireless communications. From then on, the mysteries of radio provided intellectual sustenance, but a dangerous, secret ambition – nothing less than the independence of Poland – possessed his soul. Now, with disruption and chaos breaking out across Germany, was the time for action. Polish leaders had taken control in Warsaw; civil government in the 'Prussian Partition' could not go on without the support of local, Polish, people. The Polish People's Guard was needed to keep order in Posen, or, to call it by its non-German name, Poznań, and Maksymilian Ciężki found himself elected to the local Soldiers' Council. Perhaps it was the beginning of the end of German rule in the Prussian Partition.

The Prussian Partition was a dark spectre from history; and history, in Poland, has a baneful tendency to repeat itself. On the horizon in 1918 was a post-war peace conference, and the last one of those had not gone well for Poland. Following the defeat of Napoleon Bonaparte, the Congress of Vienna had convened in November 1814. The then British Foreign Secretary, Lord Castlereagh, believed he had an answer to the 'Polish Question': the re-establishment of the Kingdom of Poland. On the other side of the table, Russia was interested in the attractive towns of Cracow and Thorn (Toruń), even though these were deep in what were the Austrian and Prussian zones of influence (and had nothing whatever to do with the defeated French). Tsar Alexander I, however, was a reasonable man. Instead of insisting on Cracow and Thorn, he would settle for being King of Poland. Castlereagh should be happy with that. The British minister had been saying he wanted to re-establish Poland. So all would be well.

As it turned out, the Kingdom of Poland did not cover much 'Polish' territory, since swathes of the old Polish lands remained within the territories ruled by Austria and Prussia, or within the Russian Empire beyond the boundary of the kingdom. Nor did the kingdom have a great deal of autonomy. In 1830 and again in 1863, there were rebellions against the Russian-inspired government, and after the second one, the new Tsar, Alexander II, had experienced enough nationalist discontent. Polish institutions were closed down in the kingdom and governmental activity in the Polish language was phased out. The Tsar 'relinquished his duties' as King of Poland; what this meant was that the kingdom was annexed to Russia and by 1874 Poland had ceased to exist. Poland was, according to a contemporary satirical French playwright, 'No Place'.

Poland might have stayed unrecognised but for the man with the moustache. Certainly, in 1918, moustaches were in fashion, but this moustache was world-famous. It hung in festoons, in theatrical exuberance, in defiant luxury. It was a symbol, it defined the movement for liberation, it identified the man who wore it for those who had only heard him on the wireless and never seen him in the flesh; and it also served a practical purpose – to conceal the gap left after the teeth behind the moustache had been knocked out with a rifle butt in a Tsarist prison in Siberia in 1887.

In a country divided and ruled by three empires there were few opportunities to nurture leaders of a new republic. But one stood out: implacably hostile to Russia, a left-wing activist, and a constant advocate for Poland to regain her independence, by force if needs be. The moustache belonged to that man. He was Józef Piłsudski, and in 1918 he was in a German prison in Magdeburg. But his custodians knew they had a head-of-state-in-waiting and they had no pretensions to govern in Warsaw, where the Russians had been in control for over a hundred years. It was just a matter of working out how to win Piłsudski and a potentially independent Poland over to their side, rather than have it become an Allied puppet. So no one was surprised when, on 8 November 1918, Piłsudski was told he was free to go and a special train was laid on to take him to Warsaw, where he found 'power lying in the streets'. Within days, and without bloodshed, Piłsudski had manoeuvred himself into a position of control in a new democratic system. The Republic of Poland was born.

But not in what the Poles called Wielkopolska (Greater Poland), that place which the Germans had bundled up into provinces such as the Grand Duchy of Posen, the homeland of Maksymilian Ciężki. Despite its name and the importance of the region, Wielkopolska was at risk of being left out of the new Polish state. Power-sharing with the Germans wasn't working. The atmosphere was tense, the Germans' grip was weakening and the province was preparing for a change. All that remained was to give the signal.

On 27 December 1918 there was a VIP visit and a speech in the centre of Poznań. The visitor and speaker was Ignacy Paderewski, world-renowned pianist and advocate of Polish rights. What he said was not important: his audience fully understood the sub-text, and on the next day the Wielkopolska insurgency began. Ciężki's unit took over the railway station in Poznań. Their next assignment was to take control of Wronki, a nearby town. That was achieved without difficulty or bloodshed, but the revolution was not going so well elsewhere. The Germans had started to fight back. And just at the point when Wielkopolska needed every fighting man, Ciężki was struck down by his pulmonary problems.

Frustrated and inert, Ciężki languished on the sick list, until he thought of his signals experience. To the north of the old town at Poznań, in the early part of the nineteenth century, the Prussians had built a major fortification. The inhabitants of the two villages there had been cleared out, though their history of wine-growing was recognised in the official name by which the new fort was known, even if the locals called it the Citadel. By 1903, Fort Winiary had been modernised with the addition of a telegraph station and now it was in Polish hands. On 2 April 1919, Maksymilian Ciężki joined the Poznań radio unit at the Citadel.[1]

At the Citadel, Maksymilian Ciężki met another technician who was still in his teens. Antoni Palluth was just out of school and was one of those young men who wanted to seize his country's destiny for himself – in other words, to throw the Germans out of their country. But for Palluth there was more to being involved in the uprising than national pride. His work was just where his interests and aptitude lay.

Antoni Palluth could pull magic from the air. There was something extraordinary about wireless telegraphy. Invisible, inaudible, undetectable, the air was full of ghostly messages. Yet with modern equipment it was possible to get the air to disclose its secrets: out from the crumble of static it was possible to coax the rhythm of Morse. Sometimes the signal wavelength wandered about and sometimes the machine played up. And when the weather was bad, the chase was hard. But Palluth tended his machine and the machine responded to Palluth's talent. Antoni Palluth was a first-rate radio engineer.

Palluth and Ciężki were not stationed together for long, but their encounter was a moment of enormous consequence. For these two young men embodied the new, technically focused country that Poland would become. They were the radio men. The comradeship between Ciężki and Palluth would last twenty-five years as they proved themselves capable of being at the forefront of what would become an international effort to break the German Enigma ciphers. For the moment, however, this collaboration was on hold. Palluth was called away to serve in the north of Wielkopolska in mid May and Ciężki was sent on another course later in the year.

Meanwhile, the post-war settlement of Poland needed to be completed, to avoid a re-run of 1814. In the aftermath of ranging armies, with a ravaged economy, thousands of dead, there was a peace conference. Again, as in 1814, the helpful British were suggesting new boundaries, talking airily about the re-establishment of a vigorous, independent Polish state. This time, however, in part thanks to their own tough fighters, the Poles had actually been invited to the party. Indeed, the French were keen to have them there. From the French perspective, the principal aim of the post-war settlement was to contain the Germans. Settling the borders between Germany and Poland was crucial. But it wasn't just the French who were very positive about a Polish state. President Wilson's basis for peace, his famous Fourteen Points, included, as Point Thirteen, the following:

An independent Polish state should be erected which should include the territories inhabited by indisputably Polish populations, which should be assured a free and secure access to the sea, and whose political and economic independence and territorial integrity should be guaranteed by international covenant.

This was all very splendid. It provided fuel, of course, for the energetic conversation in the cigar-smoke-filled conference rooms of Paris. But Wilson's Point Thirteen was not much more than an aspirational statement. The shape of the western frontier of Poland was going to look, on paper, roughly like it had until the late eighteenth century. But in the late eighteenth century, Germany did not exist as a state. For the Germans, the border ought to have been where it was in 1914, when Poland did not exist as a state. What about the chunks of eastern Germany, now reverting to being western Poland, which had been settled over many decades by Germans? At whose expense was the 'access to the sea' to be provided? And who were the underwriters of the international covenant of guarantee?

The newly re-established Poland thus had everything to worry about from its still-powerful German neighbour, whose troops were still in occupation of much of the country. Unfortunately, the Poles clearly didn't understand the purpose of the conference. The conference wasn't about clearing the Germans out of Poland, or about the viability and future prosperity of Poland. It was about the borders of Germany. And as far as the Allies were concerned, that consideration alone should settle the Polish question.

Except that 'both Russia and Poland in February 1919 were states in their infancy, the one sixteen months old the other only four months old. Both were chronically insecure, gasping for life and given to screaming.'[2] Neither of these countries was waiting to be told by the Great Powers at Versailles about decisions that had been ordained for their own good. They – or, more precisely, the Soviet Union – were going to settle the business themselves.

Vladimir Ilyich Ulyanov, alias Lenin, was the man behind the Soviet plan for Poland. 'If Poland had become Soviet, if the Warsaw workers had received from Russia the help they expected and welcomed, the Versailles Treaty would have been shattered, and the entire international system built up by the victors would have been destroyed.' This fantasy manifested itself as a secret plan called 'Target Vistula', named after the river running through the centre of Poland: a cover-name which rather gave the game away, even though the Bolsheviks claimed their operation was nothing more than the defence of borders.

The Polish-Soviet War began with the Cavalry Army of Semyon Budyonny pushing Polish forces out of the Ukraine. Then, on 5 July 1920, the Red Army began an offensive in the north-east of Poland under the leadership of Mikhail Tukhachevsky, already a general at the advanced age of 27. 'Over the corpse of White Poland lies the road to worldwide conflagration', ran Tukhachevsky's stirring order of the day. The advance was rapid and spectacular. The Third Cavalry Corps – the fearsome Red Cossacks – rampaged across the north, while Tukhachevsky steadily rumbled towards the west. Russians closed up against the Vistula to the east of Warsaw. Warsaw was going to fall and the Bolsheviks would then be free to march across Europe. Lenin's dream was going to be fulfilled at last.

In the resort town of Spa in Belgium, famous for its mineral water, the Allies were preparing for another dose of cigar smoke, this time, a conference on the topic of reparations. Unfortunately for the distinguished visitors to the Spa Conference, at the end of the first week of July 1920, what water there was came entirely from the air. The rain drenched the delegates and dampened the mood. If the troublesome business of reparations were not enough, the Poles had now raised a problem that was boiling on the far eastern fringes of Europe, a problem which was self-evidently one of the Poles' own making. They had grabbed Wilno (Vilnius) and swathes of non-Polish-speaking land around Lwów (Lviv). They were being difficult about Danzig. And now the Poles wanted the Allies to help them stop the Russians.

It occurred to the British that the Russian advance into Poland might be serious: if there were no effective allied intervention to stop the Soviets in their westward drive, 'the bloody baboonery of Bolshevism', as Winston Churchill called it, could threaten the democracies of the West. The British had a democratic leader in David Lloyd George, the man who had brought victory to Britain in 1918. But Lloyd George's authority was crumbling, weakened by his inability to impose order on the conference. To stave off his own political crisis, what Lloyd George needed was to be the man who brought peace to Europe and for that he needed the man from Wola Okrzejska.

Wola Okrzejska is about a 100km south-east of Warsaw, but it is so small it doesn't feature on many maps. It is, however, a place embedded in the Polish subconscious, for it is the birthplace of Poland's answer to Sir Walter Scott. Henryk Sienkiewicz was a Nobel prize-winning novelist whose name was known across the world in the first half of the twentieth century: every household had a copy of his novel *Quo Vadis*, about love and struggle among Christians in Nero's Rome, which was translated into at least fifty languages and had been made into a movie three times already by 1924. In Poland, Sienkiewicz is probably better known for his patriotic historical novels set in the Polish Commonwealth of the seventeenth century, where dauntless Poles battled for the survival of their country against insurgent Cossacks, unstoppable Swedes and rapacious Muscovites. In 1920, the formidable Red Cossacks galloped freely across Poland, as in the bad old days described by Sienkiewicz, while the Red Army was marching inexorably on Warsaw.

It was, therefore, entirely apposite that in this political crisis Lloyd George should look for inspiration to another man from Wola Okrzejska. The man had been born in 1888 in a country house which his grandfather had bought from an uncle of Henryk Sienkiewicz. His name was, at one point, Ludwik Niemirowski, under which he had a glittering academic career, studying at universities in Lwów, Lausanne, London and Oxford. In 1907, now called Lewis Namier, he settled in Britain. When war broke out, Oxonian friends 'plucked him out of the British Army (where his poor eyesight and guttural accent seemed likely to get him shot by his own side if not by the Germans) and placed him in the intelligence service at the Foreign Office.'[3] Later Namier participated in the Versailles treaty discussions. In 1920, he was the established Foreign Office expert on Polish cartography. It is the time-honoured role of the British at international peace conferences to propose lines on maps to deal with disputatious peoples and Namier had been busy with his pencil. The British proposed the boundary between the Russians and the Poles, one that they thought would put to bed the annoying problem of Poland's eastern boundary and bring the war to a rapid end. The line was named after Namier's boss, Lloyd George's foreign secretary Lord Curzon. Given that he had nothing to do with it, it's unfortunate that Lord Curzon is the man whose name this border bears and it is ironic, too, that the boundary was actually the creature of an expatriate Pole.

The Curzon Line runs roughly north and south along conveniently placed rivers, at least to the north. To the south the rivers behaved in a less convenient way and there was controversy about whether the line would go to the east of Lwów (thus placing Polish-speaking Lwów and its non-Polish surroundings in Poland) or to the west of Przemyśl (so giving both cities to the Ukraine, or to be more exact, the USSR). Both choices were bad: huge tracts of the country would be given up, whichever option was accepted. Under diplomatic pressure from the British, and with the news from the front getting worse every day, the Polish delegation caved in. The less bad version of the Curzon Line, with Lwów on the Polish side, would just about do. The Polish state was not yet two years old and already many hundreds of square miles were being ceded to the Russians. It was partition all over again. If the country was going to survive at all, the state needed something extraordinary, a modern miracle.

Lieutenant Stanisław Sroka worked as a radio man in Warsaw, handling the boring business of assessing intercepted Russian radio traffic, rather than finding glory at the front. It was tedious and depressing, but even in times of war, life goes on. Lieutenant Sroka's sister was going to get married and as he was to give away the bride, the lieutenant asked for a leave of absence to carry out this important duty. The Russians, inconsiderately, did not order a ceasefire or a cessation of movement during the nuptials, so it was necessary for someone to cover the good lieutenant's dull duties in military intelligence while the vodka was drunk and the dancing went on. There must have been a lot of vodka, because the officer whom Lieutenant Sroka chose to fill in for him was asked to cover for two weeks. His choice was another army lieutenant, but unlike Sroka, the replacement was a man who had read Edgar Allan Poe's short story *The Gold Bug*. In *The Gold Bug* a simple cipher led the hero to buried treasure: fabulous stuff and something which captured the imagination. Jan Kowalewski, the replacement lieutenant, put his reading to good use. In those two weeks, he turned radio interception into a different sort of treasure which captured the imagination of the most senior members of the Polish General Staff.

For, having received a bundle of intercepted messages which were in some sort of numerical cipher, Kowalewski was not content with analysing the call signs and potential evidence of troop movements: he wanted to know what the messages were actually about. He determined to attack this puzzle and soon found that the cipher was a simple enough bigram substitution system with an overlaid twelve-digit key. And the messages were certainly worth reading.

What the messages revealed was not just what the Reds were thinking, but their appreciation of the Whites. The threat to Poland was not just from the Bolsheviks: if the Russian imperialists regained power, they would want to get their old empire back, right up to the German border. But Kowalewski's decrypts showed that General Deniikin, the White commander, was being threatened in his rear by the Reds. Being able to see both sides of the Russian civil war amazed the Polish chief-of-staff, General Rozwadowski. The gift was an eagle's-eye view of the entire strategic situation. It wasn't good news, but it was just what General Rozwadowski needed to know. From now on, monitoring and decryption were a priority.

Jan Kowalewski looked like something of a bear, with his imposing physique, but people who got to know him valued him for his sense of humour and his extraordinary, intuitive mind. By putting Kowalewski in charge of Polish decryption a crucial step was taken that would lead to Poland becoming world leaders in the art of code-breaking. For Kowalewski's first request was to ask for all volunteers who were mathematics professors to be assigned to his team. Before Kowalewski, code-breakers were supposed to be linguists and psychologists. But Kowalewski was an engineer and he was redesigning the profession of cryptology.

The new, scientific approach soon showed its power. Over three days in early July 1920, crucial messages revealed new Russian operational orders given to coordinate the operations of Budyonny with the other Red Army forces invading Poland:

An order for the Army of the South-Western Front … The 14th army, taking into account the tasks of the Cavalry Army, will break the resistance of the enemy on the line of the River Zenic and will use the full force of its assault team when carrying out a decisive offensive in the general direction of Tarnopol-Przemysl-Gorodok …

[signed] The Commander of the South-Western Front YEGOROV
Member of the front's Revolutionary Council STALIN
Chief of Staff of the South-Western Front PIETIN
24/VII-1920
Deciphered/checked against original: Kowalewski[4]

These orders spelt out a new offensive:

> The enemy himself informed our headquarters precisely of his moral
> and material state, his strengths and losses, his movement, of victo-
> ries attained and defeats sustained, of his intentions and orders, his
> headquarters' stopping points, of the deployments of his divisions,
> brigades and regiments, etc ... We were able to follow the whole oper-
> ation of Budyonny's Horse Army in the second half of August 1920
> with simply incredible precision ... On 19 August we monitored, and
> on 20 August read, an entire operational order from Tukhachevsky to
> Budyonny, in which Tukhachevsky states the tasks of all his armies.[5]

The intelligence went straight to the Chief of Staff and some even into
the hands of the Commander-in-Chief, Józef Piłsudski himself.

It just got better and better. The radio men intercepted messages
that told of the Bolsheviks' order of battle, the dispositions of their
forces, and even details of new ciphers they were going to use. They
could overhear the arguments about the gap between Tukhachevsky's
army and Budyonny's. The Red Army under Tukhachevsky was entirely
stretched out: it might make sense for the Russians if they were going
to encircle Warsaw, but it made them vulnerable, providing Piłsudski
could move his troops into position. Piłsudski raced his troops through
the gap, leaving Warsaw wide open, so he could encircle Tukhachevsky
from the rear in a classic Napoleonic manoeuvre. Badly outnumbered,
Piłsudski was taking an enormous gamble based on the intelligence
supplied by Kowalewski.

On 12 August 1920, Kowalewski's unit picked up a message several
pages long. It was obviously important, not just due to its length, but
also because it was in a new cipher. Kowalewski's team were at the top
of their game: it took them just an hour to work out the new system

Ściśle tajne.

Tłumaczenie szyfrogramu.

Od: **Pr.Południ.Zachodn.** Do: **D-ców armji XII.**
I-j konnej,XIV. Przejęt **24/VII** dczytan **25/VII**

Uwagi	TREŚĆ
do 5" (Nowa Aleksandrja Puławy)	ROZKAZ do armji Południowo Zach.Frontu. ..2).........(początku brak).......5-g sierpnia ...Dubno,...............(przerwa)........ ....rejonem LWÓW-RAWA RUSKA,wyrzuciwszy przednie swoje oddziały w celu zajęcia przepraw przez SAN w rejonie SINIAWA-PRZEMYSL. 3) XIV-a armja biorąc pod uwagę zadania konnej armji , złamie opór nieprzyjaciela na linji rzeki ZBRUCZ i całą siłą swojej grupy szturmowej poprowadzi decydująca ofenzywę w ogólnym kierunku na TARNOPOL-PRZEMYSL-GORODOK. 4) Linje graniczne między : XII-ą armja i Frontem Zachodnim:na 24/VII DOMBROWICA-RATNO-WŁODAWA-NOWA ALEKSANDRJA,wszystkie te punkty,oprócz pierwszego - dla frontu Zachodniego. XII-ą armja a Konną armją: St.KIWIERCY-ŁOMACZI-MIRCZE-ŁABUN-RUDNIK,wszystkie te punkty dla XII-j armji. Konną armją a XIV-ą armją : ....(przerwa)............. Głównodowodzący południ.zach.Frontem JEGOROW Członek Rady rewolucyjnej frontu STALIN Szef Sztabu Poł.Zach.Frontu PIETIN Z oryginałem zgodne - Sz.Op.Wydz.XII arm. KRAUKLIS Zaszyfrował WANIN. 24/VII-1920 roku.
Deszyfrował:	Za zgodność z oryginałem: *Kowalew* Naczelnik Wydz. 2.

NACZELNE DOWÓDZTWO W.P.
(SZTAB GENERALNY)
Oddział II. Biuro Szyfrowe
Sz. № 31724 /II.

Warszawa, dnia 25/VII 192

Rozesłano według rozdzielnika Nr. I

Kapitan i Szef Biura Szyfrowego.

Zakł. Graf. Nacz. Dow. Nr. 1480. 10000. 8.VII.20.

29

Miracle on the Vistula. A Russian telegram, countersigned by Stalin, and decoded by Jan Kowalewski, during the Russo-Polish War of 1920. (Instytut Piłsudskiego w Ameryce – Piłsudski Institute of America) and to decipher enough of the message to get its gist. The decisive attack on Warsaw was due on 14 August and there was only just time to react. Being strung out over hundreds of miles, communication between the Russian units was dependent on radio. The crucial goal was to keep Tukhachevsky where he was while Piłsudski completed his own manoeuvres. To shift the odds, if only fractionally, Piłsudski ordered that the Russian radio communications be jammed. It would cut off the supply of intelligence but cause delay and confusion among the enemy, and a couple of extra days was all that Piłsudski needed.[6]

The troops were moved. Spearheaded by General Władysław Sikorski, the great roll-up of Tukhachevsky's army began. The surrounders were themselves exposed to locally superior numbers, which allowed them to be defeated in detail. A hundred thousand prisoners were taken by the Poles; in fear, the Red Cossacks galloped away into East Prussia, where they were interned by the Germans. And Tukhachevsky escaped with the remnants of his army back to Russia to face a grilling from Trotsky and Lenin.

In Poland, these events were called the Miracle on the Vistula. In August 1914, three very different forms of government had existed on Polish territory. There were six currencies, four legal codes, two railway gauges, and countless languages (even if Russian and German were the only 'official' ones). Now, with the country unified and at peace, the nation could become a state and fly its own flag once more: a crowned eagle, with an exuberant tail, on a red and white field. Radio and cryptology had put Poland back on the map. The vital role of Kowalewski's decryption team had been understood by the authorities and they, perhaps more than any other government in the world, appreciated the importance of supporting a modern approach to the profession. Thanks to the Polish radio men, Europe would remain free of the Bolshevik menace. For the time being.

2

ENTER THE KING

SHEPHERD: Sir, there lies such secrets in this fardel and box which none must know but the king.

William Shakespeare
The Winter's Tale, Act 4, scene 3

Jan Kowalewski was a little older than Maksymilian Ciężki, so his impact on Poland's existential struggle of 1920 had been greater. Ciężki himself had been in Poznań, still in radio. His friend Antoni Palluth had been closer to the action, in the front line for much of the conflict, but also in radio. After the war, Kowalewski, the man at the top, was in demand for many roles, political and diplomatic as well as those based in the shadowy world of intelligence. In 1922, he was seconded to Tokyo to help the Japanese improve their own codes and ciphers, to the irritation of an American code-breaker who then found his attacks on Japanese codes thwarted. It was necessary to find a replacement for Kowalewski as head of signals intelligence. So in 1923 – shortly after Maksymilian Ciężki was assigned to the Radio Intelligence Unit – Kowalewski handed over the reins to an agreeable successor, Franciszek Pokorny. At least Ciężki had been under Kowalewski long enough to be noted by the man whom all the authorities revered. For Ciężki to have his appraisal form marked 'good' by Kowalewski was no light matter.[1]

Following the war, Maksymilian Ciężki had been pursuing a traditional military career. After his father's death in 1920, although only 21, he'd found himself responsible not just for his own upkeep but also that of eight siblings, five of whom were girls. He needed a stable source of income. For a young man with his record, army life provided a straightforward opportunity for this. Ciężki was commissioned as a lieutenant, completed his interrupted secondary education, and was posted to various places around the country, always specialising in communications. Now, settled into radio intelligence, he could also settle into family life, marrying Bolesława Klepczarek in 1924. That year, Ciężki's first son, Zdzisław, was born, followed by Zbigniew in 1926 and Henryk in 1929. Life was relaxed. Ciężki could spend his spare time in the garden. He had a good job, working with good colleagues.

Antoni Palluth's path into radio intelligence was somewhat different. In the Bolshevik war he'd been posted to a radio intelligence unit, where he'd been introduced to traffic analysis and cryptanalysis as skills to add to his existing radio interception abilities. He had been on the reserve list since 1921 and was setting himself up in business. When he had returned to civilian life after his own part in the defence of Warsaw in 1920, Palluth had studied civil engineering at the Technical University in Warsaw. Palluth had not given up his interest in radio with the end of the war. Far from it, he'd become a radio ham, with his own call sign (TPVA), a subscription to a number of radio magazines and a love of sending crackly messages from his house through the ether to his friends. Being an amateur radio-ham was not just good fun. There was money to be made in radio too. The military signals branch of the Polish Army needed long-range short-wave radios; masts; interception equipment; transmitters; amplifiers; you name it. Palluth's friends Ludomir and Leonard Stanisław Danilewicz (call sign TPAV) were thinking of going professional and their mutual friend Edward Fokczyński had already set up shop making walkie-talkies and radio equipment in a small workshop in the centre of Warsaw.[2]

In this way, a new business was born. With Palluth and the two Danilewicz brothers providing financial capital and Fokczyński throwing in his premises and existing business goodwill, the new partnership took over a little factory in 43 Nowy Swiat. It was called AVA, by amalgamation of the Palluth and Danilewicz call signs, and the first orders for radio equipment came from the Polish Army's signals intelligence section. Radios the size of a credit card holder were made for use by Polish agents in foreign territory: AVA technology was miniaturised, sophisticated, and extremely secret.

Yet Antoni Palluth was no ordinary young entrepreneur. He was a paid-up member of military intelligence and his role as factory manager was a cover for a wider range of clandestine activities. Poland's need to keep a close eye on Russia and Germany had not disappeared with the Treaties of Versailles and Riga: only an optimist would assume that either of those neighbours was comfortable with the new order. Foreign ciphers were every bit as important now as they had been during the war and Antoni Palluth was one of the secret team whose job was to find out what evils lay in the plans of the Germans. In the evenings, an officer would come round to the Palluth household with cryptological problems for Antoni to work on. For, since June 1924, as well as his ostensible day job for as a radio factory manager, he had been working for the Second Department – the intelligence section – of the Polish General Staff, and he held a post in Maksymilian Ciężki's German section of the Biuro Szyfrów, the cipher bureau.

Despite the help he was getting, Ciężki had a problem. Until 1928, the German section of the cipher bureau had been operating smoothly; indeed, one might say it had been going by the book. The book in question was by General Marcel Givierge, the head of French military cryptanalysis in the Great War, who had done the unthinkable and written up the cryptographic techniques of his era and published them for all to read. The book begins with the simplest form of cipher (in use since Caesar's time) and details substitution systems, transposition systems, bigram methods, double-key substitutions, book codes and even some mechanical methods for coding. It also covered code-cracking techniques, such as frequency analysis for substitution ciphers, along with methods for finding key lengths. The toughest problems were known to the Poles as *Doppelwürfelverfahren*, or double dice, and these arose from a hand-based cipher system in current use by the German military. Double dice involved reshuffling the letters of a message according to a predefined scheme – a bit like a giant anagram – and then reshuffling them again using a different scheme. In Givierge's book the double dice system was laid bare. That didn't necessarily make it easy to crack: the code-breakers needed to find the two keys to the double-transposition system in order to tease the plain text out and this took sweat, concentration, and plenty of squared paper.

Ciężki's team could get results against *Doppelwürfelverfahren*, at least until 1928 when matters suddenly became a great deal tougher. In February 1926, the German Navy had started sending messages that were obviously not enciphered using a transposition method at all. You could tell this just by looking at them. With a transposition cipher, letters occur with the same frequency as in regular German, but the frequency of letters in these new messages had the purity of randomness. Some form of substitution was going on. Old-fashioned substitution ciphers had, over the centuries, yielded to frequency analysis, but not these new ones. There could be only one explanation for the perfect equality of the letter count in the intercepted signals. As foreseen by General Givierge, the substitution was being done by a machine. The affairs of the German Navy were of little interest to the German military section of Polish Army radio intelligence, but then, in 1928, the German Army started doing something similar.

Polish intelligence had heard that the machine was called Enigma. But what was this thing, the Enigma machine? The cipher seemed resistant to all the usual methods cryptanalysts could bring to bear. First Ciężki and then Palluth had a go at breaking it. Then they called in their colleague, Wiktor Michałowski, to see what he could do. Michałowski had been born in 1895 and, like Ciężki, had been in the German Army and later participated in the Wielkopolska uprising as a communications officer. His subsequent career had been a bit more colourful than Ciężki's: Michałowski had spent a period accompanying silent films in cinemas on a piano with his home-composed scores and also in trying his hand at business, with a pencil factory which had failed. In 1928, just as Ciężki was wrestling with the new mysterious machine cipher, Michałowski joined the Polish General Staff and was assigned to military intelligence. Coming from Wielkopolska, Michałowski was another natural German speaker and therefore an ideal fit for the German ciphers section under Maksymilian Ciężki.[3]

In about 1926, the Second Department of the Polish General Staff invested in an Enigma machine. Enigmas were commercially available, and internationally many intelligence services were considering the advantages of mechanical ciphers over the old-fashioned code books and pencil-and-paper ciphers which had been used – and successfully broken – in the Great War. The Polish purpose in obtaining an Enigma machine was not for encrypting their own messages, however. They wanted to study the assembly and mechanism of the machine with the goal of breaking the German codes.

At first glance the Enigma machine appeared to be like a typewriter, but instead of a roller with paper the machine had an array of small lamps: little torch bulbs illuminating the letters of the alphabet. When a key was pressed, one of the lamps lit up and the letter was always different from the letter on the key which had been pressed. The conversion of letters happened as a result of the wiring in the machine: pressing the key down activated an electrical circuit which flowed through three cylindrical rotors, then around a 'reflector' which turned the electricity back through the rotors again but on a different path, and thence to the lamp. If every signal behaved in the same way, the resulting cipher would be simple enough to break, as each letter pressed down would have a fixed letter that had lit up. But the beauty of the machine for those wanting to create a near unassailable encryption was that the path of the wiring changed with every single keystroke.

The physical action of pushing down on an Enigma key caused the rightmost of the rotors to rotate by one place. Press a letter, T, say, once and a bulb might come on the B. Press T again and instead of B, you might light the U. There was no obvious continuity at all between the letter T and its various appearances in the coded message. Moreover, once during the full 360-degree rotation of the first rotor the second rotor would turn on one place. And likewise the third rotor moved on too, impelled by the turning of the second. With this mechanism the path of the electrical wiring was different for each new letter in the message until, after $26 \times 26 \times 26 = 17,576$ keystrokes, the three rotors returned to their initial position.

Buying an Enigma machine helped the Poles not one jot.

Together with Antoni Palluth and Leonard Danilewicz, Ciężki and Michałowski tried a pencil-and-paper method for attacking Enigma, mapping out the transformations done by the coding rotors in the machine on to strips of celluloid, which could be slid one against the other to copy the path taken by the current in the machine. But this was no good. The celluloid maps followed the wirings of the commercially available Enigma machine but yielded no results when applied to the German military traffic. The German military Enigma machine had been modified in unknown ways. The Enigma company's marketing material said they'd make you rotors to order, so it was a fair guess that the German military were using different rotors; perhaps also they had changed the wiring in the reflector or the way the plugboard was connected up to the unit containing the rotors. And they could have added some sort of extra contraption to the machine to make the encipherment jumble even more complicated. Those changes were unknowns and something special would be needed to help understand the new type of box which the Germans were actually using for the impenetrable radio messages being received in Poznań.

The problem was serious and a solution was far out of reach. But Kowalewski was not far from the scene. Having returned from Japan, he was back in Poland in 1925, meeting with Ciężki and his boss Pokorny and, crucially, his philosophy of code-breaking prevailed. Perhaps bringing on some young mathematicians might produce new insights for a new type of cipher? In May 1926, Ciężki was given authority to 'seek information and data concerning the possibility of employing professors of mathematics that are fluent in German to do some strictly confidential work.'[4] It was time to get hold of those professors and get them working.

Poland in the 1920s already had an honourable place in the study of mathematics. The brightest stars in the mathematical firmament might, arguably, be Germans. But an important region that had once been under German control was now Polish and immediately after independence the Poles had established a technical mathematical university in Poznań, in the heart of Wielkopolska, where the older generation all had fluent German. There – the principal city of Maksymilian Ciężki's youth – is where he would find his professors.

Professor Zdzisław Krygowski had come to Poznań in 1919 to join the mathematics faculty. His specialism was the elliptical function, but he was not too specialised to try something new, even if it was rather a way out of his main field; after all, Krygowski also wrote about Frederic Chopin and his family. More importantly, he was not too grand to teach his students. Cryptography could be regarded as a case of applied permutation theory, for shuffling letters around is exactly that. Ciężki had no difficulty recruiting Krygowski to participate in a long-term project to crack Enigma. His job would be to train the cryptographers, something which could be fitted comfortably into the existing programme of algebra lectures at twelve noon, with general seminars in the evening at six.

On 30 November 1927, a detailed, costed proposal for a cryptology course was drawn up. Just over a year later, on 15 January 1929, the course began. At this stage, Ciężki couldn't be too explicit about what was going on, so the whole thing was dressed up to look and feel like extension work for keen students, no different from the routine evening seminars at 6 p.m. As well as Krygowski, the tutors were the Polish Army's head of cryptology Franciszek Pokorny, Maksymilian Ciężki himself, plus Ciężki's comrade from their teenage days, Antoni Palluth. The textbook was General Givierge; the subjects were substitution ciphers and double dice. So there was nothing secret in the course, nothing secret at all, except that it was, secretly, as much a selection process as it was tuition. Twenty-three mathematics students were accepted for the two-month course, which covered traditional subjects based on the textbook. Palluth and Ciężki each gave forty-two hours of tuition. Twenty students completed the course, of whom five achieved one of the top two grades. All the students, except four who failed, were put on the mobilisation list as cryptographers in case of hostilities.[5]

The course had been a success. The challenge for the radio intelligence section of military intelligence was to keep the budding code-breakers on board. Since these bright, technical students were mainly based in or around Poznań, far from radio intelligence, they were likely to go off and find interesting jobs and all the investment of those two months of intensive training could evaporate. The answer was to move radio intelligence to Poznań. And that made a good deal of sense, for it was in Poznań that interception of German signals was taking place. Ciężki was authorised to set up a branch office of the Biuro Szyfrów in the city and to hire the best students to work for him.[6]

● ● ●

Winters in Warsaw have a tendency to be cold. Not that they were particularly cold in the 1920s, but January 1929 was wintry enough for people to want to stay indoors. It was Saturday and the job of processing international parcels – which Shakespeare called fardels – was going on, as usual, at the central railway station. The customs label said that this particular parcel contained radio equipment, which seemed credible enough given the size and weight of the box. Then the German Embassy phoned up. There had been a mix-up. Terribly sorry, and all that, but this fardel, this box, it really wasn't supposed to be in the post at all. Could it please be found and sent back to Germany? It was actually quite important.

All that to-do seemed far-fetched for an everyday package and the customs officer decided – to draw from a different play by Shakespeare – that the Germans were protesting too much. Perhaps someone ought to be told. Meanwhile, the Germans were fed some flannel: as you know, it's the weekend, not to mention the terrible weather, nothing is really possible before Monday, but it will of course be number one priority, as and when, *et cetera, et cetera*. The customs officer's next call was to Polish military intelligence. And, as the box had radio equipment in it, they called in the radio men.

AVA was the obvious place to send the peculiar box for analysis. Ludomir Danilewicz took the call and lugged the parcel round to the AVA workshop. It was fortunate that Antoni Palluth was in the office and knew all about ciphers, because what was in the box was clearly no sort of radio. First of all, it had a keyboard like a typewriter, but instead of a normal roller and type, the machine had a set of light bulbs which lit up letters on a translucent panel. If you pressed down on a key, one of the lights would come on, but for a different letter than the one you pressed. If you pressed the same key again, a different letter again would light up. It was a ciphering machine. It was the Enigma.

Palluth and Danilewicz spent the whole weekend prising apart the different components of the Enigma machine to see how it worked. Then they carefully put it all back together and put it back in its box. Then the box was parcelled up again in its brown paper. The Germans were told their package had been found and all was well.

Though no doubt Danilewicz had found it interesting to dismantle a piece of precision cryptographic technology, all that kerfuffle and dissembling over the weekend had, unfortunately, taught the Poles absolutely nothing. The thing was an example of the commercial variety of Enigma machine which had been available on the market for years. But what they did learn from this episode was that the Germans had become very sensitive – very sensitive indeed – about the Enigma. And that meant that it was right to give priority to the effort to prise open the secret of the military Enigma machine.

● ● ●

In 1929, the reorganisation of the Polish Army, initiated by Józef Piłsudski in 1926, reached the Intelligence Corps. Piłsudski's reform movement was called *Sanacja*, which meant something like 'Clean-up'. His primary concern was the creation of a lean and efficient army. The marshal was sweeping cobwebs out of the General Staff. Empty posts were left unfilled. Cosy staff jobs were axed. At first, radio intelligence seemed to have escaped the marshal's gaze, perhaps because he remembered its usefulness in the Russian war. But perhaps not. Ciężki's name came up for a stint in regimental duties, just at the time his boss Franciszek Pokorny was being reassigned to other duties himself.[7] The broom had reached their corner now. Piłsudski himself, however, became interested in the question of appointing Pokorny's successor, wondering whether Kowalewski would be willing to come back in. But Pokorny recommended a different man, someone from the old pre-war Austrian Army whom he'd known when they trained together in military school.[8]

Gwido Langer was a Pole who had grown up in the Austrian partition and served in the Austrian Army. He was born in 1894 and, at the age of 17, enrolled in the Austrian military academy at Wiener Neustadt. He graduated on 1 August 1914 with the rank of lieutenant, four days after Austria had declared war on Serbia and on the day that Germany and Russia declared war. Gwido Langer picked up two wounds on the Eastern Front, a promotion and a medal, but his involvement in the Great War came to an end with capture in 1916. At the end of the war, he joined the Polish Army in Siberia. During the Bolshevik war he was captured again, but managed to escape, travelling over 1,000km to rejoin the Polish forces. He was a career army officer, he was a disciple of General Max Ronge, the wartime head of Austrian military intelligence, and in 1929 his new job was to squeeze the best out of the signals intelligence section.[9]

The Austrian Army man had, in a way, the perfect background to lead the signals intelligence section of military intelligence. Austria's pre-war relationship with Serbia had created a thirst for intelligence and in the Balkan Wars the Austrian military command had set up a code-breaking unit. As tension grew, the Austrian capability grew as well. Both Russian diplomatic traffic and intercepted Serbian material were being read. The act of state-sponsored terrorism that took place outside Moritz Schiller's café in Sarajevo on 28 June 1914 was just the most provocative example of Serbia's devious behaviour and the Austrian code-breakers knew exactly who was behind it. That intelligence may have given Austria the confidence of the righteous in how they reacted.

Although it had all gone horribly wrong in the end, at the beginning the war went Austria's way. The Eastern Front was long. Very long: the Austrian sector alone stretched 600km from south of Warsaw to the Romanian border. So the Russians had resorted to radio to organise themselves. After the defeat of Tsar Nicholas II by the Germans at the Battle of Tannenberg, partly attributed to Russian plain-language radio communication, the Russians quickly recognised their mistake and encrypted their signals. A steamroller of sixty Russian infantry divisions headed into Poland, straight for the border with the Austrian Empire. To avoid being completely overwhelmed, Austria had to fight an intelligent war. 'What joy, as radiogram after radiogram came to us in plain speech! What even greater joy, as several phrases were given in cipher. My trained cryptanalysts fell on to these puzzles with enthusiasm,'[10] crowed General Ronge. Forewarned of Russian movements, the Austrians could target their response precisely to points of Russian weakness and achieve disproportionate success. With the Austrian counter-attack in the harsh mountain winter, the steam went out of the Russians and the roller ground to a halt. On 6 December 1914, the

Russians called a retreat. The achievement was down to the Austrian Radio Interception Service. Ronge's trained cryptanalysts, like many of his Intelligence Corps and many of the fighting men, had come from the Austrian-controlled partition of Poland.

The situation inherited by Gwido Langer in Polish signals intelligence in 1929 was not perfect. The generals were preparing for the previous war: the focus of interception was Russia, with the radio masts and direction-finding equipment primarily directed eastwards. Moreover, the system was static and inflexible and would not be able to cope with a war of rapid movement. It would take Gwido Langer a year or two to get his programme for reform into motion, but the first step was obvious. Radio intelligence was, apparently, understood by the marshal and it was made into an autonomous division in 1930. The next step would be to centralise the code-breaking and reintegrate it into intelligence. One important existing positive in the situation, however, was that Cieżki was confirmed in his position as head of the German ciphers section.

• • •

1930 was an interesting year for military intelligence and not just in Poland. In France, another country with an honourable tradition of radio-based code-cracking from the Great War, it had dawned on the intelligence service that an integrated approach to signals intelligence would be wise. Sure, there was a ciphers section – the Section du Chiffre – but the officer responsible for the section's successes during the war was now on the reserve list and writing textbooks. And what remained of the section was no match for the mechanical ciphers which Germany had started to use in the mid 1920s. A new division was created, Section D of the Service de Renseignements, the intelligence division of the Deuxième Bureau of the French Army General Staff, which, when understood practically, meant that on 1 November 1930 the French Army had a dedicated team of one active and two reserve officers focused on interception and decryption, with specific responsibilities for obtaining intelligence on foreign cipher and exploiting enciphered intelligence.[11]

The sole officer on the active list was one who may, to borrow from the title of the book he later wrote, be described as the greatest enigma of the war. Gustave Joseph François Marie Alfred Bertrand weaves in and out of the Enigma story in a most unpredictable way and his uncanny skill for survival attracts suspicion as much as admiration. To begin with, Bertrand's military career was about as unorthodox as Gwido Langer's had been old school. When the Great War broke out, Bertrand enlisted, aged 18, as a private soldier and was sent off to fight in the hopeless Gallipoli campaign. Bertrand was wounded, but along the way he discovered an interest in radio intelligence, signals interception, direction-finding and the unravelling of enemy secrets through the mysteries of code-breaking. Bertrand was spotted by Colonel Bassières, number two to the former French cipher chief (now turned text-book author) Marcel Givierge, and a post-war career in the army beckoned. By the end of the war, Bertrand had joined the victorious French Army on a permanent basis, with an officer's commission, and by 1926 he had succeeded in his wish to be transferred to the Section du Chiffre. In 1930, Bertrand became the sole active officer of the new, dynamic Section D. The philosophy of this new section was built around the old-style techniques of spying: good agents, clandestine meetings and the timeless lubricant of success deals, a plentiful flow of cash. Bertrand's section was a business. It was about buying and selling, with a brisk trade in the code books of foreign powers.

Good, old-fashioned intelligence work meant contacts and relationships with like-minded intelligence services. Over the course of the next few years, Bertrand built up an information exchange network, liaising with the General Staffs in Czechoslovakia, Japan, Lithuania, Poland and Britain. Gustave Bertrand could show the mettle of his Section D by scoring a few victories against its greatest enemy. The enemy was not Germany, nor even England. The enemy was the Section du Chiffre. The Section du Chiffre had a large staff: twelve officers, one under-officer and seven administrative staff. It was headed by Lieutenant-Colonel Jean Marie Antoine Edouard de France de Tersant, who signed his reports in magnificent style with the single word 'France'.[12] Unfortunately for France the man, and worse still for France

the state, the magnificent reports contained absolutely nothing of interest. For the Section du Chiffre was achieving nothing. 'The output of
the Section du Chiffre was of little importance, as – be it apathy or be
it incapacity – they only attacked what was easy to decrypt: everything
else was put away or thrown away.'[13] Perhaps Bertrand's judgement was
rather unfair, because the Section du Chiffre was also responsible for
the French Army's own codes and ciphers and its signals security. But
its other duties left the field of cryptanalysis clear for Section D and
Gustave Bertrand.

As winter began to bite in late 1932, Bertrand's network was still
building and two liaisons were particularly promising. First was one
with the British. Earlier in the year, a Captain Tiltman had come to
Paris, bearing gifts.[14] John Tiltman was foremost among the cryptanalysts of World War Two, breaking codes and unravelling secrets of
a bewildering variety and with astonishing intellectual agility. In 1932,
though, the British were obsessing about the Bolshevik threat and
Tiltman's mission was to see whether the French could help fill gaps in
the British appreciation of the Soviet Navy. The French couldn't help,
but Britain's willingness to share suggested that a partnership on codes
and ciphers might be profitable.

The other liaison that might be worth the trouble was Poland.
Since 1921, a formal Franco-Polish Military Convention had been
in place. This committed both General Staffs to keeping communications open, and the Poles to keeping the French informed on all
current matters. An intelligence pact was a neat fit for this structure
and Bertrand got the go-ahead from General Maurice Gamelin, the
French Chief of Staff, to make arrangements with his Polish counterparts. So, in March 1931 Gustave Bertrand got on the train and
went to Warsaw. His opposite number there was Lieutenant-Colonel
Gwido Langer and the head of intelligence was Colonel Stefan Mayer.
It must have been daunting for the Frenchman, for although compa-
rable in age to Bertrand, Langer was far senior to a mere captain, and
Mayer even more so. Nonetheless, Langer spoke competent French
and the two were soon at ease. Bertrand saw an Enigma machine
– the commercial model the Poles had bought – for the first time
and was told of the major problem with breaking the encryption it

created. The German military had a modified version of the Enigma machine and until these modifications were understood, there could be no progress.

Amid all the bonhomie of the ad hoc liaison, Bertrand proposed a more structured arrangement: the French would supply all German military documents which allowed for exploitation of transcribed intercepts. In return, the Poles would give all similar documents on the USSR and all results of decryption of enciphered German Army traffic. Bertrand thought they had a deal, albeit a somewhat theoretical one, as there was no decryption of enciphered German Army traffic, at least not Enigma traffic, which is what they both cared about. From Langer's viewpoint, the French had made only a proposal, whereas for Bertrand, both of them had made a promise and in honour it was rightly one they both should keep, or be very explicit about their inability to do so.

Despite the ambiguity the liaison was fruitful. During 1931–32, Bertrand (cover-name Bruno or Bolek) and Langer (Luc) had four meetings in Warsaw and exchanged knowhow on current problems.[15] The biggest current problem for both of them was mechanical encipherment on the German military Enigma machine and neither of them had an answer.

Except that Gustave Bertrand still had a secret trick to play in the shadowy market for codes. He was going to deal a new card from the pack. The card was well used and slightly bent and one which might not withstand fastidious scrutiny, but it was at the top of the deck. Bertrand was going to play his king.

● ● ●

Back in March 1913, the Baron von König was preparing to defend himself in a fraud trial.[16] The allegation was that a game of cards had been rigged. The baron was a habitué of gambling salons across Europe and was thus an ideal witness. Suave, immaculately dressed, with all the confidence of aristocracy in middle age, the baron knew that the court in Imperial Berlin would eat out of his hand. The whole affair was a mistake, in his opinion. The victim of the alleged fraud was a young man, who had, perhaps, taken a little too much drink. The atmosphere of the casino had clouded his judgement; it was only to be expected that he hadn't stopped betting when he was on a losing streak. In due time, the young man would learn from his experience.

The baron gleamed coolly at the court through his round spectacles:

Judge: So, how is it that you became known to the police in several countries as a swindler?

Baron von König: I explain it in two ways. First, this opinion was put about by the French Government as rumours peddled by the press. I am still a member of all the gaming clubs of Paris. Secondly, I have the firm conviction that the name of von König is that of a swindler who won large sums of money at Davos and Chiavenna. I have become the object of all sorts of blackmail, to the point where it has become untenable. I have even asked to be confronted by the persons concerned, and they immediately said 'Hold on! this isn't the same man. The von König who we saw had an aquiline nose!' …

Judge: The central police of Paris say you are the head of an organised gang living off thefts in luxury trains, deception and rigged games.

Baron von König: It's completely untrue!

Judge: Furthermore, it is stated that you participated in the theft of a post-bag full of jewellery in September 1908 in Münster.

Baron von König: Clearly, there the police are the victim of a bad joke. I have never been to Münster …

There was a problem with the baron's testimony. It was, from start to finish, a fabrication. He wasn't a baron, he wasn't even called von König and he was guilty as hell:

Judge: How did you come to be called by this name?

Baron von König: I don't really know.

Judge: So you are using a false name?

Baron von König: All gaming houses keep a roll of their members, and it is sent to all similar clubs in Europe. For me it is disagreeable if the name 'Rudolf Stallmann' were to appear.

Judge: Why do you use a title of nobility?

Baron von König: Because these days it gives many advantages: for example, a better prospect of being well received in hotels.

The charming and sophisticated non-baron whose name wasn't 'King' had honed his skills over many years of deception. Born in 1871 to a Berlin jeweller, Rudolf Stallmann had quickly become bored with the pleasant import–export job which he took on leaving school. He'd travelled to South America, picking up languages, false names and money with ease, along with a criminal record for larceny. The biggest danger to his career-plan was being banned from casinos, which were venues where he could befriend the innocent before fleecing them at the tables where they played at *rouge et noir*. By 1913, he'd managed to get himself arrested in London, which led to his being extradited by the Bow Street Magistrates and sent to trial in Germany, from where newspapers around the globe covered the story:

King of Card Sharpers

Rudolf Stallmann, alias Baron Korff Koenig, known as the king of the card sharpers, who was extradited from London, was sentenced at Berlin to one year's simple imprisonment for fraud, nine months being deducted from this sentence on account of his imprisonment during the inquiry ... Owing to Stallmann's astute defence and the difficulty in proving card sharping when practised by an expert, it was generally thought that Stallmann would escape altogether.[17]

The learned judge in Berlin saw past the stiff collar and the ill-gotten suit and silk tie. Rudolf Stallmann, once the King of the Tables, was sent down and sentenced to three years' 'loss of honour'. It was time for the Baron von König to get a new name and a new direction to his career.

Needless to say, an experienced card player like the baron had an ace concealed up his sleeve. In 1908, the French police had their eye on him. The cause of suspicion was that Stallmann was passing large sums of money to a man called Wehrpfennig who was almost certainly a German spy. Stallmann soon found himself in the hands of Jules Sébille, head of the French security service. The false baron was surely headed for a long period of imprisonment. Yet, through some switch of the cards which we cannot hope to understand, there was an unexpected twist to the story. Stallmann became a legitimate and surprisingly effective operative for French intelligence work. 'In the course of the year 1908, I entered into contact with Monsieur Sébille ... From this moment I carried out frequent tasks for Monsieur Sébille.' The king had become an agent of the French intelligence service.[18]

'All my staff are blackguards,' remarked Captain Mansfield Cumming, the head of Britain's intelligence service, in 1911. Working for Sébille was no defence to a charge of card fraud, but once Stallmann found out how to work his way in the murky world of intelligence, it soon became clear to this particular blackguard that the underworld was tailor-made for him. The former Baron von König was now turned out as the well-dressed Rodolphe Lemoine. He 'loved life, money, good meals, risqué stories, cigars "rolled on the naked thighs of Havana girls" ... Always acting the great lord, with a sweeping gesture and easy money.'[19] In the French Security Service, Lemoine could bring his talents of charming people into revealing their secrets, and then blackmailing them, into full bloom. For the French, it was even better. Lemoine didn't need a salary. Years of gambling fraud meant that he could work on expenses only – although with Lemoine, the baronial habits of top-flight hotels, Havana cigars and the choicest vintage wines made the distinction between salary and expenses a somewhat foggy one.

In his new career, Rodolphe Lemoine had all the paraphernalia of a traditional spy. He was taught the use of secret inks and false letterheads. After a period of coercing officials in post-war Catalonia to work secretly in French interests, his job had settled down. Now he was to find and bring in contacts, to provide fake passports, to lubricate transactions involving foreign code books and secret documents. So the dealings with Wehrpfennig in 1908 (which had brought Lemoine to the attention of French intelligence) was by no means his last dealing with a German traitor. As a native German speaker, he was the perfect agent for bringing Germans into the fold. Lemoine/Stallmann was no longer the Baron von König. He was now a French agent with the cover-name Rex.

• • •

It is the last week of May 1932. A German of the officer type, though not in uniform (neat moustache, military bearing, decently cut hair, sensible suit, ought to have a monocle), walks into the French Embassy in Berlin and asks to speak to the military attaché. Within ten days an operative of French military intelligence – the Deuxième Bureau – writes to Herr Lustig, in a slightly obscure way, offering a business meeting in Paris. The operative is a Monsieur Lemoine, aristocratic and suave. He speaks German like the native he is. He is Rex. Within a short while, Herr Lustig has become Source Traurig and he knows someone who might be useful, a Dr Martin who was something in codes and ciphers during the war.[20]

This new contact sounds quite promising, but the Deuxième Bureau aren't particularly impressed. Dr Martin doesn't appear in their files. Source Traurig is, sadly, rather small fry. After all, the previous year, Rex netted the Deuxième Bureau a very large fish. It was the same story – man walks into Embassy and so forth – but this other man was not so snappily dressed, and his connection was much, much better than some unknown Dr Martin. In June 1931, Hans-Thilo Schmidt had walked into the French Embassy in Berlin. And the connection he offered was with none other than the man who had just been appointed Chief of Staff of the communications intelligence division of the German Army. This officer – Lieutenant Colonel Rudolf Schmidt – had been in command of a communications intelligence unit during the war, going on to a position on the Imperial General Staff. Colonel Schmidt was the brother of the walk-in, Hans-Thilo Schmidt. Source Asche (or, in the French version, 'H.E.') was about as big a fish as you can imagine in the spy business. No wonder Herr Lustig was transmuted into Source Traurig (cover-name 'Sorrowful'); he didn't stand a chance in this game.

Rex had handled the recruitment of Hans-Thilo Schmidt and the process had been just the same: a check with Paris, some obscure correspondence, a clandestine meeting. On 1 November 1931, Hans-Thilo Schmidt checked into a hotel in Verviers, a Belgian town not far from the German border. The hotel clerk handed him a note, while concealed in a deep club chair behind a newspaper and a cloud of cigar smoke, a well-heeled gentleman, 6oish, confident, looked on comfortably through his glasses. The gentleman was sizing up the business contact ahead of the meeting. The note invited Schmidt to the gentleman's suite, number 31 on the first floor, any time after twelve o'clock. By twelve o'clock the gentleman had gone upstairs. The only thing wrong with the gentleman was that he was no gentleman at all. In suite 31, whisky in hand – and with an envelope containing Schmidt's travel expenses nearby – was Rodolphe Lemoine, alias Rex. Rex's job was to win the confidence of Herr Schmidt (whose real name was so boringly 'Smith' it couldn't be made up) and to vet Schmidt's ability to play a cool game.

There was no ideology involved in Hans-Thilo Schmidt's coming forward for the great play. Perhaps it was because he felt overshadowed by his older brother, perhaps because his Iron Cross had failed to open doors for him after the war, or perhaps because his mother had been a baroness who'd lost her 'von' – that so-important badge of German aristocracy – when she married a mere Schmidt. Whatever the reasons, Hans-Thilo felt that he was not doing well enough in the world. Married with two children and with a failed business or two behind him, Hans-Thilo Schmidt needed money. Lots of it.

One reason Schmidt needed the money was his enjoyment of the good things in life, like whisky and cigars. Other financial pressures came from his affairs. Mrs Schmidt had got wise to Hans-Thilo's habit of seducing the maids and nannies. Each time she fired one, the next one was selected for her lack of physical charms. This stratagem, however, had apparently failed to discourage Hans-Thilo. (Even the children had noticed the stunning ugliness of the girls and their father's behaviour when mother was out.)[21] These affairs cost money. So did the holidays and the nice suits which Hans-Thilo coveted. From the comfort of his armchair, Rex took all this in with one scan of his steel-blue eyes. He now proceeded to bring in Hans-Thilo himself, and in doing so, Rodolphe Lemoine completed his own journey from card sharp and prisoner to one of France's most valued intelligence agents.

Rex ordered cigars and whisky for Hans-Thilo Schmidt. Perhaps it was nerves, or perhaps it was a premonition about where this path would lead him, but the walk-in downed several whiskies in short order while Rex attempted small talk to put him at ease. Schmidt explained his brother's new job. Until 1928, Oberst Rudolf Schmidt had been the officer in charge at the Chiffrierstelle: the German Army's own cipher office. Hans-Thilo was out of a job and his brother, the colonel, had put in a word with his successor at the Chiffrierstelle, who needed an assistant. Thus, Hans-Thilo himself had become privy to the innermost signals secrets of the German armed forces. In other words, the new contact could offer far more than a fraternal relationship with Oberst Rudolf Schmidt, he could offer highly prized intelligence in his own right. And then Hans-Thilo Schmidt began to describe to Rex the most secret secret of all: the German armed forces had converted a commercial ciphering machine called Enigma. Hans-Thilo Schmidt had access to the operating procedures and how the machines were set up. And on him, right now in suite 31, Hans-Thilo Schmidt had a selection of documents which looked as if they proved everything he said.[22] The game was on and it was the biggest game yet of Rex's long career.

3

MIGHTY PENS

On mighty pens uplifted soars the eagle aloft.

Gottfried van Swieten
Libretto for The Creation, Part II

Marian Rejewski was never cut out to be a spy. Nothing could have been further from his life than the skulduggery enjoyed by Rex and the wheeler-dealing by Bertrand. Indeed, it would not be until he was 40 years old that anyone would put Rejewski forward for a course on intelligence and even then that probably did not include modules on trafficking in code books.[1] What made Marian Rejewski tick was mathematics and he looked and lived the part. Number seven of seven children, wearing glasses, he was as serious as he appeared. Perhaps a little shy, he was a natural student for the cryptographic course at Poznań – except for the fact that he was already past it. In 1929, when the course was beginning, he was 23, had already completed his Master's degree with a dissertation called 'Theory of Double Periodic Functions of the Second and Third Kind and its Applications' and was hardly a student any more. Marian Rejewski was set to become an academic in Professor Krygowski's department, not an owlish apology for a spy. First of all, though, it was necessary for the aspiring mathematics professor to go to Göttingen for a two-year course of postgraduate study. Göttingen was *the* place to go: it was where the masters of twentieth-century mathematics and physics all were (Hilbert, Born, Courant, Heisenberg, Wigner, von Neumann, et al.).

Despite his having been well set on an academic career as a mathematician, Rejewski was diverted into code-breaking. Krygowski himself had been asked to put forward the best candidates for the cryptology course. Rejewski was clearly the best (as well as being bilingual, the legacy of a childhood growing up in German-controlled Wielkopolska). So, regardless of his previous studies, or maybe because the Master's dissertation had already been done and graded and the course at Göttingen didn't begin for a few months, Rejewski did the new course. And because he was Marian Rejewski, he came out top, the only student to get a distinction.

Still, there was no career in cryptology, so Rejewski went to Göttingen and his name went on to the reserve list. The reserve list was not where Enigma was going to be cracked. Moreover, you cannot let young chaps straight out of university, however bright they are, on to the biggest cryptological problem of the century without some sort of vetting, and if the young chap in question has gone off to the very country that is the origin of the problem, that's the end of the matter. So much the worse for Maksymilian Ciężki and his plan to get the best Poznań mathematicians to decrypt the Enigma.

Although Marian Rejewski wasn't going to serve an apprenticeship in the Biuro Szyfrów, it was nevertheless possible that some others in the same cohort might do. The others were necessarily chaps slightly younger than Rejewski but two of them, still working towards their Master's degrees, stood out. They were more buzzy and sociable than Rejewski and less committed to the academic life. Henryk Zygalski was a 21-year-old, from near Poznań, and Jerzy Różycki, the same age, came from Wyszków, a town a few miles outside Warsaw. Zygalski liked music; they both liked parties; they both liked girls; and they both liked the mind-bending puzzles of double-transposition ciphers. So, as well as being put on the reserve list in case of hostilities, they were both invited by Maksymilian Ciężki to see if they might care to do a little puzzle-solving in their spare time.

● ● ●

Rex looked at the documents that Hans-Thilo Schmidt had brought with him to Verviers. They might be the genuine article. Discreetly fingering the envelope with the travel expenses, Rex suggested another meeting.

Sunday week, same location. With as many documents like this as you can provide. Your present salary? Five hundred Reichsmarks a month? Well, here's three times that, to cover your travel for both journeys.

On 8 November 1931, Hans-Thilo Schmidt, now code-named Asche, was back in Verviers. This time he was there to make the acquaintance of a Monsieur Barsac, a gentleman who could supposedly tell a fake code book from a real one. 'In the salon, smoky from cigars, float the "flon-flons" of a radio. Rex introduces his man. Schmidt is standing, glass of whisky in hand. A smile lights up his face ... "M. Barsac, you will, I'm sure, be satisfied."'[2] Monsieur Barsac was the cover-name for the man from Section D. As Section D only had one man, that man was Gustave Bertrand.

Agent Asche – Hans-Thilo Schmidt – produced his goods. Bertrand the deal-maker could disguise his identity but not his surprise. From the large cardboard container an astounded Bertrand drew out, one after the other: an organisation chart for the German Army Cipher Office; a code book for coordinating the wavelengths and other technical matters for transmitting Enigma signals by wireless; instructions for a hand cipher, with settings, for use by the German Army General Staff; a Reich War Ministry study on poison gas procured from Schmidt's unwitting brother; a technical note on the Enigma machine model with plugboard connections; the *Gebrauchsanweisung* [Instructions for use] for the Enigma machine; the *Schlüsselanleitung* [Guide to settings] for the set-up of the Enigma machine.

Every one was rubber-stamped *GEHEIM* – secret.

But the time for admiring this magical bounty was short. Like his namesake Cinderella, Hans-Thilo Schmidt had to catch his train back to Berlin and put the documents back where they belonged before the final strike of the clock. So, while Rex and Schmidt listened to the flon-flons, talked over the price, added more cigar smoke to the air, and sloshed around some more brandy, Bertrand was despatched upstairs, where his colleague Bintz was waiting in the bathroom with a camera. No cigars or brandy for them, in a dark room, where they were to make history in photographic form.

• • •

Göttingen was turning out to be less rewarding than expected for Marian Rejewski. The course on actuarial problems was interesting enough, but he missed home. In particular, back in Poland, in Bydgoszcz, there was a girl he had known since he was quite small: Irena Lewandowska. Marian could get to Bydgoszcz easily from Poznań; it was only about an hour and a half away on the train. He could visit his mother regularly and check on the lottery shop that she ran and then he would also be able to see Irena. But Göttingen was too far away for that.

There were three other Polish students at Göttingen with whom Rejewski struck up acquaintanceships, but none of them was particularly close. There was also a current of anti-Semitism, which would culminate at Göttingen within a couple of years with the expulsion and emigration of the lifeblood of the faculty in what was called a 'great purge'. Rejewski could not avoid getting caught up in this; it was the main political debate of the time. Everyone, it seemed, blamed the woes of Germany on Jewish influence, and the 'Jewish problem' was a theme which echoed in Poland as well. Göttingen seemed to be as much about toxic politics as imaginative mathematics. As for the mathematics, none of the other Polish students at Göttingen thought much of Marian Rejewski. So much for them as well. Marian Rejewski had better options than to spend his 1930 summer holidays in Göttingen.

Back home in Bydgoszcz, Marian Rejewski found a letter waiting for him from his old tutor Professor Krygowski at Poznań. He was being offering a post as teaching assistant at the university, but Rejewski would have to give up the second year of the Göttingen course. It wasn't hard to make the decision: the railway timetable said it all. Rejewski took up his duties in September 1930, but before long he was wondering about that old cryptology course. Professor Krygowski explained that there was no plan to re-run the course, but two other 'graduates' had, apparently, been invited to work for the Biuro Szyfrów.

There were two ways of looking at this. Either it was a disappointment that Zygalski and Różycki had been taken on but Rejewski had not, or it was an opportunity: perhaps the only reason Rejewski hadn't been asked was because he was away. So Rejewski decided to test whether the opportunity to join the Biuro Szyfrów was still there.

He got in touch with Zygalski, who asked the boss. The boss was Gwido Langer, who came down to size up the candidate for himself. The candidate was unassuming and unmilitary, exactly what they needed. Rejewski was hired.

Down in the basement of the City Garrison Headquarters, next door to the Kaiser's old palace, the three alumni of the Poznań University Mathematics Faculty were set to work. The palace was conveniently close for Rejewski's day job, even if the basement was not the most elegant part of the complex. Here, the three cryptologists worked on problems of double transposition, the textbook challenges explained in General Givierge's book.

There was also the code book of the German Navy to reconstruct. For some communications, the German Navy were still using old-fashioned codes in a four-letter format, but slowly Rejewski and his partners began to unravel its structure. It seemed to be alphabetical – lots of sentences began with groups like YOPY and YWIN – maybe those were questions, which typically in German begin with 'W' (*wann, warum, wie*, and so forth). Then one day there came a giveaway message comprising only six groups, beginning with YOPY, and the response which came back was clearly a four-digit number. It was a practice message. A question with an answer that every self-respecting German should know, probably a history question. The German-educated Poles could guess what this had to be: *Wann wurde Friedrich der Grosse geboren?* [When was Frederick the Great born?] Answer: 1712. They now had the first groups of the code and began to reconstitute the entire book.

● ● ●

Over the years, Gustave Bertrand had learned a lot about intelligence, a great deal about signals and radio and a fair bit about codes and ciphers. But he would be the first to admit that he was no match for machine ciphers. To squeeze the value out of Hans-Thilo Schmidt's Enigma manuals he asked the experts. He went to talk to his old friends at the Section du Chiffre.

Bertrand recorded what the Section du Chiffre thought:

> At the Section du Chiffre of the Army General Staff ... the question 'Cipher Machine' was still at zero: anyhow, the old cryptologists ... had decreed that this method was unassailable and that there was no capacity to deal with it. *A fortiori*, the young cryptanalysts relied on the advice of the older ones and all the texts enciphered in this way went straight into the waste-basket ...[3]

The apparently priceless documents, which he had photographed in the bathroom, were not so much priceless as useless. Completely useless. The Engima problem was unsolvable without the actual machine. The manuals explained how the machine worked; how it was set up; how the information about settings was transmitted; how it was operated; how you send a message; and how you decrypt an enciphered signal. All that is fantastically good. But it was all useless if you don't have the machine. Without knowing how the coding rotors are wired and without knowing the internal wiring, it was just not possible to apply this information.

So the solution to Enigma was to get a machine. It might just be possible that Schmidt could get hold of one and photograph its innards, but that would be too much to ask of him. There was, however, another possibility: to turn to France's sniffy friends across the Channel.

John Hessell Tiltman was possibly the greatest cryptanalyst they had across the Channel. He was working at the Government Code & Cypher School (GC&CS), which had been glued together from the British Navy and Army code-breaking departments at the end of the Great War and put under the control of the Foreign Office, with MI6 sandwiched in between. Tiltman had joined in 1920 as a two-week secondee from the army to help out with a backlog of Russian decrypts and then stayed for the rest of his life. In 1932, he had been in Paris, asking the French to help with a perennial problem – that Britain's precious navy might be under threat from the Soviets. Tiltman came with an incomplete set of materials on Soviet naval codes, which he hoped the French might be able to complement. Alas, the answer was no, but the potential for cooperation had been established. So it might be, a little later, that the British could help the French with a somewhat different problem of incompletely understood ciphers: the problem of the machine.

The British had sniffed around the Enigma machine before.[4] Knowing what they did about signals intelligence, the idea of machine encryption was appealing. The military attaché in Berlin went to have a look and got hold of a prospectus for Enigma. At the World Postal Congress in Stockholm, the British brought home the daily bulletin for 7 August 1924, which included a report on a demonstration of the machine, with a nicely incomprehensible piece of cipher text and its solution. The machine was demonstrated in London to the Foreign Office. The manufacturers caught the scent of an order and took out British patent rights in October 1925. Then GC&CS got involved. An Enigma machine was purchased and delivered up to the boffins for a once-over.

The boffin was Mr Foss. In his report, Mr Foss coolly explained how you could decipher Enigma messages, even if you didn't know how the machine had been set up. Sure, you needed to know the wiring of the rotors and you needed to have an inspired guess at the likely content of some of the message. (Mr Foss called the guesswork a 'crib': having endured years of translating Latin at school, he knew that schoolboys could make sense of gibberish if someone told you what at least some of it meant. At school, they called the cheat translation at the back of the book a 'crib'.) Mr Foss concluded his analysis with a section, General Remarks. The Enigma had some weak points. But if you had to use it, he would suggest that you should have several rotors at your disposal, choosing three each time, and you should encipher and conceal the information which had to be sent to the recipient about the starting positions of the three rotors.

Like so many technical reports, Mr Foss's study was put in a file. The British would not be buying the Enigma machine for their own secure communications. But now Captain Tiltman had made the diplomatic link between GC&CS and Captain Bertrand's Section D, perhaps the boffinry might be extracted from its file and put to good use. The question was duly put, via the proper channels, which is to say MI6's liaison officer in Paris.

Bertrand's bathroom photographs were carefully evaluated at MI6. The photography was good, but MI6 independently came to the same conclusion as the Section du Chiffre. The documents were, unfortunately, useless. Useless, that is, unless you happened to have the German modified version of the Enigma. And in any case, on proper reflection, it would not be the done thing to get too close to the French. The photographs were carefully filed and carefully forgotten, and carefully worded expressions of lukewarm thanks were carefully passed back to the Deuxième Bureau. In sum, the British were a dead end.

Having now held the documents for nearly three weeks, despite the unenthusiastic reaction of his French and British peers, Gustave Bertrand was sure they had some value. There must be someone who could squeeze some information out of them. Bertrand had one option left. His boss agreed. Through the military attaché in the embassy in Warsaw, Bertrand requested a meeting with Lieutenant-Colonel Langer of the Polish Biuro Szyfrów. The precious photographs were packed and sent in the diplomatic bag and Bertrand took the long train journey through Germany to once again renew his acquaintanceship with his Polish friends.

Bertrand and Langer met on 8 December 1931.[5] The photographs were greeted by Langer, and Stefan Mayer his boss, with stupefaction and delight. Mayer asked for forty-eight hours to make an evaluation, to see what could be done with them. Meanwhile, the impatient Bertrand had to kick his heels in his hotel, wander around the sights of the Citadel, the mediaeval quarter and the wide, elegant eighteenth-century district now known as the Old Town. Finally, at the appointed hour, Mayer and Langer saw Bertrand once again.

The documents from Verviers were the real deal. '*Vous avez fait donner l'artillerie lourde*' [you brought out the big guns], said Langer to Bertrand.[6] 'The Schmidt documents were welcomed like manna in the desert, and all doors were immediately opened,' said an overjoyed Bertrand.[7] At last, he had found someone who understood these things and could put the information to proper use. Thanks to the bathroom photographs, the modifications made from the commercial machine were clearly apparent: in particular, it was evident that there had been an addition of a plugboard to the front of the Enigma machine, one which swapped over pairs of letters as the electric current entered and left the bank of three rotors. Alas, this precious material was not enough to fully solve the puzzle of Enigma, as Langer explained: the documents did not disclose the wirings inside the machine; how the rotors were wired; how the plugboard was connected to the contacts on the rotor housing; what the connections were in the 'reflector' which returned the electric current back through the rotors. If only – he continued – if only we had the monthly charts which informed operators of the settings …

So there was no immediate prospect of a breakthrough on the Enigma, but nevertheless the meeting between Bertrand and Langer was enormously significant in building a rapport between two teams with different and complementary areas of expertise. Not only were the Poles actually showing their technical abilities to be streets ahead of the French and British experts, but the tentative grafting of French-acquired material on to Polish stock was now showing buds which might, in time, bear fruit.

On his return to France, Bertrand was thrown straight into another meeting with Hans-Thilo Schmidt, once again in Verviers, the week before Christmas 1931.[8] This time, Bertrand was trusted with the camera alone, and off to the bathroom he went while Rex and Asche, together with Bertrand's superior, Major André Perruche, cover-name Alison, went off to sink a few glasses of wine. This time the photographs included a description of different types of Enigma machines in use since 1928 and a table of settings: just what the Poles had put on their Christmas list! And in the new year there were more meetings. The first was in May, which yielded more tables of Enigma settings, as well as numerous other secret military materials. Following the May meeting, Bertrand went again to Warsaw. As before, Langer was enthusiastic; as before, the materials provided were not quite enough. This time it was Maksymilian Ciężki who explained the problem. The settings tables alone did not give them what they needed to reconstitute the wirings. Ideally, they'd like the actual wiring diagrams. But failing that, maybe some examples of coded messages, together with their plain text equivalents?

It was beginning to feel like a thankless task, but Bertrand had faith in his Polish colleagues. At least they were making the effort. But to ask Hans-Thilo Schmidt for the wiring diagrams or messages requested by the Biuro Szyfrów would put him in the most extreme danger.

Hans-Thilo Schmidt was proving himself France's most valuable asset, not because of the Enigma documents, but because of the other things he was producing, such as a note on the mobilisation of the German Cipher Office; the manual cipher keys used by the German Army; an appreciation by the army about the use of tanks, motorisation and the transportation of armoured units; and a senior insider's view of the situation in Germany as the Nazi Party grew into Germany's most potent political force. There was more of this to come; to endanger the source by asking for specifics on a gamble for Enigma would be foolish in the extreme. All the same, Bertrand sensed that they were close to a breakthrough on Enigma. The head of the French intelligence service, Colonel Louis Rivet, intervened: leave it to Rex to decide. If Rex could coach Schmidt in the fine arts of tradecraft, perhaps the critical materials could be obtained without undue risk. This was an extraordinary responsibility to give to Rodolphe Lemoine, but his roguish past was entirely submerged in his new identity as Rex, the talented intelligence agent trusted at the highest levels.

On 2 August 1932, Rex met Hans-Thilo Schmidt at the Hotel Adlon, a stone's throw from the Reichstag building in Berlin. The mesmeric charm of Rex – and the lure of cash – outbid the need for caution. Schmidt agreed to see what he could do. A fortnight later, Rex left Berlin having deposited a stash of papers for transmission to Paris in the diplomatic bag. These contained the Enigma settings for the forthcoming months of September and October and an all-important enciphered message, together with its plain text for comparison. For bonus, there were also technical notes on Enigma for the German Army and Air Force; a study on the German Officer Corps; and a twenty-page secret report on the potential build-up of Germany's forces and resources. It was another incredible haul.

Bertrand once again sent the Enigma documents by diplomatic bag to Warsaw and once again went himself to the city, where the staff of Gwido Langer's radio intelligence section were being concentrated. The need for an outpost at Poznań had passed – interception could be carried out where it was needed – but for cryptographic research and evaluation of intelligence, it was better that the personnel involved were located together and closely connected with the Second Department of the General Staff. The extra-mural personnel – Ciężki's precious mathematicians – had all graduated by mid 1932 and were free of the ties to the University at Poznań, which had previously kept them at the town. So the Poznań team had come to Warsaw.

The move was made at the beginning of September 1932, a couple of weeks before Bertrand's visit. For Marian Rejewski, the move was not so convenient. Irena was still in Bydgoszcz and the train journey to her from Warsaw was a lot longer than from Poznań. For the other two code-breakers, the change was a positive one. For them, Warsaw was a vibrant, exciting and attractive place. For Henryk Zygalski there may have been some wry enjoyment in the idea that the new offices assigned to the German Cryptographic Unit were located where Frederyk Chopin had spent part of his childhood: the elegant colonnaded Saxon Palace in the recently renamed Marshal Józef Piłsudski Square.

About the beginning of November 1932, Maksymilian Ciężki walked into the room where Marian Rejewski worked in the Saxon Palace.

'Good morning.'

'Good morning, Mr Captain.'

'How are you finding it, Mr Rejewski?'

'Most agreeable, thank you, Mr Captain.'

It was all very polite. In fact the new offices were nothing remarkable. Civilian supernumeraries attached to a special sub-section of a department whose function nobody knows are not going to be allocated the swankiest offices, particularly if they are working in intelligence, which is well known to be the lowest form of military life.

'Could you come to my office, please, Mr Rejewski. There is something new I should like to discuss.'

'Certainly, Mr Captain.'

Ciężki closed the door of his office. 'Mr Rejewski, do you have any spare time, during the evenings?'

'Yes, indeed, Mr Captain.'

'Good, good,' said Ciężki. 'In that case, I would like you to come into the office in the evenings. I have something which might interest you. In fact it is something quite difficult: our best men have not got anywhere with it.' There is nothing better calculated to stir up the ambition of a mathematician than to tell him that a problem is too difficult. Captain Ciężki had the full attention of Civilian Supernumerary Rejewski. 'I need not mention, Mr Rejewski, that nobody else must know about this work, nor must they even know what you are working on.'

Actually, the one thing better calculated to stir up the ambition of a mathematician working on an impossible problem is to tell him that the work is also deadly secret. In a separate cubicle, away from his morning workplace, Marian Rejewski began to study the problem of Enigma after hours. Each component of the Enigma machine swapped around the letters of the alphabet. And that, as Marian Rejewski could see, was a problem in permutations.

Professor Krygowski had taught a module at Poznań on Group Theory, of which permutations is an amusing subcategory. With normal algebra, you can divide a number by two and then multiply it by two and you finish up with what you started with. If you tried that sort of thing with an egg, however, you would finish up not with a reconstituted egg but with an urgent need for a saucepan. Manipulating permutations contains the same idea: you have to treat permutations like eggs, since reversing an operation doesn't put you back where you started. Rejewski had enjoyed permutations at Poznań and Captain Ciężki had just served up a nice problem in permutation algebra. Marian Rejewski was going to get to work on some equations and descramble the Enigma.

For his first step, Marian Rejewski was able to discern how the 'indicator' of each message – the starting position of the three rotors in the Enigma machine when the cipher clerk begins encryption – was arranged. There were repeating patterns, showing that the first six letters in every transmission were in two groups of three. Three letters implied something, something like the three starting positions of coding rotors. He had reached this degree of understanding without even seeing an Enigma machine.

Maksymilian Ciężki could see that his faith in Rejewski was not misplaced. After his success with the message settings, Ciężki brought Rejewski a wooden box. Inside the box was the commercial Enigma machine which Polish intelligence had bought a few years back. 'And, Mr Rejewski, if you would be so kind, I should like you to work on this problem in the daytime as well. I'm afraid you will still not be able to discuss the matter with any of your colleagues, though.'

'Yes, Mr Captain.'

Now Rejewski had a room of his own. It was small and somewhat less agreeable than the shared space which he had had at first, but better than a cubicle and he could concentrate. Rejewski was also told that the machine which the Wehrmacht were using was different: there were differences in the wiring and in the rotors, and, most difficult of all, there was a plugboard on the front of the machine. Rejewski was given a copy of the operating instructions – part of the haul from Hans-Thilo Schmidt, of whose existence Rejewski remained wholly unaware.

Now equipped with the basic structure of the machine, Rejewski could assign labels to each of the parts that scrambled the letters of the alphabet. There was the plugboard. There was the wiring connecting the plugboard to the ring of wires where the electric current entered the bank of three rotors. Then there were the three rotors themselves and finally there was the reflector which turned the current round and back through the rotors. Representing each element of the scrambling mechanism by an algebraic label, Rejewski could then draw up a set of simultaneous equations in several unknowns, where the unknowns were the permutations carried out by the different elements of the machine.

Rejewski was puzzling over his equations when, on 9 December 1932, once again Maksymilian Ciężki came to call. In his hand he was bearing a photographic copy of the actual daily settings used by the Germans during September and October. 'Now,' recalled Rejewski, 'the situation changed radically.' Since the table of settings included the connections of the plugboard, one of the unknowns had dropped out of the equations.

There was, however, still one feature of the machine which was – at that time – beyond the analytical genius of Marian Rejewski. This was the way the plugboard was wired up to the ring of twenty-six wires at the right-hand end of the bank of three rotors. In the commercial Enigma machine, the typewriter keyboard letters Q, W, E, R, T, Z etc. were wired directly to the letters A, B, C, D, E, F etc. on the entry ring. Not so with the military machine: some other arrangement had been chosen. In the first place, there was a plugboard interposed between the keyboard and the entry ring. The twenty-six wires leaving the plugboard were connected in some fashion to the twenty-six contacts on the entry ring. There were twenty-six factorial ($26×25×24×23×...$) possible ways of doing that: a horrendously large number containing twenty-seven digits if written out in full. Marian Rejewski, however, guessed that a simple arrangement might have been chosen; after all, the Germans were, if nothing else, methodical. Maybe Q was wired to Q, W to W, E to E, etc. And, miraculously, that seemed to have been the choice the designers had made. 'The very first trial yielded a positive result. From my pencil, as by magic, began to issue numbers designating the connections in [the right-hand] rotor.'[9]

At the end of September, the Germans swapped around the rotors in the machine, so during October a different rotor was in the right-hand slot. More magic, and the connections of another rotor were disclosed. Marian Rejewski's mighty pencil had started to bust the Enigma box wide open.

● ● ●

Mürren is a small village, clinging unsteadily to a rock terrace above a vertical 900m drop into the Lauterbrünnen Valley in Switzerland. It's a tourist trap, with hikers in summer and skiers in winter. The scenery is stunning, with the Jungfrau and the Eiger and the Schilthorn all within easy distance. The only problem is getting a hotel room – let alone three of them – at short notice in January.

The aristocratic gentleman with perfect German had a commanding mien as well as ample charm. The hotel staff would be only too happy to oblige. Perhaps the gentlemen and his lady wife would like to sit in the lounge while everything was made ready? Rex took a large brandy and settled into a large armchair to admire the view. Soon enough, two more gentlemen arrived: Messieurs Barsac and Saint-Georges from France. And, eventually, on the very last cable car up from the valley, a third, bearing an elegant suitcase of fawn-coloured leather.

The 1930s were being kind to Hans-Thilo Schmidt. His liaisons with the French were paying off. Handsomely. Each package of documents he brought netted about 10,000 Reichsmarks and there seemed to be two or three opportunities a year to deliver these. By 1934, the pattern of payment was well established. Schmidt would receive a bland postcard; then he would know to take his false ID to the post office and claim an envelope from the poste restante service. In the envelope there would be a left-luggage receipt and this enabled Schmidt to collect a holdall from one of Berlin's railway stations. A holdall containing his cash. Meanwhile, he'd been taught to write letters in invisible ink (no more complicated than dissolving salt in water; steam and starch would reveal the writing), to arrange meetings using more blandly worded postcards and to conceal the source of his unexpected wealth.

The French were worried about the cash. Too much cash might draw unwanted attention to their asset. And there was no chance that Hans-Thilo Schmidt would save his cash. For him the cash was there to be spent: on wine; on girls; on nice clothes; on all those things which showed just how he was making a success of his life. So, between them, Rex and Schmidt manufactured a laundering scheme. Hans-Thilo had studied chemistry. He borrowed some money from the bank (and from his ever-compliant military brother) and bought himself a soap factory. All the cash could now be explained as profits from the business. And the real business, the really exciting business of lifting secret documents, could now be done using a smart, expensive case of fawn-coloured leather.[10]

While Bertrand was once more banished to the bathroom, Rex, Hans-Thilo Schmidt and 'Saint-Georges' (in fact Major Guy Schlesser, a fluent German speaker from French intelligence) enjoyed a brandy in Rex's suite. Rex asked politely about the soap enterprise; Schmidt wanted to talk about something else. He had a new role. The French looked disappointed. The flow of information might be about to dry up just as they had got the plumbing fully operational. Schmidt smiled, 'I have been given responsibility for liaison between the Cipher Office and the Forschungsamt.' Neither Rex nor Schlesser had the first idea what the Forschungsamt might be. None of the belligerent nations that made up the Allies in World War Two – a war which, in January 1934, was a world away from anyone's imagination – ever found out about the Forschungsamt until after the war was over. Except the

French, who found out on 5 January 1934. The Forschungsamt had been set up in 1933 as the, 'research bureau of the Reich air ministry'. It reported to Hermann Göring, who wore so many hats it was probably irrelevant whether he was Commissioner of Aviation, Minister without Portfolio in the Reich government, Minister of the Interior for Prussia, or just the second most powerful man in the country. The Forschungsamt was Göring's own personal intelligence service, 'the richest, the most secret, the most Nazi, and the most influential' of all Nazi Germany's proliferating intelligence services.[11] In being brought into the Forschungsamt, Hans-Thilo Schmidt had been given access to Germany's highest-level secrets and here in Mürren he was offering to get those secrets for the French. Schlesser and Rex hardly knew what to say. Rex ordered more brandy.

From now on, Hans-Thilo Schmidt was the number one asset of French intelligence. 'He enabled us to follow step by step the German rearmament, to get intelligence on the highest level of German military policy, to know in advance all the most important projects until the war began.'[12] Schmidt's clandestine deliveries had just become much, much more important.

The deliveries were sometimes bizarre. In September 1933, Schmidt had hiked over the border into Switzerland with the secret codes in his rucksack. On a later trip, Schmidt brought papers which contained the new procedures for the Enigma machine, as well as the most recent monthly settings and a set of the army high command's plans for neutralising the Czechoslovakian defences. In case he should be discovered with this incriminating material on him, Schmidt had asked the conductor on the train to take care of his bag – a wiser move than might be imagined, as Schmidt had also packed a selection of Bavarian salamis and charcuterie. As the central heating in the train wrought its effect, the temptation to look inside the bag diminished accordingly. One feels sorry for Captain Bertrand, stuck in a small hotel bathroom a few hours later with a camera and the documentation, delicately marinated in garlic and herbs.[13]

● ● ●

The first breakthroughs into Enigma had all happened very fast: Rejewski's work had all been completed within a matter of weeks. Then he could turn to a rather more important personal problem, which was how to cement his relationship with Irena Lewandowska. It was 1933 and Marian had known Irena for years and years, but distance and work challenges had stood in their way. Rejewski's persistence eventually paid off, though, and they were married, in Bydgoszcz, on 30 June 1934.

Unlike his celebrations with Irena, Rejewski's cause for happiness over his progress against the German encipherment machine was, in fact, incomplete. Not a single message would be deciphered unless the Poles could find out the order in which the three cipher rotors were being put into the machine, as well as which of the twenty-six starting positions each rotor was in. The easy solution was to look into Hans-Thilo Schmidt's rucksack to find the monthly settings which he routinely supplied in his meetings with Bertrand. But the more recent, more aromatic gifts finding their way to Gustave Bertrand did not continue their journey to Rejewski's office in the Saxon Palace. For reasons we no longer know, Ciężki and Gwido Langer had decided to keep the team up to the mark using wits alone, rather than the materials procured by French intelligence.

Marian Rejewski was not daunted by the challenge of the settings. He had already observed that the preamble of every German message was structured as an 'indicator' of three letters, repeated and then enciphered. The idea behind repeating the indicator was that bad atmospheric conditions or other difficulties with radio reception might garble the indicator. Having it sent twice provided a back up. However, repetition of the indicator – enciphering the same three letters twice – gave Rejewski a tiny chance to discover what the indicator was. He noticed that he could follow a trail of letters from one encrypted indicator to another, and that the trails would eventually join up into loops he called cycles.* These cycles were 'characteristic' of the combination of rotors and the order in which they had been put into the machine. Finding the characteristics was the way the Polish code-breakers would uncover the settings being used by the Germans to keep their signals safe from enemy eyes.

---

* See Appendix for a more detailed explanation.

Moreover, the German operators were being daft. They seemed to be an unimaginative bunch, choosing for their three-letter indicators adjacent keys on the Enigma keyboard, like QWE, or even repeated letters like QQQ. Such simple indicator patterns could be guessed by Marian Rejewski and other members of the team. After Rejewski's great breakthrough, it became clear to Maksymilian Ciężki that Enigma decryption was a real possibility and the ban on sharing the nature of Rejewski's special problem was lifted. It was only lifted by a tiny amount, but now Rejewski was not working on his own. His erstwhile Poznań classmates Jerzy Różycki and Henryk Zygalski were brought in on the secret and began to contribute their own thoughts to the problem of indicator-finding and the decryption of intercepted radio telegrams.

They rapidly realised that the potentially huge complexity of the Enigma machine could be distilled into something much simpler. If you examined only a short sequence of encrypted text – like the indicator, for example – the chances were that only one thing was changing from one letter to the next and that was the 'fast' right-hand rotor of the machine. The other two rotors and the reflector were just processing inputs in the same way, every time. So if what came out of the right-hand rotor went into the middle rotor at 'K' and came out at 'P' in position 2, anything coming out of the right-hand rotor at 'K' must always get converted to 'P' (and vice versa) at any other position in the sequence.

The 'static' behaviour of the middle and left rotors between turnovers (turnovers occurred only when the right-hand rotor had rotated enough to cause a simultaneous rotation of the middle rotor) allowed the code-breakers to devise new techniques for finding the rotor order and revealing the content of encrypted messages. The first technique they devised was called the 'grille method' because it used a sheet of paper with slots cut into it. Written on the paper was the transformation which the static part of the machine would make, given an electrical input at any one of its twenty-six electrical connections; through the slot another piece of paper was visible, showing the possible transformations of the right-hand rotor. If the code-breakers could trace actual encipherments through the transformations shown by the two sheets together, and find common pairs of letters, that told them they had found the right-hand rotor and its starting position. A by-product of the grille method was that it indicated some of the switch-arounds done by the plugboard as well. To get the most out of the grille technique, the code-breakers began to put together a card catalogue of the permutations brought about by all combinations of the left and middle rotors and the reflector: incredibly tedious, detailed work, but worth it to get the results.

• • •

Antoni Palluth was also doing rather well in the early 1930s. His electrical factory, producing radio equipment and other high-tech kit for the Polish military, was (in contrast to Asche's soap factory, which held itself together only through the munificence of the French Deuxième Bureau) a commercial success. It had exhibited an innovative 50-watt transceiver at a public exhibition in Warsaw in 1930. With the wow factor of miniaturisation, the transceiver brought in orders from the Biuro Szyfrów and the navy. The orders came in regularly, including large contracts for the installations of radio telegraphy stations in Gdynia and Bydgoszcz, for Hughes type-printing telegraphy apparatus in Wilno and Lwów, and more. The relationship between one of AVA's owners and their primary customer might seem a bit cosy for some tastes, but the products were of good quality, were good value for money and were produced on time. Palluth's competitors could not match all that. And the whole thing was above board: senior officers in the Second Department of the General Staff knew all about the role of Palluth and they were signing off the requisitions. With the orders flowing in, AVA outgrew its city centre premises, ending up in a new facility in the southern district of Warsaw called Mokotów, a location that would prove to be very convenient in future years.

In among the radio equipment, the factory was making some rather unusual machinery. These special machines needed squat, fat wheels with twenty-six contacts on either face, with finger-grips and the letters of the alphabet printed around the rim. Inside the wheels the contacts were connected by criss-cross wiring. The wheels were, in fact, not wheels at all, for, having found a way to unravel the set-up of the Enigma machine, the Poles had wanted to get on with the useful business of actually reading the intercepted messages. And to carry out decryption they needed a bit more than just Rejewski's mighty pen and knowledge of the settings: they needed an actual Enigma machine. They had one, for sure, but it was the old commercial machine with the wrong type of rotors. So an order was placed with a secret, privately run electrical factory to make some machines which would behave just like the Enigma. The factory was AVA, and it could be trusted with these top-secret orders because it was run by Maksymilian Ciężki's friend and colleague, Antoni Palluth.[14]

So, apart from the fact that Adolf Hitler had come to power in 1933 and begun the transformation of his country into a vicious war machine, everything seemed to be going rather well. Perhaps still appreciative of the value of being able to decode enemy signals in their wars for independence, the Polish authorities recognised what they had in Ciężki and his team of specialists. Ciężki was decorated with the Gold Cross of Merit in 1933 to add to his 1928 Silver Cross and his war and regular service medals. The code-breakers were also paid handsomely. Little did they know that the fat pay cheques would leave a trail which might expose their secret work and even put their lives and those of their colleagues in mortal peril.

4

THE SCARLET PIMPERNELS

I have heard speak of this Scarlet Pimpernel. A little flower – red? –
yes! They say in Paris that every time a royalist escapes to England,
that devil, Foucquier-Tinville, the Public Prosecutor, receives a paper
with that little flower designated in red upon it.

Baroness Orczy, *The Scarlet Pimpernel*

In 1934, rearmament and belligerence still lay in the future. Who, apart
from Hans-Thilo Schmidt, could tell what Hitler's new political programme would bring? Certainly, his first year of power showed that
the election speeches had not been all bluster, but the policies imple-
mented by the Nazi Party had, so far, been all domestically focused:
suspending constitutional protections for citizens; removing Jews
from public offices and schools; introducing a eugenics programme for
people with disabilities; establishing concentration camps; and burning
un-German books. However unpleasant all that might be, it was not,
apparently, a threat to other countries.

Nonetheless, Poland was worried. With East Prussia to the north,
the rest of the Reich to the west and the twin problems of Danzig
and the 'Polish Corridor', there was plenty to worry about. A non-
aggression pact was the obvious way to go and one was signed in
1934. Paradoxically, the pact had a destabilising effect: the French saw
it as backsliding by the Poles, weakening their own alliance, which
was designed to keep Germany under check from two sides. Now
the French felt threatened. So they put out their own feelers to the
Soviets. A Franco-Soviet pact followed in 1935 and now it was the
Poles' turn to feel threatened again. What if the Soviets tried a replay

POLAND 1922–1939

of the 1920 war? The close relationship between France and Poland had begun to crumble.

The Franco-Polish relationship faltered just at the moment Hitler upped his game. In 1936, Germany reoccupied the wide swathe of land between France, Luxembourg and the left bank of the Rhine. Just as Hans-Thilo Schmidt had reported, the Germans had jettisoned disarmament.

The seedling of intelligence cooperation, planted by Gustave Bertrand and Gwido Langer, might have so easily wilted in the new climate of mutual suspicion. But their own personal relationship was founded on discretion. If something should not be divulged, it would not be. 'When [Bertrand] saw you about to ask a question that he couldn't answer, always he'd say "*Ne pas demander!*"'[1] Sometimes, though, there was a sticky moment. Bertrand had been invited by Langer in May 1933 to observe an exercise in the Polish Corridor, the most vulnerable part of Poland, in which the Poles were deploying their mobile interception and decryption group. The number of German messages which could be read seemed remarkable given that the Poles could, by their own account to Bertrand, do nothing with Enigma. Maksymilian Ciężki had an explanation ready, though. The Germans were extraordinarily lax: they were sending the same message in clear and in cipher! Bertrand was convinced. The fact that numerous messages said '*Maschine defekt*', which did not need any translation, was indication enough that the Germans were struggling as much as, apparently, their observers were.[2]

Despite the cooling-off in the upper atmosphere of foreign policy, then, Bertrand was able to carry on his liaison with Langer. He made eight visits to Warsaw in the period 1934–38, and he didn't go empty-handed. For throughout these years, Hans-Thilo Schmidt continued to supply the French with an array of intelligence which was astounding in both its volume and its quality. In 1932–33, there had been five handovers; in 1934 another three; and then three each in 1935 and 1936. And there were more to come. Gustave Bertrand was nearly always present and at nearly all those meetings Schmidt had Enigma materials to hand over.[3]

• • •

Hitler's Germany was changing not only in the way people thought and behaved, but also in the rigour and discipline it was bringing to all aspects of its resurgent military. First, the slackness which allowed Enigma machine operators to use lazy indicators like AAA was stamped out. That was just the beginning. In 1936, the rotor order was changed monthly, and the number of cross-pluggings used on the front of the machine was varied to between five and eight. In October, the rotor order started changing daily. The old grille method developed by the Poles was now too difficult to apply: new thinking was needed.

Jerzy Różycki was 27 in 1936. Now fully engaged as a member of the Enigma team, he was at the peak of his intellectual powers. His response to the disaster of the daily rotor change came from a completely different approach to cryptology: it was an application of good old-fashioned letter-counting, coupled with mathematics.

For centuries it has been known that the easiest cipher to break is a simple letter-for-letter substitution, because each letter in plain language occurs with a particular frequency. In German, for example, the letter E is the most frequent (appearing 16.9 per cent of the time) and Q is the least (0.02 per cent). But if an Enigma machine is used for encryption, the letter frequency flattens out, to the dismay of those trying to do code-breaking by counting. Unless, that is, the Enigma machine is used with identical settings for two different messages, in which case a different theory applies.

Różycki's had a brilliant insight based on the thought that while letters were not distributed randomly in a normal sentence, they ought to be when encrypted with Enigma, and if they were not, then you had an important clue to work with. If you line up two different pieces of regular German, one underneath the other, the probability that two identical letters appear one above the other is about 1 in 13. And if you line up two different Enigma intercepts, the probability drops markedly, to 1 in 26, which is what you'd expect for sequences of randomly chosen letters. But, if the Enigma settings were identical, this probability went back up to 1 in 13, because the transformation was identical in both cases. And that, concluded Różycki, gave a way in to identify which rotor was in the right-hand position in the Enigma machine. For a run of letters (where there had been no turnover of the middle rotor), the transformation effected on a given day ought to be the same and you could spot the point of a turnover when the rate of coincidence switched from 1 in 13 to 1 in 26. And that switch-over was enough to identify the right-hand rotor setting, since where the turnovers happened was different for each rotor. It was like watching for the turnover on the taxi meter of a cab, or the step-up to the next hour after the expiry of sixty minutes: Różycki and his colleagues called his rotor-detection scheme the 'clock method'.

The pace of German changes stepped up still more: 1937 brought further modifications, this time to the technology rather than the procedure. The reflector, which turned the current round after it passed through the three rotors before it went back through them in the reverse direction, was changed that year. The methodical German military had sent out a helpful reminder – in an Enigma-ciphered message, which the Poles could read – about the changeover day, giving the Polish team information about what was going to change. Rejewski's technique for recovering wirings needed to be brought back into operation to find the innards of the new Enigma part. Then the painstakingly assembled catalogue of permutations had to be redone. Yet the achievements of the secret team were enough for more official recognition and encouragement. Marian Rejewski was awarded the Silver Cross of Merit in 1936 and the Gold Cross of Merit in 1938. Henryk Zygalski and Jerzy Różycki each also received the Silver Cross of Merit in 1938.[4] The Poles were keeping up. Just.

● ● ●

The post-war order was crumbling in 1936. It wasn't just the Rhineland. In the same year, a group of conservatives mounted a military coup on the socialist government of Spain. The Nationalists failed to seize total control and the struggle degenerated into a civil war. The intelligence services of Great Britain began to monitor Morse Code messages being sent by the Nationalists, messages enciphered on the commercial model of the Enigma machine. The man who was assigned to work out what the messages said was an associate of the GC&CS known to his family as Erm.

Erm was born, the second of four brothers, into a family of hyper-achievers. The eldest was editor of *Punch*, then Britain's most popular satirical magazine. The youngest was an ostentatious convert to Roman Catholicism, a monsignor and translator of the Bible into English for the Catholic Church: the twentieth century's counterpart to Cardinal Newman. The other brother was 'an Anglo-Catholic priest in the East End, a dedicated socialist, a fearless motorbike rider, a welfare worker, an eccentric recluse and just possibly a saint'.[5] Unbeknownst to any of these stellar brothers, Erm – so called by them because of his awkward hesitancy in social settings – was the most brilliant star of this small galaxy. His real name was Dillwyn Knox, Dilly for short, and his achievements would remain a secret for another half-century.

Dilly Knox had been one of the stars of 'Room 40', the British Admiralty's code-breaking operation in the Great War. Knox liked to think in the bath; a bath was conveniently installed. There he broke the German flag officers' code and that told the British where the predatory U-boats were located, making the convoying system a success. Knox had also cracked a different sort of code. A set of irreverent poems called the *Mimes of Herodas* survived only in tiny fragments of rolled papyrus, which someone had tried to stick back together in the wrong order. Knox's day job, as a fellow of King's College, Cambridge, was to reassemble, edit and translate Herodas for the modern world. 'The language of the Mimes is precious, with unpleasant affected archaisms, and an honest translation, it seemed to Dilly, must be the same … "La no reke hath she of what I say, but standeth goggling at me more agape than a crab."'[6] Heaven knows what the goggling modern readers were supposed to make of that.

The Mimes appeared in this crabwise form of English in 1929. By 1936, Knox was declining invitations to the King's College Founder's Feast, an annual gathering of intellect which he greatly enjoyed. 'The reason was simple; the dinner was noted, even among Cambridge colleges, for its hospitality and its fine wines, and, in consequence, for the occasional indiscretions of the guests. These, to be sure, were heard by Kingsmen only, but the time had come when Dilly could not risk even the hint of a shadow of a reference to what he was doing.'[7] For what he was doing was an attack on the Spanish Enigma.

The challenge for Knox in 1936 was to know how the Enigma machine had been set up – in other words, which of the three coding rotors occupied the three places in the machine and what the starting positions of the rotors might be. Soon he fathomed out the principle which had guided Marian Rejewski several years before: as long as there was no turnover of the middle rotor, the transformation effected by the wiring of the two rotors on the left and the reflector device remained constant. That made it easier to figure out which rotor was being deployed in the right-most position, along with its starting position. Using strips of paper he called 'rods', Knox began to tease out the Enigma traffic.[8] If they were ever to meet, it was just possible that Knox and Rejewski might speak the same language, a language of cryptology if not of Polish, English, or ancient Greek.

• • •

Antoni Palluth was leading a complicated life.[9] He had far too many jobs. In the daytime, Palluth acted out the role of partner in a small engineering firm. It was his night jobs for the army that made for the trouble. The code-breaking problems set by Maksymilian Ciężki had to be done after hours in the family's apartment. And a family there was: he had got married to Jadwiga von Kessel, who came from an aristocratic family, and in 1931 and 1934 there were children, Jerzy and Andrzej. But there was a third job as well and it was dangerous. The third job obliged Palluth to make 'business trips' overseas to fix equipment: if AVA was to maintain its credibility with the military, its after-sales service had to be spot on. It wasn't exactly secure for a Polish spy to walk into a radio store in a German high-street and ask them to repair a secret radio not much larger than a prayer book, so AVA's rep, Antoni Palluth, had to go. Jadwiga didn't like it when her husband had to reach into the cupboard for his handgun and include that in his luggage on these trips. The handgun proved that the third job was too dicey for comfort.

Building and servicing micro-sized transmitters and Enigma analogues was only part of the AVA brief. There were also commissions to build normal radios and aerials and all the other peripherals that go with wireless telegraphy. One of the larger projects was to construct a giant radio mast at a Polish intelligence service station in the Kabaty woods in the outskirts of Warsaw. Among the young trees, not far from the mast, the Second Department of the Polish General Staff was building a bunker. Inside the bunker, below ground, the code-breakers were going to have new offices. The place was called Pyry and the cover-name for the operation going on there was *Wicher*, the Polish term for a tornado.

Maksymilian Ciężki moved his team into the bunker in 1937. A team, but strictly demarcated according to traditional lines. Langer and Ciężki, commissioned military officers, hailed from the upper echelons of Polish society, as did Antoni Palluth. The class differential, coupled with a slight disparity in age, kept the group from socialising as a unit. The younger non-establishment technicians, Rejewski, Różycki and Zygalski, rubbed along together in a friendly enough way. But the invisible line between officers and others meant there was no question it would be anything other than 'yes, Mr Major' when the boss, newly promoted, came to call.[10]

The radio mast above the bunker at Pyry was no ordinary aerial. Opened in 1938, it was the visible part of Radio Station G, the hub of a network of eight listening stations across Poland. Radio Station G could itself pick up signals from as far away as Tehran and even Manchuria, which the Polish high command wanted to do in order to keep an eye on the USSR. It used state-of-the-art technology that only the AVA factory could master. Radio Station G was also called 'Jedynka', meaning Number One, probably because it cost a fortune: $1 million in 1938 currency values. It was undeniably the best in Europe, but it was also undeniably a peculiar way to spend the shrinking Polish defence budget when Hitler was sabre-rattling next door. It also made the code-breakers' offices something of a target. In short, it was a vanity project. Some people thought there should be an inquiry, as the radio men would, sooner or later, find out.[11]

● ● ●

In October 1937, Colonel Stewart Menzies, not yet the head of MI6 but tipped as a possible successor to the incumbent, met Lieutenant

Colonel Louis Rivet in Paris.[12] Rivet had been in charge of the French intelligence and counter-intelligence services, part of the Deuxième Bureau, since June 1936. Menzies was mainly interested in Italy and Spain (as a result of its history, Britain thought of strategy in terms of oceans, and the Mediterranean was Menzies' focus). The French wanted to talk about Germany. Menzies admitted frankly that the British knew next to nothing on that subject, but then he went on to predict that it would take only three weeks for the Germans to achieve *Anschluss* with Austria and that the Sudetenland in Czechoslovakia would suffer a similar fate. The British policy towards Germany was 'wait and see'. Despite this official discouragement (suitably dressed up as Menzies' personal views and not official at all) there were some practical results, the first drips of a thaw. MI6's man on the spot, Commander Wilfred Dunderdale, would have more frequent meetings with Rivet and, from now on, to minimise the risk of compromise, Dunderdale would go under the cover-name 'Dolinoff'.

It was about time. The drumbeat of rearmament was sounding more and more like a *pas de charge*; it would be imprudent to assume that Hitler's aggressive posturing was only that. There was a real need by both parties to have some solid information to go on.

Bydgoszcz is a pleasant town in north-west Poland. Until 1918, it had been part of the Kaiser's Empire and called Bromberg. Bydgoszcz was the home town to Marian Rejewski and Irena Lewandowska. After their lengthy engagement and struggle to maintain the relationship over long distances, the couple had married on 30 June 1934, and Bydgoszcz was never far from their thoughts. Although they lived in Warsaw, Irena wanted to have the family around when her first child, Andrzej, was born in 1936 and thus Bydgoszcz became Andrzej's home town as well. It was the same when Janina, the Rejewskis' daughter, came along a couple of years later.

Bydgoszcz may be a pleasant place for a family, but, primarily because it was right in the middle of the Polish Corridor, it was also home to an out-station of Polish military intelligence. The head of Polish Secret Intelligence Station III was called Major Jan Żychoń and in 1938 Żychoń could sense the Nazi threat becoming stronger. In the summer of that year, one of his agents reported that in case of an imminent war the German Command intended to make changes to the way they used the Enigma machine. The information was reliable: it had come from an agent who was a member of the signal section of the German Air Force.[13]

September 1938 was a time of European crisis. It was six months after the absorption of Austria into the new German Reich, which had (as foreseen by Menzies) been a business taking only a few weeks. On 12 September 1938, Adolf Hitler made a speech in Nuremberg that voiced specious complaints about Czechoslovakian atrocities, aggression, belligerence, and so forth. There were riots in Czechoslovakia. Neville Chamberlain asked Hitler for a meeting: their first session at Berchtesgaden began on 15 September. The Czechoslovakian government found itself sidelined as the Germans, aided by the British and the French, carved up their country. Its borderlands were ceded to Germany, placing Czech defences behind German lines.

While Chamberlain was settling in at the Berghof on 15 September, the dramatic events that subsequently became known as the 'Munich crisis' became a crisis for the Enigma code-breakers of Pyry. The Germans changed the procedure for transmitting the settings of Enigma-enciphered telegrams. Up until then, all users of Enigma machines on a particular radio network had set their machines up the same way in the morning with what they called a 'ground setting' and then used the same ground setting all day to encipher the six-letter indicators which Rejewski had found so useful in his virtual dismantling of the machine. The use of a single, daily ground setting had given the Poles a substantial volume of material to work with each twenty-four hours, all of which was enciphered in the same way. From now on, however, there was a different ground setting for each message. The German authorities instructed their operators to arrange the three rotors afresh for every single message. There were 17,576 ways they could do that.

And the technical problems were not the real significance of this change in procedure. According to Major Żychón's agent, this change signified the imminence of war.

● ● ●

Like almost everyone else, the British had not really been paying attention. Britain had an Empire to protect and the Empire was protected by a navy and the navy was not threatened by Germany. Apart from a has-been backbencher called Winston Churchill, whose Cato-like croakings about Germany were thoroughly tedious, nobody in Britain wanted to get engaged in anything to do with defence in Europe.

So the British were not ready for a war, imminent or otherwise. Nor were they ready for a new alliance, particularly with the French. The Prime Minister, Neville Chamberlain, said that the French, 'never can keep a secret for more than half an hour' and thought that staff talks would recreate the insanity of 1914.[14] The one reliable thing about 1914 had been the network of alliances, which with the oiled efficiency of Edwardian engineering had swung into action when the starting lever was pulled. By contrast, in 1938 the old alliances were cold and the non-aggression pacts shifting and unreliable. French objectives were as clear to the British as a glass of pastis and as likely to have unwanted consequences. They wanted to pull the British into another continental entanglement and the way they would do this was via intelligence talks, which would become joint staff talks and then joint operations. And as to the Poles, since the fiasco over the Curzon Line during the Russo-Polish War, the British had been so unenthusiastic about relations with Poland that they could almost be considered hostile. When Sir Austen Chamberlain, half-brother of prime minister Neville, had been foreign secretary in the 1920s, he had said, 'for the Polish corridor, no British government ever will or ever can risk the bones of a British grenadier.'[15] British involvement in military operations to thwart Germany, it would seem, was wholly out of the question.

At the Government Code & Cypher School in London, though, it was more obvious that Germany was a threat, but the German Armed Forces Enigma was a closed book. Perhaps, given the new atmosphere of cooperation with the French, there might be a possibility of getting something that would help with Enigma? On 9 September 1938, Captain John Tiltman of GC&CS prepared a shopping list:

Can the French be asked to give us *all* the information they have with regard to the following points?

Full details of all devices additional to or differing from the market model.
What is the Army practice with regard to the following:-
Fitting new drums.
Changing the order of drums.
Moving the tyres (bands) on the drums ...[16]

Wilfred Dunderdale (cover-name Dolinoff) duly put the question to Colonel Rivet. The French had no hesitation in establishing cryptology cooperation with the British. It was an essential part of the plan, in fact, to develop a relationship that became so close that the British could not escape from it. The French opened the tap and a flood of information immediately began to flow across the Channel.

25 – *Renseignement a/s des moyens de chiffrement utilisés par la Wehrmacht* [Intelligence report on means of encipherment used by the Wehrmacht]
29 – *Gebrauchsanleitung für die Chiffriermaschine ENIGMA* [Guide to use of the Enigma cipher machine]
30 – *Schlüsselanleitung für die Chiffriermaschine ENIGMA* [Guide to settings of the Enigma cipher machine]
44 – *a/s de la machine à chiffrer ENIGMA (Marine-Modell)* [Concerning the Enigma cipher machine (Navy model)]
79 – *Renseignement sur l'organisation de la Section du Chiffre du R.K.M.* [Intelligence report on the organisation of the Cipher Section of the Reich Navy]
80 – *Renseignement sur l'organisation du Service d'écoute de la Marine allemande* [Intelligence report on the organisation of the Monitoring Service of the German Navy][17]

Along with reports under these titles, came many, many more. Gustave Bertand later wrote that 925 intelligence reports were sent to MI6 and GC&CS between September 1938 and August 1939. For each delivery, he obtained a receipt, signed by Dunderdale in the name of 'Dolinoff'.[18] The British code-breakers were enthusiastic. The materials were highly praised: 'of very great interest'; 'of very considerable value to us'; 'with these pinches [enemy material acquired by whatever means] came pictures and diagrams of the Steckered enigma, from which we were able to establish [what] previously had been only surmise'; 'the value ... was enormously enhanced when the French communicated to G.C. & C.S. in 1938 a series of documents on the German W/T networks'. The British, however, could not entirely stop themselves from being sniffy, also writing that 'French cryptography does not appear to be of the highest class'.[19]

The British code-breakers called these reports from France 'Scarlet Pimpernels'. The Pimpernels were typed using a purple ribbon and each of them was numbered, in red ink, in the top right-hand corner, in a characteristic French font. They were stamped TRÈS SECRET, also in red ink. No wonder the British thought that these *billets doux* evoked the secret communications with the French underground – sealed with a red monogram in the shape of a flower – as seen in the 1934 film of Baroness Orczy's novel.

Tiltman's 'shopping list' memo had been written days before Munich and only a week before the Germans made their changes to the Enigma operating procedures. If the British had been nowhere on German military Enigma before, they were even further in the dark now, despite the help they were getting from the Pimpernels. A face-to-face meeting with the French might provide even more information and it was also time for the British to trade something back in return for the Pimpernels. So on 21 October 1938, Alastair Denniston, the head of the Government Code & Cypher School, invited Bertrand to a meeting to take place in London in early November. The agenda: a British officer would give his theory of how the Germans communicated the set-up of their Enigma machines, along with a method of finding that set-up, as used before the 15 September change of procedure; what, technically, the September changes actually were; and the method of solving the commercial Enigma.[20] The British also agreed to supply copies of the intercepted German signals which they had picked up. They also had Tiltman's list of outstanding questions.

Not surprisingly, the French were unable to answer any of the questions which Knox – for it was he who was now the British officer dealing with Engima – had posed. But Bertrand knew who could. On

5 December 1938, Bertrand wrote to Denniston, saying that 'he had found someone who believed he could get access to an army Enigma machine' and suggesting that Denniston send across a questionnaire.[21] Bertrand never revealed the identity of his source and did not even describe French intelligence's relationship with Hans-Thilo Schmidt until 1972. But Bertrand was happy to mention 'the agent' again in his next letter to Denniston two weeks later. Rather than wait over a month for the possibility of new material arriving from Hans-Thilo Schmidt (the next meeting between Bertrand and his crucial source of intelligence on Engima did not, in fact, take place until 29 January 1939). Bertrand had another way of helping things along. Namely, to introduce the British to the Polish code-breakers.

> Dear Colonel [wrote Rivet to Menzies on 14 December], After his meeting in London, B hinted that a collaboration with Warsaw on technical areas could offer common advantages, and asked what you thought: you indicated your consent – leaving him to put things in hand – with the assurance that the sensitivities of each party would be paramount. Accordingly, we thought to bring together representatives of each Service in Paris, with a view to putting forward the results of current researches on radio traffic enciphered with the ENIGMA machine used by the WEHRMACHT – thinking that this occasion could be the prelude of a deeper collaboration, both in peace and in war ...[22]

The vital phrase in Rivet's letter to the British was the one about each Service being subject to its own rules about secrecy (*'avec l'assurance que la susceptibilité de chacun serait placée au-dessus de tout'*). Sharing raw materials like intercepts and the fruits of intelligence where the sources can be disguised, is one thing. Sharing know-how which might be turned against you is something completely different. Although the French had no particular code-breaking insights to impart, they were fully aware of how difficult the tri-party collaboration idea could be for their partners. And those partners were not even proper allies: the Franco-Polish pact had been on ice for years, while the British were still disengaged, notwithstanding the unofficial Pimpernel deal brokered by Menzies.

From the French perspective, the game was more subtle. Bertrand was finding out rather more than it might seem. Ostensibly, as French code-breaking activity was weak, French intelligence thrived on purchases. And what better currency in which to purchase intelligence than intelligence itself? The idea of bringing the Poles and the British together, through the agency of the French, would create a perfect arrangement, where the French, as brokers, could see what the British and the Poles were willing to share. In this context, Bertrand put two apparently innocent suggestions forward to his old friend and Polish equivalent, Gwido Langer. Time was pressing, so there seemed to be two options to speed things up. Option 1: let the Germans know that their traffic was being read and thereby get them to change the system. Option 2: if there was some hope of a breakthrough, get everyone round the table and share their knowledge.[23] Langer reacted as predicted. From the Polish perspective, Option 1 was out of the question – it would, at one blow, destroy years of success. But by agreeing to Option 2, Langer was in effect signalling (despite the word 'hope') that the Poles had a reason why they ruled out Option 1. Bertrand had found something out of great significance: the Poles must have made some progress with the machine. Now the stakes were higher. If the three countries could co-operate, perhaps they could break Enigma. The question now was whether either of the groups of guests would show their cards.

Above: The founders. Jan Kowalewski (seated, right), who founded the Polish code-breaking service during the Russo-Polish War, together with his successor as head of the service Franciszek Pokorny (seated left), Maksymilian Ciężki (standing right), other members of the service and a lieutenant from the Japanese Imperial Navy, in 1925. (Barbara Ciężka)

Left: Jadwiga and Antoni Palluth. The AVA company, run by cryptanalyst and engineer Antoni, built the machines which broke Enigma in the 1930s; Jadwiga faced down the Gestapo during the war. (Krystyna Palluth-Tunicka)

Wiktor Michałowski. Photographed in First World War German Army uniform alongside members of his family, Michałowski was one of the first to try to break the Enigma cipher. (Piotr Michałowski)

Above: Palac Saski 1. Marshal Józef Piłsudski takes the salute outside the headquarters of the Polish intelligence service on Independence Day 1926. (The Józef Piłsudski Institute, 238–246 King Street, London)

Left: L'homme à tout faire. Rex, the French intelligence service's spy handler and passport trafficker, whose mesmeric gaze kept the agents producing the precious goods. (Christie Books)

Left: The magician. Gustave Bertrand pictured in 1934, shortly after the crucial handover of stolen Enigma documents. (© Service historique de la Défense, CHA Vincennes, GR 14YD 755)

Below: An expensive holiday. Hans-Thilo Schmidt relaxing with his wife; the holidays and other habits were funded by the French in payment for stolen secrets. (Gisela Schmidt)

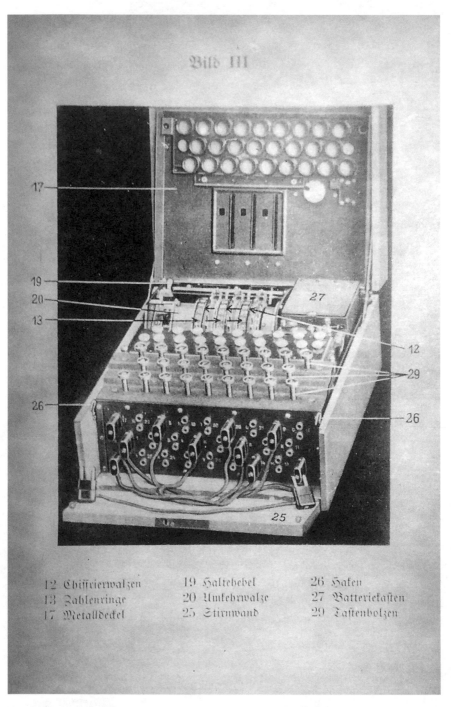

Bild III

12 Chiffrierwalzen	19 Haltehebel	26 Haken
13 Zahlenringe	20 Umkehrwalze	27 Batteriekasten
17 Metalldeckel	25 Stirnwand	29 Tastenbolzen

Secrets from the bathroom. A page from the Enigma operating manual, showing the special features of the Wehrmacht model, as photographed by Gustave Bertrand (© Service historique de la Défense, CHA Vincennes, DE 2016 ZB 25/5)

The code-breakers: (*Top left*) Marian Rejewski; (*top right*) Marian and Irina Rejewski in Warsaw in 1935; (*below left*) Jerzy Różicki; (*below right*) Henryk Zygalski. (Janina Sylwestrzak/The Enigma Press)

Dilly Knox, the British code-breaker who made a successful attack on the no-plugboard Enigma before the war.

The Commander. Alastair Denniston, who had to keep Knox from upsetting the fragile X-Y-Z co-operation. (Reproduced with kind permission of the Director, GCHQ)

007. Wilfred Dunderdale, aka 'Biffy', was the liaison officer behind Anglo-French intelligence.

Bomba. A replica, on display at Bletchley Park, of the Polish Bomba, the first machine designed to find Enigma settings. (© Andy Stagg)

Bunker in the woods. The unassuming building in the woods at Pyry, beneath which the code-breakers worked and where the July 1939 revelations took place, photographed during the German occupation of Poland.

Hotel Bristol. The British delegation to the Pyry conference stayed in Warsaw's poshest hotel. (Author's collection)

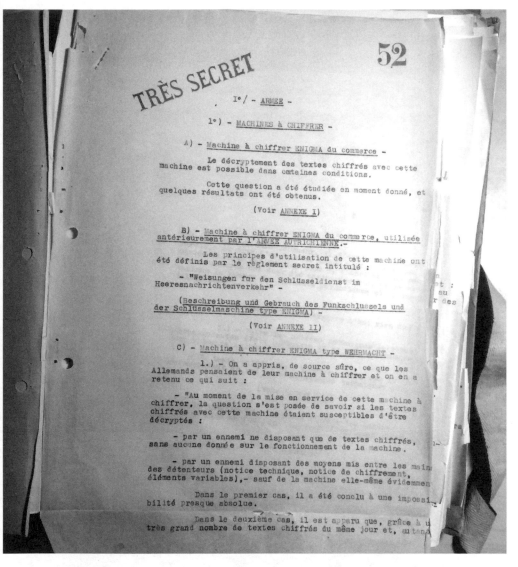

TRÈS SECRET

I°/ - ARMEE -

1°) - MACHINES à CHIFFRER -

A) - Machine à chiffrer ENIGMA du commerce -

Le décryptement des textes chiffrés avec cette machine est possible dans certaines conditions.

Cette question a été étudiée en moment donné, et quelques résultats ont été obtenus.

(Voir ANNEXE I)

B) - Machine à chiffrer ENIGMA du commerce, utilisée antérieurement par l'ARMEE AUTRICHIENNE.-

Les principes d'utilisation de cette machine ont été définis par le règlement secret intitulé :

- "Weisungen für den Schlüsseldienst im Heeresnachrichtenverkehr" -

(Beschreibung und Gebrauch des Funkschlüssels und der Schlüsselmaschine type ENIGMA) -

(Voir ANNEXE II)

C) - Machine à chiffrer ENIGMA type WEHRMACHT -

1.) - On a appris, de source sûre, ce que les Allemands pensaient de leur machine à chiffrer et on en a retenu ce qui suit :

- "Au moment de la mise en service de cette machine à chiffrer, la question s'est posée de savoir si les textes chiffrés avec cette machine étaient susceptibles d'être décryptés :

- par un ennemi ne disposant que de textes chiffrés, sans aucune donnée sur le fonctionnement de la machine.

- par un ennemi disposant des moyens mis entre les mains des détenteurs (notice technique, notice de chiffrement, éléments variables),- sauf de la machine elle-même évidemment

Dans le premier cas, il a été conclu à une impossi-bilité presque absolue.

Dans le deuxième cas, il est apparu que, grâce à u très grand nombre de textes chiffrés du même jour et, autan

Pimpernel No. 52 (© Service historique de la Défense, CHA Vincennes, DE 2016 ZB 25/5)

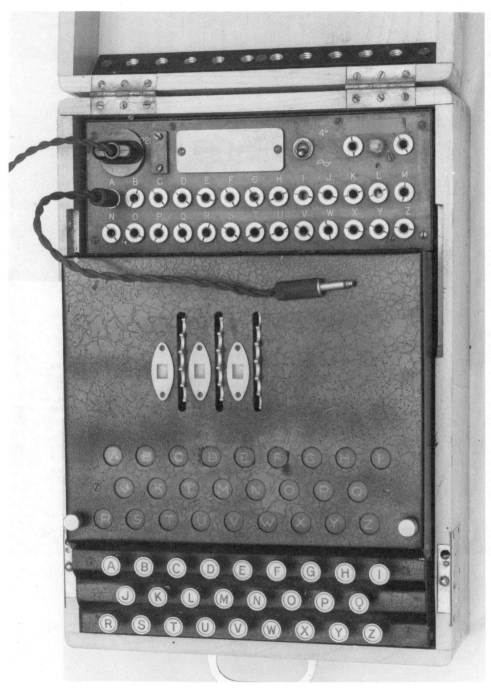

Enigma reborn. A reconstituted Enigma machine, made in France to the Polish design based on Marian Rejewski's reverse-engineering. (The Józef Piłsudski Institute, 238–246 King Street, London)

Der OBERSTE BEFEHLSHABER bei seinen Truppen in Warschau

Palac Saski 2. Führer Adolf Hitler takes the salute in October 1939, presumably unaware that the Enigma machine had been reverse-engineered in the building behind him.

14 – Gretz
Armainvilliers
Château de Vignolles

Souillet, éditeur, Gretz

The Château de Vignolles. Located near Paris, the elegant château was the home of the exiled Polish code-breakers until the invasion of France in 1940. (Author's collection)

Before the deluge. Left to right: Gwido Langer, Gustave Bertrand, and Kenneth 'Pinky' Macfarlan in the sunshine of the phoney war.

Team photo. Michałowski (1), Smoleński (2), Szachno (3), Paszkowski (4), Ciężki (5), Sylwester Palluth (6), Gaca (7), Langer (8), Antoni Palluth (9), Bertrand (10), Marie Bertrand (11), Graliński (12), Captain Honoré Louis (13), Różycki (14), Rejewski (15), Fokczyński (16), Zygalski (17), photographed in 1941. The others are unidentified. (Anna Zygalska-Cannon)

REPUBLIQUE FRANÇAISE

SAUF-CONDUIT

(Partie à détacher)

Indication de l'Autorité qui a délivré le sauf-conduit : B.M.C. 19ª Région

Sauf-Conduit N° 24

Valable pour (1) Un voyage , du 7 Septembre au 8 Octobre 19 40
(Dates en toutes lettres)

Mode de locomotion autorisé : (2) Chemin de fer Compagnie Maritime

Localités ou périmètres de circulation autorisés :

M. MULLER Maximilien

N° de la carte d'identité : Charleville N° 10.609 Nationalité : Nationalité Française

Profession : Directeur Commercial

Né le : 24 Décembre 1898 à : Strasbourg (Bas Rhin)

Domicilié à (adresse complète) : à Alger Hotel de Bordeaux.

Est autorisé à faire usage du présent sauf-conduit dans les conditions ci-dessus indiquées.

Fait à Alger , le 7 Septembre 19 40

Le Général de Corps d'Armée
Com... (Autorité qui a délivré le Sauf-Conduit)

Signature du Titulaire P. O. Le Chef du Bureau Militaire de
Circulation de la 19ª Région

Alexis Semenoff

Autorisé à conduire l marque n°

Carte grise délivrée le à M par

Permis de conduire n° délivré le par

Sauf dispositions spéciales, le présent sauf-conduit servira de permis de séjour dans les limites des dates fixées. Si le sauf-conduit, une fois périmé, n'a pas été retiré au porteur à la gare de retour, il est à rendre par l'intéressé à l'autorité qui l'a délivré.

(1) Mettre, selon le cas, la mention « un » ou « plusieurs ». Le retour est de droit, sauf mention spéciale. (Voir au verso pour les séjours dépassant 24 heures).
(2) Modes de locomotion autorisés : à pied, à cheval, en voiture hippomobile, à bicyclette, en chemin de fer, en véhicule automobile ou en bateau affectés à un transport public.

21

Fake ID. Maksymilian Ciężki becomes 'Maximilien Muller', born in Strasbourg, for his safe conduct to Algiers. (The Józef Piłsudski Institute, 238–246 King Street, London)

5

HOW THEY BROUGHT THE GOOD NEWS FROM GHENT TO AIX

I sprang to the stirrup, and Joris, and he;
I galloped, Dirck galloped, we galloped all three;
'Good speed!' cried the watch, as the gate-bolts undrew;
'Speed!' echoed the walls to us galloping through;
Behind shut the postern, the lights sank to rest,
And into the midnight we galloped abreast.

R.B. Browning
'How They Brought the Good News from Ghent to Aix'

In 1938, Antoni Palluth began to receive some strange commissions in his capacity as partner in the AVA radio and precision electrical equipment business. One of the strangest was to build, on behalf of the Biuro Szyfrów, a sex machine.

The machine had six wheel-like objects, arranged in two sets of three. The machine also had a bank of switches and lightbulbs and a variable resistor to ensure that the current did not blow the bulbs if only one or two were lit up. Once again, the wheels were synthetic Enigma rotors, but this machine was not a duplicate Enigma machine.

The machine was nicknamed the 'sex machine' because its job was to find females.[1] Roughly 40 per cent of the time, a repeated letter showed up in the encrypted version of the six-letter indicator sequence which the Germans used to tell the recipient of a radio message how to set up the Enigma machine for the incoming signal. These repeats were called females as a play on words, since in Polish they were called *samiczki* for 'the same', while *samica* means 'female'.

Officially the device was called the cyclometer, because its job was to find the length of cycles (trails of letters) that could be traced from message 'indicators' enciphered using the same rotors orientated in the same starting-position. As early as 1932, Marian Rejewski had noticed that indicators had a characteristic cycle-length depending on the combination of rotors being used. From the catalogue of characteristics – one for each of the 17,576 possible orientations of three rotors, multiplied by six for the six different ways you could put three rotors into the machine – it was possible to narrow down, even to identify exactly, which three rotors were in use. The cyclometer was designed to speed up the process for matching cycle-lengths to a rotor setting by lighting up a number of bulbs corresponding to the length of the cycle. Single-letter cycles were particularly prized, because they could be seen in a single intercepted message, giving the code-breakers a quick way to create a short-list of the possible rotor settings. Single-letter cycles equate to 'females', and so in time cyclometers came to be called sex machines.*

Palluth received an even odder commission later in the year. This time he was asked to make a 'bomb' and this time the peculiar name was not even a nickname. The Biuro Szyfrów was not getting into explosives and AVA was not an armaments factory: the odd name was something the code-breakers had given to a new cryptological device.

We will probably never know for sure how the cryptological bomb (in Polish, *bomba*) came to be given that name. There are various theories.[2] One is that it made a ticking noise, as it had rotors, just like Enigma rotors, which were driven around all 17,576 possible positions by a central motor and it stopped when it found a possible solution to the problem of how the Germans had set up their Enigma machines for the day. Another is that the machine was designed while the Poles went out, as was their habit, for an afternoon dessert. They enjoyed chocolate-coated ice cream, a famous black spherical confection designed in France to look like the explosive and thus called a *bombe*. A further possibility is that *bomba* is a colloquial exclamation when something really good is done. Maybe all three are right. The

---

*   See Appendix for a more detailed explanation.

code-breakers themselves seem to have treated it as something of a secret. Różycki got blamed for naming the machine and Rejewski said it was called bomb 'for lack of a better idea'.

What the *bomba* did was to exploit the doubly-enciphered indicator once again. By grinding mechanically through all the 17,576 possible rotor positions, it could check whether there was a single position where the machine could give out the observed cipher-text at all six positions of the indicator. If so, that implied the choice of rotors, their order in the machine and the start position for the message. It was a novel approach to the increasingly complex problem of Enigma code-breaking: using technology to attack technology.

● ● ●

The British had not begun to consider the possibilities of machinery to tackle machine ciphers. They were still stuck on a more fundamental question, which was how the Wehrmacht version of the Enigma was internally wired. Fortunately, they were less stuck on the question of how to respond to Gustave Bertrand's invitation to a conference. On this technical matter of signals intelligence, there was little to lose. The Pimpernels were chock-full of valuable material on German radio networks, information gathered from Polish listening stations, which could not be obtained in any other way than through the channel established by Bertrand. The Poles or the French could possibly teach the British something about Enigma. So it was agreed. Commander Denniston would go to Paris and meet with Bertrand and the Poles. To show the Poles and the French just what could be done on the technical side, Denniston would bring on his version of the *artillerie lourde*.

The British were going to bring out Knox.

● ● ●

For the Polish Biuro Szyfrów, the decision to go to Bertrand's conference was prompted by a swathe of radical changes to Enigma encipherment methods brought in by the Germans in the weeks before the invitation arrived. Despite mechanising the tedious, mind-numbing repetition of code-breaking routines, keeping up with the Germans had become much harder. Until the autumn of 1938, the Biuro Szyfrów had matched them pace for pace. But what came at the end of 1938 almost finished them off.

Another change – one far nastier than the decision to re-set the rotors to fresh starting positions for every Enigma-enciphered message – was sprung by the Germans three months after Munich, on 15 December 1938. Major Żychoń's agent had warned them it was coming. Two new rotors were added to those available to the German Enigma users, giving them much more flexibility as to which three to pick and in what order to put them into the machine.[3] The first problem for the Polish team was to discover the internal wiring of the new rotors – that is, to reverse-engineer them by cryptanalysis. And then copies would be needed (made by the AVA factory) to give their *bomba*s a chance.

Fortunately, while working intensely in their bunker beneath the Number One listening station at Pyry, the Poles realised that the *Sicherheitsdienst,* one of Nazi Germany's numerous security organisations, had made a screw-up when the new operating procedures were applied by the Wehrmacht the previous September. In a typical display of inter-service independence, the SD had continued as before while the Wehrmacht changed to using a fresh starting position for every message. When the SD stayed on the old system of a single start position for all messages of the day even after the two new Enigma rotors were introduced in December, it was a fatal error. Because with sufficient quantities of messages enciphered at the same setting, the Poles could use the reverse-engineering technique discovered by Marian Rejewski to unravel the wirings of the new rotors. So, for the time being, the Poles were not left behind by the new German encryption techniques. The question remaining was whether their technology could keep pace with their brainwork.[4]

The technological problem arising from the use of two new rotors by the Germans was that the number of possible ways to put three rotors into the Enigma machine had increased tenfold. The cyclometers ordered from AVA were desperately needed to assess the characteristics of all the new rotor combinations, of which there were nearly 950,000. That was bad, but the biggest blow was to the *bomba* machine. Each *bomba* – the code-breakers' most up-to-date AVA-made technology – was dedicated to testing a single combination and order of rotors. On the top of the *bomba* were six axles, each mounting the same three synthetic Enigma rotors in the same order. To carry out an exhaustive test of all possible rotor combinations, the Biuro needed a *bomba* machine for each one. With six combinations, that was six machines. But five rotors meant sixty combinations and that meant sixty *bomba* machines, which was way beyond the resources of the Biuro. There was a blackout. Except when they were very lucky, the Poles could no longer read messages enciphered with Enigma.

The sixty-permutation problem could be solved with more technology, but the Second Department's technology budget had been blown on the Radio Station G project, that massive Jedynka radio tower which was a monumental daily presence as the code-breakers went to work in their bunker in the Kabaty woods. Maksymilian Ciężki's team could only soldier on, slowly compiling a new catalogue of characteristics and using their limited *bomba* capacity to get some results when by chance they got the right combination of rotors on to the *bomba*s early enough.

On top of the message-specific ground setting and the additional rotors, the Wehrmacht made another change on New Year's Day, 1939. From now on they would use ten connecting cables on the plugboard. Now only six of the twenty-six letters of the alphabet would remain unchanged by the plugboard, instead of twelve. This was a disaster for the techniques previously employed by the Poles: the card catalogue of permutations was useless and even the use of the *bomba*s was frustrated. This time the Germans had outmarched the Poles. Without a radically different approach, the Poles would be locked out of Enigma permanently.

In early 1939, with only one-tenth of the machine capacity they needed, the results being obtained by Maksymilian Ciężki's German section of the Biuro Szyfrów were a woeful fraction of what they had achieved the previous year. From a success rate of 70 per cent of messages read before the Czechoslovak crisis they were now producing 10 per cent of their previous output.[5] The Enigma was slipping away from them. To get back on form, they needed help. The French conference, with its subtext of wider cooperation, made good sense. Colonel Tadeusz Pełczyński, head of the Second Department, was persuaded.

The successes of the Enigma team could be the 'Polish contribution to the common cause of defence and divulged to our future allies.'[6] And at the right time too.

Under no obligation to reveal anything sensitive, the Poles had nothing to lose by taking up Captain Bertrand's suggestion of a conference. As well as possibly leading to advances on their challenge to Enigma, such a conference would enable the Poles to see what the British knew and thus judge the value of their potential contribution to an allied defence initiative. So it was now the turn of Gwido Langer and Maksymilian Ciężki to get on a train and go to Paris.

● ● ●

The British were characteristically snobbish and ill-behaved at the Paris meeting. Hugh Foss was there – the boffin who had previously attempted to crack Enigma in the 1920s – together with Denniston and Knox. According to his account:

> The French cryptanalysts, in January 1939, showed Denniston, Knox and myself their methods, which were even more clumsy than mine, ending with a flourish and dramatic '*Voici la méthode française*'. They asked Knox if he had understood and he replied in a very bored way '*Pas du tout*' [not in the least], meaning (I think) '*Pas tout à fait*' [not entirely]. Denniston and I rushed in with some conciliatory remark. The French were, however, delighted with the rods when Knox explained them and by the next interview had made a set of 'réglettes' of their own. At these interviews the Poles were mainly silent but one of them gave a lengthy description in German of the recovery of throw-on indicators when the operators used pronounceable settings. During this exposition Knox kept muttering to Denniston, 'But this is what Tiltman did,' while Denniston hushed him and told him to listen politely. Knox went and looked out of the window.[7]

The Poles kept their cards tight against their chests ('*The Poles.* Practical knowledge of QWERTZU enigma nil'); the British had found the

French, with their meagre cryptanalytic resources and achievements more impressive ('*The French.* Captain Braconnier [actually Braquenié]. Quite capable').[8] Bertrand would probably have been pleased with that. He himself noted, with barely suppressed pleasure, that his rival organisation in French intelligence, the Section du Chiffre, had sent a so-called expert for the first day who had declined to attend the second day of the conference.

Know-how changed hands, but in tiny amounts. The British had heard definitively from Ciężki that the Germans had added two new rotors to the range available for use. In turn, they had shown the French and the Poles Knox's rodding technique and his own method for reverse-engineering the wiring of rotors using only a collection of messages enciphered on the same setting. The French had demonstrated that they were working on the same problems as the British and had offered to ask their secret agent to get hold of answers to their principal questions.[9] These were:

1) How the plugboard was connected to the entry ring where the current enters the first rotor (a problem which the British called the 'QWERTZU' and the French called the 'couronne fixe'. The fact that the British called the problem the 'QWERTZU' reveals their unfamiliarity with the machine. QWERTZU is the layout of keys on a German typewriter, but between the keyboard of a military Enigma machine and the entry ring lies the plugboard. The problem was how the plugboard, not the keyboard, was connected to the entry ring. In the autumn of 1938 the British were still trying to understand what the plugboard was).
2) The interior wiring of each rotor.
3) The wiring of the reflector.

The Poles did not let on that they knew the answers to all these things and had already known them (apart from the wiring of the two new rotors) for several years. Although nothing much had been learned, it was agreed that if something came up – if '*il y a du nouveau*' – the others would be notified. But the sharing of know-how was not the point of the meeting – Colonel Rivet had made that clear in his invitation – the point was to initiate a relationship. The most important result of the meeting, and the primary objective sought by the French, was that certain key people had been given a chance to size each other up.

Soon after the Paris meeting, on 18 January 1939, Dunderdale, using his cover-name 'Dolinoff', signed a receipt for Pimpernel number 212, the French note of the Tripartite Conference. Pimpernel number 213 was the agreed questionnaire for the French agent (i.e. Hans-Thilo Schmidt). Now the three countries' intelligence services knew each other, the French could broker exchanges between the other two, all the while improving their own relative position.

Pimpernel number 211, again, signed by Dunderdale, recorded the decision for French, British and Polish intelligence to collaborate against Enigma and the shorthand by which the three countries were to be known:[10]

> *TRÈS SECRET. – NOTE pour 'Y' – Pour plus de commodité et de discretion, il est proposé d'utiliser désormais les abréviations suivantes* [For greater convenience and discretion, use of the following abbreviations is proposed]:
> *X = PARIS*
> *Y = LONDRES*
> *Z = VARSOVIE*

Documents and knowledge began to move between the three services. In May 1939, X asked where Z might have got to on Enigma: a four-page paper in German came back, explaining how the doubly-enciphered indicator could be exploited.[11] The Poles almost certainly thought they were giving away nothing that the British had not already figured out for themselves. Nothing really vital was being shared. That was not the point. The trust was being built and from that trust developed the most consequential intelligence-sharing arrangement of World War Two.

The partnership of X, Y and Z had been born.

• • •

In January 1939, Hitler's government began work on tearing up the Munich settlement. On 15 March 1939, the remainder of the Czech part of Czechoslovakia was seized and a puppet government was installed in the rump of Slovakia. Poland was therefore enveloped by Germany and its clients on three sides: the west, the north and now the south. Hitler's response to the outcry which followed was to seize Memel, a port on the Lithuanian coast, on 23 March. Memel, just to the north of East Prussia, may not have been part of Poland, but any threat to Lithuania was bound to elicit strong feelings in Poland. Centuries ago, the Grand Duchy of Lithuania had been united with the Kingdom of Poland to constitute the largest and strongest empire in central and eastern Europe. In the post-war period Józef Piłsudski had tried to recreate a defensive bloc including Lithuania. Although his plan had not come to fruit, the Poles were bound to see a threat to Lithuania as a challenge to their own interest. It did not take genius to see that the moves on Czechoslovakia and now on Lithuania posed a most serious threat to Poland. On the day Memel was captured by the Germans, the Polish Army mobilised.

Appeasement had failed. As Britain saw it, Germany's power was now free from limits. The road south-east led Germany to limitless natural resources and friendly governments that would supply them. Dismantling Czechoslovakia had, in practice, dismantled Britain's only defence against Germany, namely the threat of blockade. It was time for a new policy. It was time to talk tough.

On 31 March 1939, a thin man with an uncomfortable collar rose in the House of Commons in London to do the tough talking. Prime Minister Chamberlain stated:

> in the event of any action which clearly threatened Polish independence, and which the Polish government accordingly considered it vital to resist with their national forces, His Majesty's Government would feel themselves bound at once to lend the Polish Government all support in their power ... I may add that the French Government have authorised me to make it plain that they stand in the same position.'[12]

The Enigma changes of 1938 had been signal enough to Poland that Germany planned war. Now, it was the turn of the French to hear the threatening drumbeat. Hans-Thilo Schmidt was the most effective, the most informative, the best value spy the French ever had. As 'Asche' he furnished not only code-breaking materials but top-level news about the thinking of the German high command. There was a meeting between Schmidt and his handlers early in 1939, followed by a series of letters in invisible ink, which showed that Hitler was simply ignoring the Munich Agreement. Colonel Louis Rivet, head of French military intelligence, received a letter in secret ink on 27 May 1939, reporting on a conference held by Hitler at which it was decreed that Poland would be attacked whenever the occasion presented itself.

The French and British statements of March were no doubt encouraging to the Polish government, though their worth was difficult to judge. Hitler, for one, was not impressed. On 28 April 1939, the German non-aggression pacts with Poland and Britain were unilaterally rescinded. On 9 June another secret ink letter arrived in Paris from Schmidt. This one was significant enough for Rivet to note it in his diary: *attention à la fin d'août.*[13] There it was. The Germans were going to present their own occasion and attack Poland at the end of August.

United, the new allies might be able to face down the German Army's 100-plus divisions. While Poland could call on thirty infantry divisions plus reserves, the French Army was three times the size, even ignoring those troops stationed outside metropolitan France. Britain had only a meagre ten divisions, but the world's largest navy and a growing air force. The Polish state, however, faced the same problem that the French had been facing for years: to convert polite diplomatic blandishments into joint staff talks and a credible plan of defence. To bring the allies to the table, Poland needed something valuable to put up as a stake.

There was one asset which could be contributed on the Polish side to make Britain–France–Poland a meaningful alliance. Although this vital intelligence was of priceless value in the struggle with Germany, the cost of parting with it, even to a trusted ally of long standing, was not to be taken lightly. In the Europe of the 1930s alliances changed with the seasons, friends rapidly changed into foes. Divulging the golden secret of Enigma would be extremely dangerous, a desperate measure even. The British and the French had proved, in the January meeting in Paris, that they were far behind the Poles. So the contribution would be of real value. The allies might be able to solve the technology resources problem as well. So the Poles would do this dangerous, desperate, unprecedented thing, and teach the French and the British how to break Enigma.

● ● ●

On 30 June 1939, Gustave Bertrand received a telegram from Gwido Langer. *Il y a du nouveau.*[14] Something was up; the Poles wanted another conference. And, of all people, they specifically wanted to see Knox.

Rousing the interest of the sceptical British team would certainly be hard. Knox and Denniston did not think their trip to Paris had been much use. The Poles had been friendly enough, but there was nothing of any technical interest to show for it. On another level, the meeting had been a great success. The Poles had sized up Knox. They had seen the light of his genius, despite the language barrier, the mutual unpronounceability of names, and the cultural gulf between an academic classicist and career army officers like Langer and Ciężki. Although there was no real exchange of detail, enough had transpired to give them the confidence that the British knew what they were working with, even though it was apparent that they had not yet got anywhere with the Wehrmacht Enigma.

Knox was not in the best of moods. Another journey to see the incompetent Poles, with the bumptious and only slightly less incompetent French in tow? Worse, this journey was going to be longer. Not just the boat-train, but a horrible *wagon-lit* carriage all the way across Nazi Germany. Days and days of it, all the way to Warsaw. But the Poles had asked for Knox specifically and so Knox had had to go. Denniston had planned to send Tiltman instead of going himself,[15] but Knox's behaviour on the previous occasion suggested that he needed a minder. When you thought about it, the only candidate for that particular job was Denniston himself, who, having known Knox for twenty years, was the only one in the GC&CS who could actually face Knox down and tell him what was what. Thus, Denniston was on the train too, trying to make the best of what they both knew was likely to be their last look at Germany before the conflict began.

By special request of the Admiralty, a third man joined the party. The third man went by air, which implied some sort of special importance. He was introduced as 'Sandwich'. The Poles were duly impressed. They thought the mysterious personage going under such an obvious cover-name as 'Professor Sandwich' might be 'C' (the head of MI6) or, more likely, his deputy, Stuart Menzies, who seemed to be running C's show in Europe. By contrast, Henri Braquenié, Bertrand's own deputy, thought it was hilarious. Marian Rejewski recalled, 'Braquenié nudged me with his elbow and said: "Sandwich – his name is Sandwich!"'[16] Braquenié understood Professor Sandwich to be the Earl of Sandwich, descendant of an eighteenth-century First Lord of the Admiralty and inventor of a form of fast food. To send an aristocratic stuffed shirt with a silly name would perfectly fit the way the British did things.

The identity of the third man remained mysterious for many decades, but in truth there was no mystery whatever. Denniston had told his allies exactly who he was. The British had no means of covering the radio traffic of the German Navy on the Polish side of the Kiel canal, leaving a sizeable gap in their strategically vital understanding of German naval operations. So the Admiralty placed great value on those Pimpernels which described the German radio nets along the Baltic. As this information came straight from Poland, they wanted their own radio man, Commander Humphrey Sandwith RN, to be at the party. Although the cryptanalytic liaison was bound to be a washout, information of real value might be obtained about radio, changes to the way the Germans were doing things, intelligence about call signs, naval strengths and deployments, and there was even a possibility that the Poles might provide copies of messages they had intercepted.[17]

The grumpy Knox and his two companions checked into the best hotel in Warsaw's old town, The Bristol. At 7 a.m. on Wednesday 26 July 1939, a car came to collect them and whisked them off, past the Belvedere Palace, through the suburbs, out to the woods to the south of the city. They were being taken to Polish intelligence's most secret installation, the number one radio intelligence site, the Pyry bunker.

Within the bunker, there was to be no stepping around the subject, as had occurred in Paris with the courtly dance of secrecy. Here they got straight down to it, albeit with a certain amount of characteristic Polish military formality which irritated the British delegation (Denniston's description is of 'pompous declarations' at a 'full dress conference'). Ciężki dropped the bombshell almost at once. The Poles had cracked Enigma. Years ago. They knew the wiring of the rotors. They were able to find the settings used by the Germans to set up the machine so that the cipher changed every day. They had done the reverse-engineering by pure mathematics and they were using machinery to discover the rotors in use and the daily settings. Here were the men who had done it and here were the machines.

Bertrand and Braquenié were open-mouthed with amazement. So, evidently, were the British, described by Braquenié as *les anglais idiots*. How feeble seemed Knox's little rods, as described in Paris, against the technological approach being used by the Poles:

> I confess [wrote Denniston] I was unable to understand completely the lines of reasoning but when, as seemed part of the conference, we were taken down to an underground room full of electric equipment and introduced to the 'bombs' I did then grasp the results of their reasoning and their method of solving the daily key [Enigma settings]. Knox accompanied us throughout but maintained a stony silence and was obviously extremely angry about something.[18]

Knox had reason to be angry. The Poles' claim to have used mathematics was ludicrous. Knox knew the mathematician at King's in Cambridge who had been working on the Enigma problem for a year now and even he hadn't got anywhere. Knox was suspicious. It had to be a 'pinch' – something acquired, through spying, purchase or stealth, or even all three. How else had they found the QWERTZU – that all-important wiring between the plugboard and the rotors? Explain that one? Well, actually, that had just been an inspired guess. They'd tried ABCDEFG … and it had worked. Knox's discontent grew. It could not have been worse. One of Knox's own staff had suggested that very idea and he had pooh-poohed it. Knox retreated into one of his black silences.

When they got into the car for the ride back, Knox's frustration exploded:

He suddenly let himself go and, assuming that no one understood any English, raged and raved that they were lying to us now as in Paris. The whole thing was a fraud that he kept repeating. They never worked it out. They pinched it years ago and have followed developments as anyone could but they must have bought it or pinched it.'

Perhaps Bertrand and Braquenié did not need fluent English to get the gist of Knox's outburst. Denniston was beside himself with shame. Priceless intelligence was being laid out for them and yet the meeting was going about as badly as could be imagined.

Back at the Bristol, Knox went to his room while Denniston and Sandwith tried, together with Bertrand, to salvage something of the plan for the following day. Upstairs, meanwhile, Knox was still furious. Ordinary folk who have something to say just say it. But Knox did not belong to the category of ordinary folk. He grabbed some notepaper from the desk and spilled out his bile in a letter to Denniston, who was, after all, just the occupant of a nearby room. Denniston, being altogether a calm and mild person, instead of crumpling this piece of ire and consigning it to the waste basket, kept it, and after his return to London, he filed it, where it is still available to see in the National Archives:

My dear Alistair,

Let's get this straight.

(a) The Poles have got the <u>machine to Sept 15th</u> 38 out by luck. As I have said only Mrs B.B. had seriously contemplated the equation A=1 B=2. Had she worked on the crib we should be teaching them ...

(c) Their <u>machine for determining</u> all ciphers ... <u>may</u> be good. If we are going to read these we should give it a detailed study: if not, we only want the broadest outline of its electrical principles.

(d) ... Even the principle of electrical selection must be viewed with distrust ...

I am fairly clear that Schensky [Ciężki] knows very little about the machine + may try to conceal facts from us. The young men seem very capable and honest.

A.D.K.[19]

Writing the letter seems to have expunged the poison from Knox. On the next day at Pyry, which Denniston and Sandwith must have dreaded, he was much calmer. Cieżki brought back in Rejewski, Różycki and Zygalski and the demeanour of all three was emollient. They continued to impress Knox with their technical ability and especially Zygalski, because he had some English to add to the quatsch of German and French being spoken. The more detail they gave on their machines – the cyclometer and the *bomba* – the more Knox was ready to listen to a thing not of his invention. Knox would return to London knowing that, possibly for the first time in his life, he had met his intellectual match.

August 1939 became a time for thank-yous and apologies:

My dear Bertrand [wrote Menzies on 1 August 1939] Having just seen [Dunderdale] on his arrival from Paris, he has told me about the huge success of the combined visit to Warsaw, and I wish immediately to take the opportunity of letting you know how appreciative I am of your role in arranging the trip.[20]

My dear Bertrand [wrote Denniston on 3 August 1939] It's possible that you understood my great difficulty – Knox. He is a man of extreme intelligence, who does not know the word 'collaborate'. Outside work, you have no doubt observed that he is a kind boy liked by everyone. In the office, he's something else. In Warsaw I had some painful scenes with him ...[21]

Serdecznie dziękujęza współpracę i cierpliwość [wrote Knox to the Poles on 1 August 1939: sincere thanks for your cooperation and patience]. *Çi inclus (a) des petits batons (b) un souvenir d'Angleterre.*[22]

Knox's enclosures with his note were, in a sense, a type of code. He sent the Poles some of his rods and a silk scarf, printed with a horse racing scene. Knox's hidden message was an acknowledgement that the Poles had won the race, by a mile or more, his little strips of paper outridden by mathematics and machinery.

The Poles had not only explained the wiring of the Engima machine and its rotors but given over the plans to their *bomba*. The *bomba* was possibly the most impressive demonstration of Polish talent. While the British had themselves devised a method to find the wiring of rotors, to use it they first needed the unknown QWERTZU. Without a 'pinch' of their own, there had been no prospect of finding the QWERTZU before that meeting at Pyry. As things turned out, the first, incomplete, 'pinch' of pieces of Enigma hardware during hostilities occurred in early 1940. The Polish revelations had shortened the British attack on Enigma by at least a year.[23]

Now Knox had some work to do. His first step was to explain what he had learned in Warsaw to Alan Turing. Alan Turing had been recruited as a reserve staffer for the Government Code & Cypher School in the late summer of 1938, when Alastair Denniston had done the rounds of Cambridge colleges on the lookout for 'men of the Professor type' to add to an emergency list of standby code-breakers.[24] Turing was a mathematician from King's College who was making a small reputation as a logician with an interest in machinery for solving mathematical problems. They hadn't thought about machines for breaking ciphers at GC&CS before the Pyry disclosures in that underground chamber, even though Turing had been sent on a course to learn about the Enigma problem in January 1939 and had been mulling over the challenge ever since. In the late summer of 1939, at Knox's house, the Polish secrets, the theory of cycles and the *bomba* were revealed to Alan Turing.

● ● ●

The *Golden Arrow* boat-train squealed asthmatically into Victoria Station during the evening of 16 August 1939. The presence of a VIP on board required the attendance of a very senior officer of MI6 to meet the train. Thus Stewart Menzies was at the station, dressed for dinner, with (as subtle as it was appropriate for the occasion) the tiny rosette of the *Légion d'honneur* in his lapel. As the train ground to a halt, Gustave Bertrand stepped from it into the cloud of steam. That their host was wearing a dinner jacket and the rosette was a fine touch, instantly appreciated by Bertrand, head of the escorting party: *accueil triomphal*, he said.[25] The importance of the VIP could not be overstated. The escorting party included Wilfred Dunderdale and his number two, cover-name 'Uncle

Tom', in fact an oversize MI6 volunteer whose business connections helpfully made border problems disappear. All these preparations were vital, for Bertrand's VIP was a large wooden box, containing a kind of Wehrmacht Enigma machine: one of two Polish replicas donated to the British at the Pyry conference, which had been sent across to Paris in the diplomatic bag.

In a different train, on the way back from Warsaw the previous month, Denniston could be forgiven if he felt a little *triomphal* himself. As the train galloped across the plains of Prussia, he felt a little like the surviving rider in Robert Browning's poem. As in the ride from Ghent to Aix, Dirck and Joris had fallen out of the party. Sandwith had gone back in his plane and Knox had had some trouble with his visa at the border and had been made to return to the consulate at Poznań to sort it out. So Denniston was on his own, thinking over the good news which he was carrying from Warsaw to London. His piece of paper, unlike Chamberlain's, listed seventeen items of enduring worth which the Poles had given up voluntarily.[26] The good news in his briefcase vindicated his decision to recruit mathematicians like Alan Turing. Maybe, just maybe, through the X-Y-Z liaison created by Bertrand, the Poles had given the British an edge, something which Turing and Knox might be able to use to find out what the Nazis were up to.

BALTIC SEA

● Wilno

● Bydgoszcz

Poznań
●

GERMAN
THIRD
REICH

● Warsaw

GENERAL
GOVERNMENT

USSR

Lwów
●

PARTITION OF POLAND
1939–1941

Poland before 1939

6

MONSTROUS PILE

A maudlin and monstrous pile, probably unsurpassed in the architectural gaucherie of the mid-Victorian era.

Landis Gores, quoted in
Robin W. Winks, *Cloak and Gown*

The tallest wooden structure in Europe is a radio mast. It is now located in Poland, but in September 1939 this part of Europe was Germany. It was not just the Poles who had radio-related vanity projects. Indeed, the radio centre at Gleiwitz was an obvious target. The Poles would, for sure, be planning to attack it. The attack would be clandestine, done at night, and its careful planning was codenamed Operation HIMMLER. It was scheduled to happen on the night of 31 August–1 September 1939.

The only thing was, the attack was not going to be made by the Poles at all. It was the task of a tiny group of SS men who dressed up in Polish uniforms, murdered a local farmer and a few concentration camp inmates, dressed these corpses to look like saboteurs, 'seized' the station from themselves, broadcast a message in Polish, and returned to their proper uniforms to tell the world triumphantly how the Polish attack on Germany's tallest asset had been thwarted. In a cynical piece of political theatre, the Gleiwitz incident provided an outraged Hitler with the excuse to invade Poland. Later on the same day, 1 September 1939, Poland was invaded from East Prussia in the north, Germany in the west, and German-controlled Slovakia in the south-west. World War Two had begun.

There are many myths about the Battle of Poland in 1939. Cavalrymen charging tanks, clapped-out biplanes fighting Stukas, and such like. Most of these stories are bunk. But there was a failure of planning and strategy. The Poles planned to fight on the border and to defend the industrial and resource-rich region of Silesia. The German Army rapidly squeezed them out of the Polish Corridor, pushing the Poles relentlessly south and east. Edward Rydz-Śmigły, the successor to Piłsudski as Marshal of Poland, was no Piłsudski when it came to the real test. Rydz-Śmigły was fighting a war of movement: movement away from the Germans. Within less than a week of the invasion, Rydz-Śmigły had taken the government out of Warsaw. All the movement left no time for actual government.

Polish strategy relied heavily on the French and the British to honour their promises. If matters worked as they had in 1914, the French and British would immediately attack Germany with all the power at their disposal. And so it was. On 7 September 1939, eleven divisions of the French Army crossed the border into Germany near Saarbrücken and approached the Siegfried Line. German resistance was weak; the bulk of German forces had been committed to the Polish campaign.

The British, meanwhile, sent bombers to Berlin. The planes bombarded innocent German civilians ... with leaflets. John Colville, a diarist close to the heart of the British establishment, observed on Wednesday 13 September 1939: 'Poland has exhausted nearly all her resources of aerial defence ... our comparative inactivity on the Western Front is causing general uneasiness. Why not bomb military objectives instead of scattering pamphlets is the question everybody is asking about the R.A.F.'

The Polish code-breakers found themselves under attack from the Luftwaffe, who most certainly had more than pamphlets to deliver. The way the German planes singled them out seemed almost personal. Jerzy Różicki had a young wife, Barbara, who kept her own diary:

September 2nd. We witness air battles over the Pole Mokotowskie [a park in Warsaw]. They tell us that the second line of Warsaw's defence now runs along our street (Ursynowska) and that they placed an anti-aircraft gun on our terrace. We're worried and our concern is growing. 'Maliznota' (that's what we called our son) will soon be only 4 months old. I use a bottle to feed him. Already it's difficult to get milk and food. Many shops are closed.

September 3rd. The airport and Raszyn are being bombed. Constant air-raid alarms – our life is now a constant journey between the basement and the apartment. Jurek (diminutive of Jerzy) came back from the office late at night. He came with Zyga (a friend called Henryk Zygalski). The events of the day shook them up. They tell us that their bureau is vacating their current place of work (Pyry near Warsaw), they're already packed, tomorrow they're taking a special train to Brześć [Brest] by the Bug river …

September 6th. Jurek arrived at 5 a.m. Their train can't leave just yet. He came just for a moment to see how we were. He's shocked to see us still here. He couldn't leave us under those circumstances. He decided he would take us on to his train – so that we can at least leave Warsaw … We start off on foot, then using different means of transportation, before eventually getting to the station. As soon as we found ourselves in the carriage, the station and the trains standing there were subjected to bombing. We're all going under the carriages to hide. There's no way we can depart now. The tracks are destroyed as are some carriages. Some of our carriages need to be replaced. Jurek left to look for milk. His colleague M. Rejewski ran home to see his wife and children. Zyga stayed with us. He was from Poznań and had no family in Warsaw. We were all back together in the evening. The train left …

September 7th. The train isn't running, it's going at a snail's pace. The tracks are broken and need to be fixed. During the day bombs target the train all the time. The train has to stop, we need to leave and hide under the trees in the nearby gardens or in the bushes by the road …

September 8th. Myself, the baby, Jurek and Zyga were in hiding during an air raid and a bomb came down very close to us. A crater opened up in front of us, luckily we were only covered by some sand … Hidden under the trees we saw, on the other side of the tracks, on a field by the forest, some 300 meters away from where we were, a German plane landing …

September 9th. Finally around midday we find ourselves at the station in Brześć by the Bug river. We are met by peace, quiet and beautiful weather. We leave the train. Jurek and I run to find milk and food ... Suddenly we hear the sound of motors, then we see a black cloud over our heads – planes just above us. During this, the first air raid on the city, 36 bombers arrived. Again, us first, then them ... We need to get back on the train – we left our child there in the care of a 16-year-old girl. However, we find ourselves running with others in the opposite direction – towards the air defence bunkers. We managed to stop when a bomb flew into a bunker in front of us. We come back to the station, to find the building already destroyed by bombs – the station building had a glass roof. We approach the train silently and in the highest state of anxiety. The tracks are damaged, as are the carriages – but our carriage is ok, underneath it we find our baby and his carer. We ask how it is that they're alive and also how the air raid was. 'The baby didn't even cry that much – we hid under the carriage straight away – I had a rosary that the baby was playing with and I was praying out loud ...' Zyga came to tell us that the three of them – M. Rejewski, H. Zygalski and Jurek – had been given a car and that they had been under an order to go to Romania as soon as possible. Everything inside me is rebelling – how come, after yet another rescue, yet another farewell. It's the third time, since the war began, that we say goodbye ...[2]

● ● ●

In one of the most significant undercover operations of World War Two, a small group of men converged secretly on a long-disused building next to the railway station serving a crummy, red-brick town. They were dressed in plain clothes and had been informed of the password in case of challenge. They had also been told that the official address of their destination was 'Room 47, Foreign Office', which was likely to deceive no one, at least not for long, for the actual place was a long way from Whitehall. It was a Victorian concoction, a fantasy building created from dozens of architectural styles through the ages and served up like canapés, all the different pieces presented alongside each other on the façade. Perhaps the most remarkable thing was a stockbroker Tudor gable poking out of an immense bronze dome. The hideous building was a 'maudlin and monstrous pile' and its name was Bletchley Park.

The secret operation was the mobilisation by Alastair Denniston of the 'men of the professor type'. Upon the declaration of war, the professors were called in, most arriving during the first week of September 1939. They included Dilly Knox and Alan Turing, who were immediately assigned to the cottages around the stable yard behind the main house. It would not do to have the administrative staff treading on the toes of the code-breakers, or maybe the thinking was that the administrative staff wished to preserve their sanity from excessive exposure to the idiosyncratic code-breakers.

Although the fighting war in Europe was soon over, it was clear that the war against Enigma had barely begun. The priceless intelligence gleaned at the Pyry meeting in July had furnished the British not just with knowledge about the structure of the Wehrmacht machine but also with ideas on how to find the daily settings. By their own admission, the Poles had not been making much headway in finding the settings during 1939. The extra rotors introduced in December 1938 were part of the problem; the switchover to a fresh ground setting for each message was another; and to cap it off, in January 1939 the Germans had added three extra cross-plugging wires to each Enigma machine, vastly increasing the number of possible cross-pluggings. All these factors contributed to the conclusion that the successful pre-war Polish methods were becoming outdated.

The Polish *bomba*s, and another method of finding settings invented by Henryk Zygalski using perforated cardboard sheets, relied on the occurrence of 'females', repeated letters showing up in the indicator which the Germans transmitted at the start of a message. But females were an endangered species. If the Germans changed their procedures again and stopped the insecure double encipherment of the indicator, all techniques based on searching for females would become redundant at once. The British knew that they not only needed to improve on the Polish techniques, they needed to create new ones which did not depend on finding females.

Alan Turing, aged 27 in September 1939, brought to Bletchley a grounding in mathematical theory coupled with a very practical approach to machines. He visualised mathematical problems and their proofs in machinery. Turing's most famous paper, published in 1936, was called *On Computable Numbers, with an Application to the Entscheidungsproblem*. It postulated a mechanical device into which instructions could be fed. This proved, in due time, to be the theoretical blueprint for a programmable computer. Since 1936, Alan Turing had not just been theorising, he had also been building various machines, such as a mechanical multiplier and a cog-wheel machine to find answers to a problem of the uneven spacing between prime numbers. His new task at Bletchley Park was to invent a machine to find the settings used by the Wehrmacht on their Enigma messages, one that did not depend on double encipherment of indicators and the existence of females.

On the upper floor of one of the cottages, Alan Turing set to work. As all code-breakers know, the process of code-breaking is immeasurably easier if you know – or can guess accurately – some of the content of the message. The Scarlet Pimpernels included materials discussing a technique called the *mot probable*, used by both Knox and Henri Braquenié to attack the commercial model of the Enigma machine.[3] The British called the probable word a 'crib', following Hugh Foss's choice of the schoolboy word for using the answer in the back of the book. Alan Turing's machine to attack the Wehrmacht Enigma was going to be based on cribs.

The basic idea was similar to that of the Polish *bomba*. Turing's machine would go through all 17,576 possible rotor configurations and look for a possible start position which could have caused all the letters in the crib to become enciphered as the gobbledegook which had been intercepted. All the letters in the crib could be electrically tested at the same time. This was essentially what the *bomba* did with the six-letter indicator, but Turing's machine could test a crib of any length. Better still, the new, powerful machine would help with the problem of the plugboard. Whereas the Poles had found it necessary to use trial-and-error to work out the cross-pluggings, Turing's machine would offer up one potential cross-plugging as part of the solution it proposed. That one cross-plugging would prise open the remaining settings for the day, would unravel the rest of the Enigma set-up. The design was completed in the first few weeks of the war and the engineers were called in. Without the priceless gift of the theory of the *bomba*, it is hard to imagine that Alan Turing's crib-checking machine would have been conceived so fast, if at all. In a small acknowledgment of its intellectual provenance, the machine designed by Turing was going to be called the 'Bombe'.

● ● ●

Major Maksymilian Ciężki had received special orders on Tuesday, 5 September 1939.[4] The constant raids on Warsaw meant that the secret outstation of the Biuro Szyfrów at Pyry was at risk. The equipment still on site was to be destroyed and explosive charges were set to blow up the radio tower at the appropriate time. Henryk Zygalski spent the day burning papers. Suddenly, it dawned on Ciężki that the orders for destruction and evacuation did not cover the AVA factory, where there were Enigma rotors and machines and documents that would compromise the Enigma secret if they fell into the hands of the German forces. Despite the bombs and chaos across Warsaw, Antoni Palluth and a team from AVA got there in time. The assets were whisked off to be hidden in the eastern suburbs. Now the time had come for the code-breakers to leave.

When, eventually, the code-breakers did get going, the train journey was even more of a nightmare than Barbara Różycka's account reveals. After a day of constant air raids, their train collided with another in the middle of the night. Some of the party – but none of the code-breakers – were hurt. Zygalski and his colleagues had to get the crushed wagons off the line. The focus of the bombing had shifted to Siedlce, the next town on their route, which was now ablaze. They had been going two and a half days and had managed a whole 80km. Even if they got as far as Brześć – and they were not even halfway there yet – the Romanian border, where they were to join the regrouping army, was still 400km further on.[5]

On 17 September 1939, the Soviet Union invaded Poland from the east.

On the same day, the French began a withdrawal from the Saarland, which they had occupied for just over a week.

The Russians moved up to a pre-agreed line, closely modelled on a historical one drawn by a Polish expert in London in 1919. With some local deviations it was the Curzon Line. The British approved then and they were hardly in a position to complain now. For Russians, it was nothing other than recapture of what they had lost in 1920. For Germany, the logic was similar. West of the line, reinvigorated German culture would bring to Poland the benefits of concentration camps, anti-semitism and hunger. To the East, the USSR would offer the Gulag, political re-education and hunger.

The Battle of Poland was over, and with it, the war. For the fourth time in its history, Poland had been partitioned. As with the country, so with the families. Barbara Różycka and little Maliznota would have to stay behind. Gwido Langer, Maksymilian Ciężki, Marian Rejewski and Antoni Palluth were all exiled, cut off from their families. Poland, and its people, had ceased to exist.

● ● ●

When, on 27 September 1939, Warsaw finally surrendered to the Germans, life for those left behind became no easier. The Poles were not going to give in, whatever their leadership might be doing. The Palluth household at Marshałkowska 19 became a focal point for the underground. Despite the Luftwaffe's best efforts, the AVA factory had not received a direct hit and valuable equipment was stocked there which could help the nascent underground resistance movement. The Gestapo reacted to the potential for an insurgency with a decree that all wireless equipment must be surrendered by a certain date, failing which any Pole found in possession would be subject to the extreme ultimate penalty. The materials had to be sneaked out of AVA. Hiding places around the city were few, overlooked, and dangerous. The aristocratic Mrs Palluth was not going to allow fear of reprisals to get in the way of her responsibility as the factory owner's wife. The apartment at Marshałkowska 19 had a long, wide hallway, wide enough for her young son to have learned to ride his bike there. The hallway would do

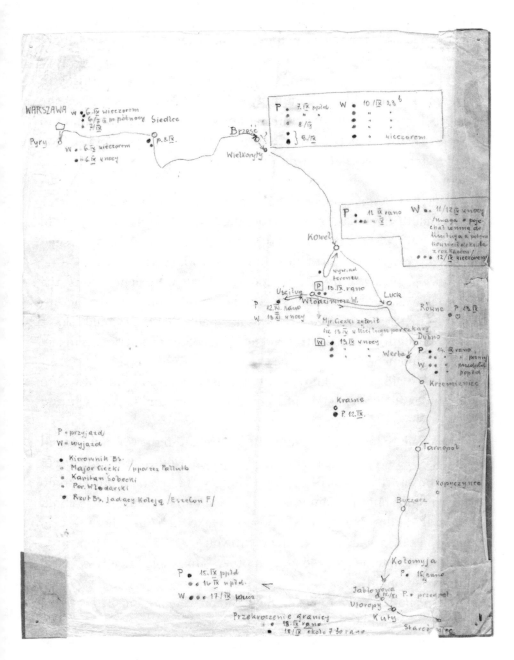

The way out. Gwido Langer's sketch map of his escape route from Poland in September 1939. (The Józef Piłsudski Institute, 238–246 King Street, London)

just fine to store the dozens of boxes of radio equipment spirited out of the factory.

The goings and comings into the apartment building in Marshałkowska did not go unnoticed by the Gestapo. One day the doorbell rang. Jadwiga Palluth told her son Jerzy what was going to happen. Most mothers would tell their 8-year-old to hide. Not her. 'You will watch and listen. It is your duty, to bear witness.' She opened the door for the scene to begin.

In perfect German, immaculately dressed and with respectful etiquette, Mrs Palluth greeted the officers from the Reich's Secret State Police. 'In this country, we have the custom that officers remove their hats and side-arms on entering a private house.' It was clear who was in charge.

Jawohl, gnädige Frau. The weapons and hats were deposited on the side table. Next to the rows of stacked boxes, all containing the incriminating material. '*Was ist das?*' It was inevitable that they would ask.

Mrs Palluth, ever in control, did not blink. 'Since you ask, it is in fact radio equipment.'

'What? Did you not know about the decree which required you to surrender all wireless and radio equipment? We could arrest you and you can be shot!'

Mrs Palluth looked the senior officer straight in the eye. 'Oh yes. Of course. There is just one problem. Perhaps you would care to lift one of these boxes?' It was far beneath the dignity of a Gestapo officer to do such a thing, but the point was made. 'Each of them must weigh about a hundred kilos. How am I supposed to take them anywhere? I'm so glad you called, you can take them with you.'

The Gestapo men looked at each other. '*Jawohl, gnädige Frau.* We'll send a van round.'

Mrs Palluth was winning, but the Gestapo were not finished yet. 'We need to know where your husband is.'

'You had better come in and sit down. Would you care for some tea? Unfortunately, in view of the situation, I can only offer you herbal tea.'

The Gestapo knew she was stalling; they stayed put. 'We need to know: where is your husband?'

'I can only tell you what I know. I last saw him in September. I have had no contact. I assume he must have perished in the war.'

It was true, but it was not an answer they could accept. 'At least you must have some of his belongings.'

'Of course. Give me one moment.' Young Jerzy sat, watching the Gestapo men, while his mother went into the room where Antoni Palluth kept his books. 'Here.' She handed the officer a leather-bound volume. It was a school prize book, extolling the glories of Kaiser Wilhelm's High Seas Fleet, which had so nearly smashed the British at Jutland. The book pre-dated that battle; it pre-dated Polish independence. Inside, in the Kaiser's own handwriting, a conventional statement of congratulation and encouragement to Antoni Palluth on coming top of his class. 'It is one of his most treasured possessions.'[6]

Like Jutland, the encounter might have been a tactical draw, but it was a strategic victory. Jadwiga Palluth was not beaten yet.

● ● ●

While the BTM company in Letchworth were trying to convert Alan Turing's Bombe design into engineering reality, on 18 October 1939, Alastair Denniston received some truly shocking news. Playing the stage magician as always, Gustave Bertrand had produced a rabbit from his *képi*. To be precise, a whole family of them: the Polish codebreakers had magically appeared from nowhere and they were working in his unit in Paris.

Like all good magicians, Bertrand had been unwilling to reveal the secret of his trick. For the previous month or so, Knox had been sending notes to Denniston about dealing with the French. The first problem was lunch:

> It has been a great pleasure to me, though somewhat testing to my knowledge of French, to bear-lead Captain B. from 8 a.m. to 10 p.m. I have taken the line, though he offered to pay generously, that entertainment is *une affaire de bureau*: that is, from my angle, that I should get a billeting allowance ...[7]

Then there were the niceties of dealing with the people. 'Liaisons. Braquenié. Admirable. We are great friends ...' Knox had invited Henri

Braquenié to stay at his house, which tested the limits of Braquenié's admirability and friendship. 'Dilly was no wine connoisseur and one can only wonder how the *entente cordiale* survived ... even the odd admiral would be entertained with just a half-bottle of plonk.'[8]

Denniston wanted the Polish experts for himself. It was understandably galling that Bertrand the bear had achieved his coup, but to punish him and Braquenié with peculiar versions of hospitality was perhaps unfair. But what was the explanation for the mysterious reappearance of the Polish code-breakers in his team?

The ghastly train journey had, eventually, come to an end for Marian Rejewski, Jerzy Różycki and Henryk Zygalski.[9] They switched to a truck after arriving at Brześć and then travelling became less dangerous, if no simpler. A week into their journey they reached Łuck (Lutsk). Here a deviation was ordered and they headed west again, towards the town of Włodzimierz (Volodymyr-Volynski). Just outside Włodzimierz is a tiny place then called Uściług. In 1939, the only thing this place was remotely famous for was that Igor Stravinsky had a house there; even today its population is microscopic. Possibly by reason of its remoteness, the intelligence officers stopped the convoy in Uściług. Kazimierz Gaca was one of the civilians employed in the Cipher Bureau, and, at 19 years old, the youngest of the code-breakers, but he also held a commission in the reserves. He was ordered out of the truck and told to dig a deep hole. It was a bit demeaning for an officer to be involved in grave-digging, but the saddest part was not the labour. To take the code-breaking secrets out of the country would be too dangerous, so into the hole went the fruits of years of intellectual sweat and all their precious kit: six *bomba*s; Polish-designed Lacida cipher machines; unburnt papers; no fewer than seventy replica Enigmas; in fact, almost everything that had escaped the flames the week before.[10] Then, back into the truck and back on the road south. On Sunday, 17 September 1939, they heard the news about the Russian invasion and the same evening they reached the border town of Kuty and crossed into Romania.

Scores of refugees were on the road. The Romanian border guards were trying to separate military personnel from civilians: under the theory of neutrality, Polish military personnel were supposed to be interned. The military truck in which the code-breakers had bumped uncomfortably for hundreds of kilometres was 'interned', but in the chaos Rejewski, Różycki and Zygalski, not being uniformed members of the armed forces, blended into the crowd and quickly found their way to the railway station. The three arrived in Bucharest the next day. The others would have to fend for themselves.

It was chaos in Bucharest too. The code-breakers decided to try the British Embassy. The French Army had proved itself unequal to the task of supporting Poland, or unwilling to try, but the British code-breakers seemed to have some real talent. Perhaps the best way to help Poland win back its independence would be to join the British war effort.

Just as the three men arrived at the Embassy, a bus pulled into the yard. It disgorged a disorientated and stressed group of diplomats who had fled from Warsaw and made the long journey on the refugee-congested roads to Bucharest. The British Romanian mission was overwhelmed. Three civilian mathematicians, trying to communicate in German, trying to explain who they were without actually telling anyone anything, was a complicated, low-priority problem. They were told to come back the next day and meanwhile the British officials would try to contact London to check out their story, if time permitted.[11]

But time was running out. If the Romanian security police found out who the code-breakers were, there was every chance they would be handed straight over to the Gestapo. Waiting even twenty-four hours was a very unattractive option. They would have to try the perfidious French, even though that nation had abandoned its feeble invasion of Germany.

The French Embassy was calm and bureaucratic, but the Poles knew the key to this particular diplomatic lock. Years of liaison with Bertrand meant that simply mentioning the name 'Bolek' – the code word for Bertrand known to the Deuxième Bureau – opened the way. A quick check back with Paris assured the fugitives every support: passports in false names and visas to go with them would be provided right away, together with special additional documentation essential for the three to get to France. Maybe, after all, the French were not quite as perfidious as it had seemed.

After two days the three mathematicians left the French Embassy. Despite all the preparations there was an initial hitch: the Romanians were not convinced about their permit to travel. Here the French officials' familiarity with Romanian procedure came to the rescue: the special additional documentation, slipped in between the regular papers, consisted of a 500-lei note. It seemed there might not be a problem with the code-breakers' departure after all. Finally, they were on their way to France. The long journey by train took over three days, via Yugoslavia and Italy. At the French-Italian border there were more problems. At Modane, on the French side, a clearing centre had been set up. A new army was being formed out of the wreckage of the flight from Poland, under the charismatic leadership of General Władysław Sikorski. The post-Piłsudski government had collapsed along with the failed defence of Poland. Sikorski was ideally placed to take control: with a strong war record from the Russo-Polish conflict of 1920, and some experience of government, he had briefly served in government but latterly had been the leading figure in the opposition. Now Sikorski was trying to extricate as many men from Poland and Romania as possible to continue the fight. The three code-breakers were going to have to wait while the Franco-Polish officers worked out who was who.

Then another of Bertrand's magical moments occurred. A French officer appeared. There was no need for the three gentlemen with the fake IDs to wait in line. They were expected. Perhaps they would care to come this way. The French officer took them straight back to the station and, without further fuss, they were on their way to Paris.

Meanwhile, Bertrand was trying to get hold of Langer and the rest of his team. Having been separated from the civilians at the Romanian border, the uniformed members of the Cipher Bureau were due to be interned. Internment in Romania, however, in the boiling political climate of September 1939 was not the measured and orderly process taking place in Britain (where assorted foreigners and suspected spies were being rounded up). Romania was the very opposite of measured and orderly. A dictatorship had been in place for a year, but this did not guarantee security. The prime minister was assassinated in the middle of the Polish crisis. Tens of thousands of Polish servicemen had flooded across the border. There was nowhere for the 'internees' to go and the Romanians did not want them to stay. But getting out was easier for some than others. The young Kazimierz Gaca, who was carrying the only AVA-made duplicate Enigma machine to survive the burial at Uściług, wangled his way on via Yugoslavia to Greece, eventually boarding a ship in Piraeus bound for Marseilles. His journey took five months.[12]

When Warsaw surrendered on 27 September 1939, Gwido Langer found himself in Calimanesti in the heart of the Romanian countryside. A French Army officer appeared, clutching a telegram containing an invitation in the name of Colonel Louis Rivet, for Langer, his colleagues and their families to join Bertrand's unit in Paris. Langer's boss, Colonel Stefan Mayer, was also at Calimanesti and approved the move.[13] Within four days the entire group was relocated to Paris and reunited. There, in the suburbs, where peacetime frivolities still prevailed, the Polish code-breakers could carry on the intelligence struggle.

● ● ●

As the autumn of 1939 greyed into winter, a spirit of optimism seemed to infuse the British at Bletchley Park. A tea-stained note in the British National Archives begins with an optimistic, 'we may with some hope look forward to the state when we shall be able to deal with some of the German Enigma traffic.'[14] And on the same day, Bertrand wrote to Denniston to arrange another three-way meeting. Now the secret of his capture of the Poles was out, Bertrand was ready to revive the X-Y-Z liaison properly. Queries, intercepts and ideas were flowing back and forth again, as was a seasonal spirit of goodwill. 'My dear Bertrand,' wrote Denniston on 23 December 1939, 'I am writing to wish you a very restful (?) Christmas and, I hope, a prosperous 1940, which year may, I trust, be the last for the Nazi Band.'[15] The spirit of Christmas optimism could not go much higher than that. Outside, the winter of 1939–40 was turning into the coldest for forty-five years. When the ornamental lake at Bletchley Park froze over, some of the code-breakers gingerly ventured out wearing skates. Although the *entente cordiale* was providing some degree of warmth, the fundamental problem of finding a way to uncover the Enigma keys in real time had not been solved. Poland was still ripped in two and it was far too early to predict the demise of the Nazis.

For, on 14 December 1939, Adolf Hitler had given orders to prepare another invasion, this time in the West.

7

THE MIRROR CRACK'D
FROM SIDE TO SIDE

Out flew the web and floated wide;
The mirror crack'd from side to side;
'The curse is come upon me,' cried
The Lady of Shalott.

Alfred, Lord Tennyson
'The Lady of Shalott'

The Battle of Poland was over. The British and the French found themselves in a 'phoney war'. The French called it the 'drôle de guerre'. And
against the background of an imminent threat of real war, a diplomatic
battle was underway between X and Y.

To win the war against the Germans, it was self-evident that the
Polish cryptologists should join the Y team at Bletchley Park. On
10 October 1939, MI5 had been 'asked to receive seventeen Polish cryptographers who are said to be experts in Russian and German ciphers.
We have said that we will be guided by the Government Code & Cipher
School. I gather, however, that they do not want all these people and
would much prefer to see them in France. Alastair Denniston has
already had a talk with them in Warsaw … they might be very useful.'
The idea of the Poles moving to Bletchley was suggested to Gustave
Bertrand on 29 December, but 'the French Government were paying
for the Polish Army and therefore the Poles must work in France'.
A weak excuse; it was time to try again.

Dear Menzies,

Here are the names of the three young Poles, Jerzy Rozycki, Marian Rejewoli [sic], Henryk Zygalski. If we are faced with a change on the outbreak of War (and we begin to suspect it), the experience of these men may shorten our task by months. We possess certain mechanical devices which cannot be transferred to France. These young men possess ten years' experience and a short visit from them might prove of very great value.

Yours ever sincerely, A. G. Denniston.[2]

It seemed that Bletchley Park was losing this battle. Come what may, Bertrand was not going to agree to a transfer of his star players. 'I am resigned,' wrote Alastair Denniston to Bertrand on 7 February 1940, 'to not receiving the Zs with us. You have said frankly that it is impossible, so I accept it.'[3] Alastair Denniston was unfailingly polite. When decrypted, the message meant that he did not accept it, but his hand had been forced. Perhaps it was not too intolerable. With a teleprinter link between Bertrand and Bletchley, cooperative relations could still go on. France, where the X and Z teams were playing, was not so far away, and Y had some star players of its own, whose scoring abilities were just becoming recognised. One of them was Alan Turing.

Alan Turing was not regarded as being much good at German. At one stage – when he was learning German at school – this would have been considered a fatal flaw in a code-breaker whose job was to decrypt German messages. In 1931, Turing's German teacher had said, 'he does not seem to have any aptitude for languages.'[4] By 1940, though, the schoolmaster might have had to revise his opinion, since the study of mathematics at a higher level in the 1930s obliged go-ahead students to master the German language. And Turing was also competent in French: his mother (a fluent French speaker who had herself studied in Paris and lived in France for several years) had force-fed him on French in earlier years. So, after the frozen Christmas of 1939, Alan Turing was selected for a multilingual international mission.

During 1938, while the *bombas* were still being developed, Henryk Zygalski had invented a new technique to exploit 'females' (repeated letters showing up in the indicator which the Germans transmitted at the start of a message) to find out the set-up of the German Enigma machines. The new approach used perforated cardboard sheets. Zygalski's idea was to represent the configurations of Enigma rotors on sheets of card ruled into a grid, with the vertical axis listing all positions of the right-hand rotor and the horizontal one all positions of the middle rotor. In this way, twenty-six sheets would do for all possible positions of three rotors. Then holes were punched into the sheets in positions where females were possible. When the sheets were ready, they could be stacked on a light-table, and the correct choice of rotors and their start position would be revealed by a single ray of light shining up through the holes in the stack.*

The sheets were tedious to create, complex to use, and relied on a manual process which seemed less sophisticated and more time-consuming than the modern, electric *bomba*s. But the beauty of the Zygalski sheets was that the theory removed the plugboard from contention altogether. For the sheets to work it didn't matter how many annoying cross-pluggings the Germans were using. So long as the Germans continued to encipher the three-letter indicator sequence twice over, there would be a copious supply of females and the need for machinery was postponed.

That was 1938, but with the advent of the Germans adding two rotors, so that there were five to choose from, 1,560 cardboard sheets were now needed. The Polish team had been cutting out holes from their sheets with razor blades. With around 800 holes per sheet, it was a tedious and time-consuming job. The British, however, were working on their own set and ordered a punching machine to do the task. When it arrived, it drove Alan Turing into the attic to escape the noise.[5]

Soon after Christmas 1939, the punching of the cardboard sheets was done. Thus, Alan Turing was detailed to take a set across to France, though not before Knox had lost his temper and threatened to resign unless the sheets were made available to the allies. ('Unless they leave by Wednesday night I shall tender my resignation. I do not want to go to Paris but if you cannot secure another messenger I am actually at the moment completely idle.'[6]) Having disparaged the Poles once, now he

---

* See Appendix for a more detailed explanation.

had the zeal of the convert. But Denniston was going to act cautiously. The choice of Turing for the mission may have been only slightly more cautious, given Turing's well-known eccentricities and social awkwardness, but they needed to send someone who was fully on top of the technical side.

For the Enigma team at Bletchley Park were facing some more puzzles which the intelligence from Pyry did not seem to solve. First of all, the splendid cardboard sheets were slow and inefficient to use. And on top of that there was a problem with Method Kx. Method Kx was a technique for inspired guesses at rotor-orders, which exploited 'Cillies' – the inability of humans to pick three letters at random, so allowing code-breakers to guess that the starting positions chosen by German operators were such 'random' sequences as AAA or QWE or SOS. But Method Kx didn't seem to work when the two new rotors, introduced by the Wehrmacht in December 1938, were involved.[7] Alan Turing, who understood these problems, would go to France, his school reports notwithstanding.

Marian Rejewski may not have known about Turing's 1936 paper on *Computable Numbers*, which turned the theory of mathematics upside-down and at the same time introduced a model for a programmable computer. And Turing was not Knox; he was an unknown in the Bletchley Park equation. So Rejewski may be forgiven for being slightly patronising: 'we treated Turing as a younger colleague who had specialised in mathematical logic and was just starting out in cryptology.'[8] It may have been just the way to deal with Turing; the meeting was a roaring success. Using the freshly minted Zygalski sheets, the Poles in exile showed Turing (using intercepts dating from the previous October) how to stack them up in the most efficient way and to find the rotor-settings and plugboard connections. On 17 January 1940, eleven weeks after their transmission, the first Enigma messages of the war were read by the Poles, the French, and Turing, the emissary from Britain. It was a result at last for X-Y-Z. And a further big plus for Turing's mission was that the problem of the Method Kx was solved. There had been a misunderstanding over the position of the turnover notch on the new rotors.

A celebration was in order. Bertrand and Langer hosted a dinner at a nearby restaurant. On the table was a small glass vase containing a few autumn crocuses. Flowers in a freezing January are a rarity and Langer pointed to them, giving their Polish and German names. Then, observing Turing's incomprehension, Jerzy Różycki chipped in, in Latin. *Colchicum autumnale.* 'Why! That's a powerful poison!' exclaimed Alan Turing. Alan Turing's life would end, fourteen years after that dinner, with a dose of an even more powerful poison.

●●●

In 1940, a whiff of poison was in the air, not for Alan Turing, but for the more senior members of the exiled Polish intelligence service including Maksymilian Ciężki and Antoni Palluth. The new government of Władysław Sikorski was investigating just what had gone wrong the previous autumn to allow Germany to make such a successful assault on Poland.

Professor Stanisław Kot, leading member of the Peasants' Party in Sikorski's government-in-exile, was minister of 'internal affairs' (which was slightly odd, since the ability of Sikorski, Kot, or anyone else to do much about the internal affairs in their torn country was somewhat limited). Perhaps for that reason it was Kot who went to a series of liaison meetings that took place with the British Foreign Office. It was at these meetings – for which the British wheeled out of retirement their favourite Polish expert, Professor Lewis Namier, erstwhile author of the Curzon Line –that the Foreign Office learned about the poisonous atmosphere among the Polish émigrés. On 9 November 1940, as the professors sipped their tea, Kot revealed that matters were not entirely harmonious in the State of Poland. In particular, the relations between the Polish government's undercover resistance organisation and its intelligence bureau were at a low point. The bureau was staffed with old-timers from the Sanacja régime, whose leader was Edward Rydz-Śmigły. Sanacja itself was being cleaned up, with a new head of Polish military intelligence, Colonel Stanisław Gano, due to take over.

Blame needed to be allocated. While most of the blame must rest with the unloved régime of Rydz-Śmigły, the dirt might extend deep into the army's substructure and its aristocratic officers. There was, it seemed, a good deal to investigate.

The investigator was Lieutenant Colonel Ludwik Sadowski and his brief was wide-ranging.[9] He was to name names and point fingers. He was to identify the men who should have assessed the plans of the enemy. What were the political affiliations of these men? Why did the intelligence service fail to act with agility upon the invasion? Why were budgets misspent? The Second Department of the General Staff was responsible for intelligence. The Biuro Szyfrów was part of the Second Department and there was an unpleasant contrast between the total failure of intelligence during the Battle of Poland and the Biuro's achievements with Enigma during the years of peace. This was exactly the pattern you'd expect if there were a German influence at work in the Biuro. Statements were taken, from Ciężki, from Palluth, from those employed at Pyry and elsewhere.

As for the budgetary investigation, wasn't it clear that the Biuro Szyfrów had needed more code-breakers? And an efficient system of bringing results to the command? Whereas, in fact, the money had been spent on a ludicrous radio tower which could not even relay signals to the army commanders. The mismanagement went even further: the tower had been blown up prematurely and the explanation for this seemed to be that Maksymilian Ciężki had been receiving kickbacks from Antoni Palluth's AVA company and these two had destroyed the tower as part of a scheme to cover their tracks. Self-evidently their relationship was altogether too cosy. Palluth and Ciężki said that that was nonsense, but of course they would say that. What was needed was more evidence.

Actually, what was needed was a blast of cold, common sense. Major Wiktor Michałowski gave his deposition to Sadowski's inquiry on 14 December 1939. Of course, there had been some leadership failures within the Biuro after the war broke out, but frequent relocations and a constant division of resources had hampered the code-breakers' efforts. Moreover, there was a shortage of intercepted material to work with and they had been constantly harried by the Luftwaffe. In the final analysis, Sadowski had Ciężki and Palluth in his sights for a political reason rather than a genuine concern that corruption or German influence had undermined the efficacy of the the Biuro. The cloud over Ciężki and Palluth was that since the fighting in Poland had ended, the Biuro's leaders and their staff had been working not for General Sikorski, but for the French.

• • •

While the unpleasant business of the post-mortem was going on, Team Z were settling into their new quarters. On 20 January 1940, just after the meeting with Alan Turing, the X and Z groups moved into the Château de Vignolles.[10] The château was an attractive country house with rather nice grounds in a village called Gretz-Armainvilliers, situated near enough to, but outside, Paris. The out-station was called 'Poste de Commandement Bruno', or PC Bruno for short. The garden was infested with rabbits. Bertrand designed a special letterhead for the secret out-station, with gambolling bunnies as a logo and the address unhelpfully specified as 'Somewhere in France'; whether this increased the credibility of his reports is not revealed.[11]

Antoni Palluth and Edward Fokczyński – both veterans of the AVA factory – now joined the group at PC Bruno, together with Henryk Paszkowski, a junior cipher officer. More Poles joined in February and March, devoting their efforts against Russian ciphers. Since the arrival of the Zygalski sheets from London, the Poles concentrating on German messages were having to work very hard. They were finding the Enigma settings more rapidly: in the two months after the move to PC Bruno, the average time to find the settings fell from over eighteen days to five. In some cases the Enigma team could work out the settings just two days after the associated messages were sent. As they caught up with the older traffic, the workload went up. Bletchley Park solved about fifty Enigma settings between mid January and the end of March; for PC Bruno the number was about forty in the same period.[12] Most importantly, every month, they were now reading thousands of messages, some of which might reveal still-current facts not yet known to the Allies.

With many coded messages, when the fun of finding the secret key is over, there can be a sense of anti-climax. The disappointment when the content of an Enigma-enciphered telegram turns out to be nothing more than, say, congratulations on the promotion of some unknown officer to the rank of major, can easily be imagined. Despite an intense effort, the content of messages deciphered during February and March 1940 was of limited strategic worth. Bertrand's boss, Colonel Louis Rivet, thought the increasing volume of material about the Luftwaffe showed promise, and some feedback from air intelligence in London on the scraps they were sent was mildly encouraging.[13] At least the Allies were getting a bit better at handling the traffic. If the phoney war turned into a fighting war and Enigma messages contained tactical information, they would need to be.

Gustave Bertrand ran PC Bruno according to slightly strange rules. For one thing, the working environment was a bit weird. Équipe Z – Langer's Z team – were put into an artist's studio at the very top of the château, where the walls were daubed with attempts at landscape painting by its former occupant. The furnishings, however, were very basic. And then there was segregation: each nationality was required to eat separately from the others. In addition to the Poles, Bertrand was accommodating a group of Spanish refugees, Équipe D, who were tackling the codes of the Franco régime (and its ally the Italian fascists) with success, so that meant there were three dining rooms, for no obvious reason that the code-breakers could see.[14]

In addition to the Spanish residents, there was a British liaison officer; we are not told whether he was expected to eat alone or with one of the other groups. He was Captain Kenneth MacFarlan, nicknamed Pinky (apparently on account of his complexion). MacFarlan was not cleared to share in the Enigma secret: as a relatively junior army liaison officer his job was to speak fluent French, the language of liaison, but otherwise he was clueless. Bertrand was keeping Pinky at arm's length. The French re-nicknamed Pinky the *Le Navet Royale* [the royal turnip]. Pinky was not amused.[15]

Gwido Langer soon worked out what was going on. It was divide and rule:

Bertrand's attitude towards the English was very French. He was most displeased with the fact that in 1939 the English were simply handed over the machine and the technique of breaking the codes, whereas he had spent a long time trying to obtain the machine. He then said that if the machine hadn't cost the English a lot, they must pay a lot for it now. However, when the English submitted a proposal, according to which some of them were to come to France to help, Bertrand fought this threat of 'British colonization' with passion.[16]

If the British became fully engaged at Bruno, the French would become mere suppliers of intercepts and no more.

The Poles weren't exactly locked up, despite Bertrand's arrangements. Distraction came in various forms. There were excursions to whatever hostelries the locality could offer and plenty of laughs. A luggage label, in immaculate condition (which proves that it was never used), is in the possession of the Zygalski family. The label was supposed to be tagged to the buttonhole of Henryk and it gives directions to the reader of what to do with its drunken and unconscious wearer (including disinfection). At a special Christmas dinner on 24 December 1939, there were novelty cigarettes whose smoke turned into snowflakes; sugar lumps which contained plastic cockroaches which revealed themselves as the code-breakers drank their coffee; biscuits with rubber bands inside so that the bitten-off part sprang out of the eater's mouth; and, the *pièce de résistance*, a 'Verdun bomb'. A veritable tribute to the work of the code-breakers, the Verdun bomb was a round dark chocolate shell. When its fuse was lit, it actually exploded, showering the company with sweets and other goodies.

Marian Rejewski later confessed to having exposed a terrible secret of PC Bruno.

Once, in the hollow of a tree growing near the sluice gates to the pond in the park, I found a crank which opened the sluice. I turned the crank and opened the sluice just a bit, and I left. Next morning, all the meadows in the vicinity were flooded, and a big pile of empty wine bottles had appeared at the bottom of the pond. It turned out that Major Ciężki would take wine bottles, emptied in secret night-time drinking sessions with Lieutenant Colonel Langer, under his coat and throw them into the pond.[17]

Gustave Bertrand was promoted to commandant (major) on 25 March 1940. This helped with an anomaly. The idea of Langer, a lieutenant colonel, and Ciężki, a major with three years' seniority already, being subordinated to a mere captain, was strange enough.[18] Langer believed his unit ought to have been incorporated into the Polish Army which had been reassembling under the authority of Sikorski.[19] For his part, Bertrand was trying not only to prevent that, but also to establish his authority with the Poles and in his dealings with the British.

Periodically the British would come across to check how the relationship was going. At a meeting in February, led by Denniston's number two, Commander Edward Travis, there was a longish agenda, covering the progress the British were making with their special machinery, Russian codes, and more.[20] The British wanted to know how the Poles were getting on with their theoretical attack on Enigma, but Langer had to report that the team was already working flat out – not going to bed until 2 a.m. – on deciphering, translating, and reporting. There was no time for research. It was a contrast with the other country house at Bletchley, with its separate teams for theory, decipherment and translation, and intelligence.

The park at Bletchley was becoming less and less like a stately home with gardens. Its residents knew that with express trains only 100 yards away, belching filthy coal smoke and whistling as they passed the Bletchley junction, comparison with the country house idyll of the Château de Vignolles was laughable. Even before the professors of September 1939 arrived, carpenters had moved in and sturdy wooden outbuildings were being knocked and hammered into place all over the lawns. Soon the maze would be pulled up by its roots and the rose garden would go. Eventually the organisation would outgrow the mansion, its stable-yard cottages and the wooden huts. Bigger, more permanent buildings would be needed. The builders kept the whole site in a state of activity, increasing the sense of urgency.

The Bombe designed by Alan Turing had taken several months to develop and even then nobody knew whether it would work. On 18 March 1940, a prototype arrived in the back of a lorry from Letchworth. It was heavy and ugly. On its bronze-coloured front face, there were rows of what looked like little dartboards picked out in brass.

The dartboards were set out in columns of three, dozens of them. Each dartboard had at its bullseye a spindle, on which a small, squat cylinder would be set. These cylindrical drums would behave like Enigma rotors, each trundling round the 17,576 possible positions of the three-rotor Enigma machine. Round the back, red plaited cables connected up the sets of three drums to test a crib. It was Britain's most secret technical development. It would solve the Enigma problem once and for all. But there was just one glitch: it didn't work. Or rather, it worked a bit too well. The idea of Alan Turing's Bombe was that it would stop – literally, the drums would stop revolving – when it had found a possible setting which could cause the observed encipherment. The issue was that the machine stopped too often, finding too many plausible solutions. The method only worked efficiently if you could connect up the cables to make not just one circuit around the sets of drums, but as many circuits as possible. Having multiple electrical circuits meant that far fewer false positives would be thrown out for further testing. Until the Bletchley Park technicians could find a solution to this, the machine wasn't going to be of much help, and it wasn't going to win a war. To decipher Enigma, they would need to go on using Zygalski's sheets.

● ● ●

Gustave Bertrand understood that the solution to Enigma depended on the ability of his joint Franco-Polish team to have access to the technical equipment they had relied on before the war. The search was on for a factory which could reproduce in secret, in France, what the AVA team had achieved (in spite of Colonel Sadowski's suspicions), in Poland. Gwido Langer had saved one of his team's duplicate Enigma machines from the graveyard near Włodzimierz; with the machine previously donated to Bertrand in July, that made two to work with. Tucked away in PC Bruno, the technicians of Équipe Z were dismantling Langer's machine, to enable the French to make more copies.

The Polish Enigma machine was not a straightforward copy of a German military one. In 1939, nobody in the Allied intelligence services had yet seen a real version of the Wehrmacht Enigma, except in the photos stolen by Schmidt and copied in European bathrooms. So the

Polish machine differed in appearance: its plugboard was at the back and its keyboard was arranged in alphabetical, rather than standard QWERTZU, order. But these differences were superficial. The machine worked in exactly the same way as the German machine. It was a triumph of reverse-engineering.

By April 1940, Bertrand had found his engineering company in the shape of the Établissements Édouard Bélin in Paris and the order was placed. For a total price of 240,000 francs (something around £1,350 at then prevailing rates) he ordered twenty-five cipher machines of type 'A' and three cyclometer machines of type 'B'. The intention, in due course, was to increase the number of type 'A' machines – the Enigma analogues – to forty. The manufacturers reckoned they would need four months to make the first twenty-five.[21]

In light of what the French intelligence team had just learned, four months would prove to be a very long time.

● ● ●

The entry in the diary of Colonel Louis Rivet, the head of French Secret Intelligence, for 18 March 1940 is unexciting. He had lunch with Amédée Bussière, head of the Sûreté Nationale, the French equivalent of the FBI. And he went to see General Louis Koeltz, to discuss 'various matters'. How dull. But one should never treat the diaries of spies as documents that tell the complete story. Henri Navarre was a career army officer who had been assigned to the German section of the Deuxième Bureau in 1938, with Louis Rivet as his immediate boss. On 17 March 1940 Navarre had returned from a meeting in Switzerland; then there had been that discussion of 'various matters', and by the next day, 19 March, with Navarre in tow, Rivet insisted that he needed to see General Maurice Gamelin, the commander-in-chief, to impart intelligence of major importance. Navarre's trip to Switzerland had been an affair of the utmost secrecy. Even the self-important Bertrand was kept in the dark, despite the fact that the meeting had been with Bertrand's personal contact, none other than Hans-Thilo Schmidt.[22]

Notwithstanding the state of war, Schmidt had come to meet Navarre in the bar of the Hotel Eden in Lugano. Hotel Eden had a gorgeous view of the lake, framed by the snow-tipped mountains. The sun was shining and Schmidt needed to talk. He was on his way back from Rome. But that wasn't the reason for the meeting. Schmidt's brother, now returned from invading Poland, had been promoted again and was the general in command of the 39th German Armoured Division, which was lined up along the River Moselle and facing Luxembourg and Belgium. The tank general had learned, during a lunch with no less a personage than Adolf Hitler, the tactical outline of something called *Fall Gelb*. The person setting out the plan was General Erich von Manstein. Where *Fall Weiss* (Operation WHITE) had been the invasion of Poland, *Fall Gelb* (Operation YELLOW) was a forthcoming attack on the West. Manstein had explained that the direction of attack by the Panzers would be through the Ardennes, bypassing the French defences of the Maginot line.

Hans-Thilo Schmidt foresaw that when Operation YELLOW was put in train, it could be the end of his special relationship with the French. His business partner had already been called up and the soap-factory, which had done so well as a front for his ill-gotten funds, could no longer serve. It was going to be wound up. Schmidt was becoming a hunted man. An official investigation into a leak had been initiated and all communications with foreigners were being watched. But this wasn't what scared Schmidt. His concern was that he knew the French had revealed the existence of a highly placed German intelligence agent to Langer and the Poles. What if the Poles had left something behind which revealed who the source was? Moreover, he had learned that the Sicherheitsdienst, the intelligence agency of the SS and the Nazi Party, had found proof in Warsaw that the Poles had reconstituted the Enigma machine.

In 1940, Schmidt knew about the Franco-Polish liaison and suspected that the Poles had reconstituted the Wehrmacht Enigma. 'I hope that M. Barsac [Bertrand] and M. Lemoine [Rex] haven't given anything to the Poles which could put me in the frame,' he said to Navarre. Thus, with the war about to enter a new phase, it was with a sense of finality that Hans-Thilo Schmidt asked Navarre to pass his particular regards to Bertrand, and, additionally, to Rex, as he took his leave on 10 March 1940.

• • •

The intelligence supplied by Schmidt was beyond any price, completely impossible to value. Other agents had warned of an offensive on the Western Front to begin on 11 April 1940; then another agent produced an Abwehr questionnaire requesting of its own spies minutely detailed information about bridges, railways, roads and watercourses in the Ardennes sector.[23] The intelligence was contradictory and did not imply a new concentration of German forces. John Colville, who spent much of World War Two serving at 10 Downing Street, recorded in his diary the views of his superiors: attacks on the Netherlands and Belgium were threatened in November 1939 and again in January 1940, but nothing had come of these.[24] No surprise, then, that the French high command was becoming increasingly sceptical about reports of imminent attack by the Germans. Anyhow, an attack through the Ardennes was impracticable owing to the difficulties of the terrain, not to mention the violation of Belgian neutrality that would be involved. 'The accumulation of evidence that an attack is imminent is formidable ... and yet I cannot convince myself that it is coming,' fussed Prime Minister Neville Chamberlain.[25] But coming it was.

The Germans introduced a new Enigma network on 10 April 1940; this seemed to be focused around Norway and Denmark. The network was labelled 'Yellow' by the traffic analysts at Bletchley, who assigned the names of colours to each network for ease of sorting. Each network used its own basic set-up for its machines (ring settings, plugboard, choice of rotors) so each network had to be attacked separately. Bletchley Park broke 'Yellow' within five days using Zygalski's sheets.[26] The material was 'voluminous and highly operational', if sometimes hard going and difficult to understand owing to the copious use of military jargon, abbreviations and acronyms and the lack of context. With effort, it disclosed information about army, air force and naval movements. Better still, the code-breakers were working much faster. Compared with the months of February and March, the volume of material generated in April was significantly greater. Enigma intelligence was coming of age.

On 7 April 1940, German ships had already set sail. On the following day, the Polish submarine ORP *Orzeł* sank a German transport off the coast of Norway. German troops landed in Norway on 9 April and on the same day Denmark was occupied. An Anglo-French task force attempted a counter-invasion the following week but within two weeks they had been driven off. It was an unmitigated disaster for the Allies. The famous Royal Navy had been unable to prevent a seaborne landing by the Germans, which had cut off the Anglo-French troops. Then, on 9 May 1940, German forces marched into Luxembourg and on 10 May into Belgium and the Netherlands. Prime Minister Chamberlain was ousted the same day, his failed policy of appeasement now compounded by a bungled operation in which British troops had died for no reason. The Battle of France was about to begin and at last there was the opportunity for signals intelligence to play its part.

Except that everyone knew signals intelligence would have no role to play. The experts knew that radio silence is imposed in major operations. Certainly the major decisions would be communicated over landlines where possible. And, in any case, the French would be defending their country from the Germans by standing firm behind the Maginot Line.

The Maginot Line was a formidable defence, certainly impenetrable. It stretched all the way north from Switzerland. When it reached the Belgian border, however, it became ... Belgium. French territory from the Belgian border was, to cite an acid remark of John Colville, 'only defended by an unimpressive ditch', because there was no need to defend France from the Belgians. Behind the ditch was posted the small and subordinate British Expeditionary Force, who had spent the past six months trying to turn the ditch into a defensible proposition. In defending France from Germany, from previous experience one might imagine that a German invasion would probably come via Belgium, especially if something as inconvenient as a Maginot Line were blocking the other way.

When General Rudolf Schmidt's panzers fired up their motors their route was, sure enough, the Belgian one. That put paid to one piece of received wisdom. The next piece of received wisdom to crash was the idea of radio silence. The transmitters were buzzing with orders and reports from the front. The volume of traffic grew beyond any expected measure. During the fateful Norway campaign, PC Bruno had handled 768 messages over four weeks; during the first three weeks of the Battle of France, 3,074.[27]

Airfields were being bombed to prevent the French Air Force fighting back against the invaders. The Luftwaffe signals were prolific. April had been a large increase on March, but May saw a complete explosion of material, with dozens of pages of detail, so much so that air intelligence in London had no time any more to make supercilious remarks on the usefulness of this bit of information or that. And the Germans, baring their plans to the Allies, were wide open to retaliation.

If only the high command would actually use what they were being told. Gustave Bertrand and Gwido Langer watched the war unfold before their unhappy eyes. Langer's notes on the intercepts recorded:[28]

21 May. Key [Enigma settings] determined same day. Message received at 23h00. Message reveals intention of German forces to advance in direction Calais-Boulogne. [The trap, to cut off British and French units from retreat into France, was sprung the same day.]

25 May. Key determined same day. Message received at 22h00. Full order of battle of General Hoth's motorised corps listed. [General Hoth was commanding the right flank of the invading army, the wing that was the 'sickle-cut' which had sliced off the British Expeditionary Force.]

28 May. Key determined 29 May. Message received at 17h10. Locations of French aircraft factories specified (as well as destroyed factories).

30 May. Key determined 31 May. Message received at 01h10. German 77th Squadron requests orders from 8th Air Corps, being unaware of the operation codenamed PAULA. Message received at 01h50. 8th Air Corps responds PAULA means Paris.

31 May. Key determined same day. Message received at 10h45. Full operational details for Operation PAULA: groups involved, height to fly at, target to be pinpointed by incendiary 10 minutes ahead of main attack, inward and outward routes to be followed. [On 3 June the aerial destruction of France's remaining air force in the Paris region began. Only eighty French planes were scrambled in defence.]

Despite the successes of the joint X-Y-Z operation, Bertrand, whose views were echoed by many of his colleagues, was in despair. The General Staffs of both the French and British forces were quite unable to accept what they were being told. To protect the secret source, intelligence reports derived from code-breaking were dressed up as reports of a highly placed agent called Boniface, thereby consigning them to the same category of unreliability as the other contradictory and variable human intelligence which was already too hard to evaluate.[29] Bertrand said he had been feeding '*confiseries aux cochons*' [sweets to swine].[30]

The march of the Wehrmacht could not be stopped. The British Expeditionary Force was gone. The security situation was desperate. MI6 wrote to Alastair Denniston on 6 June 1940 that, 'with the evacuation of the B.E.F. the enemy has obtained possession of all information on Military cyphers and cypher methods' and that 'information vital to our work ... may be becoming available to the enemy'.[31]

It was even more perilous for those on the ground. On 14 May 1940, while the world began to collapse around the hopeless French defences, Lieutenant Colonel John Tiltman was at the French General Headquarters. His mission was not an easy one, to withdraw his team of British code and cipher experts from the joint enterprise before the risk of capture became too acute. It was the diplomatic mission of a rat in a sinking ship. Bertrand came to the rescue. 'We value your party very much; we'd like to keep them, but you'd better get out while you can,' he said. Bertrand's next remark widened Tiltman's eyes to the size of saucers. 'Please tell your chiefs in London that none of your secrets will get into enemy hands.'[32] How could Bertrand make such a promise? There were possibly a hundred French officers who knew about the Enigma secret. If any of them were captured, if the Germans stopped using Enigma, the fledgling operation at Bletchley Park could be stifled before it had really begun.

PC Bruno was vacated on Monday 10 June 1940. The teleprinter link to London was disconnected.

On 21 June 1940, Bertrand took his British liaison officer Pinky MacFarlan in his car to Cazeaux, where the last RAF plane was leaving France.[33] A free France was a thing of the past. By 23 June the defence of France was finished. Word had been passed to the Germans that the French would treat for an armistice. Adolf Hitler selected a location of maximum humiliation for the terms to be signed: a railway carriage in the forest of Compiègne. In that same carriage the defeated German Imperial generals had signed another armistice document on 11 November 1918. The humiliation of France was complete. The only positive aspect to the disaster was that the war in France brought an end to the investigations of Lieutenant Colonel Sadowski. The invisible men of Équipe Z had survived the bombardment from their own side, but their future was looking bleak. Gwido Langer told Bertrand that Poland was still fighting, notwithstanding the armistice, and he was going off to find his commanders.[34] Only Langer had no idea where they were and he had no transport.

For Bertrand, for the Poles of PC Bruno, the war was over, and the successes with *bombas*, cyclometers, and Zygalski's sheets had been a brief, fading spark in the dark cryptological sky which was now going to blanket the whole of Europe. The liaison of X, Y and Z was surely finished.

● ● ●

In moments of darkness, James Bond should come on to the scene. Lieutenant Ian Fleming, RNVR, spent the war reporting to the Director of Naval Intelligence and in that capacity found enough real-life inspiration to create his famous novels in his second career. One of his most colourful contacts was Commander Wilfred Dunderdale, also RNVR, who is one of the many contenders to have been Fleming's model for the suave, martini-swilling international agent of the books.

Dunderdale had a CV which came straight from a Fleming story. He was born in Odessa and grew up speaking Russian as well as English. He was 19 when the Russian Revolution began and found himself caught up in the civil war as temporary honorary sub-lieutenant in the Royal Navy, acting as interpreter and liaison officer with the White Russian naval commanders in the Black Sea. He was also a formidable boxer, on which account he was nicknamed 'Biffy' by colleagues. No doubt deploying his pugilistic skills, he is said to have thwarted a Bolshevik attempt to murder the Tsarist officers (and himself) on the ship he was assigned to and came back from this venture with an MBE ('Dunderdale remain Interpreter to [Senior Naval Officer]. Promote and decorate.') As he moved up in the world, he found himself at Yekaterinburg investigating the murder of the Imperial family and then at Constantinople in the employ of MI6. Another job as interpreter was to assist a White Russian general in a private railway carriage liaison with his mistress. As neither spoke the other's language, Biffy stood outside and interpreted, presumably until the point at which words became unnecessary for the proceedings.

The British Establishment continued to make use of Biffy's services as intermediary in similar sensitive situations: 'he always maintained that his first job for MI6 was to pay off, with gold sovereigns, all the foreign members of the sultan's harem and to repatriate them through the good offices of the Royal Navy.' Liaison involved more traditional forms of intelligence as well and Dunderdale was commended by the Admiralty for his reports on minefields, defences around Odessa, shipping, and so forth. By 1926, possibly because Paris had become a hotbed of White Russian intrigue, but certainly because he spoke excellent French, Biffy was posted there and began his long mission of liaison with the French secret intelligence services. By 1937, he was Head of Station and it is in this context we have met him before, meeting with Rivet and escorting the Polish replica Enigma machine across to London in 1939.[35]

Still under the cover-name Dolinoff, Dunderdale was busy in June 1940, trying to salvage something from the wreck of Allied intelligence in France. On 17 June 1940, contact was established with Bertrand, who from this date on is referred to in the British sources as 'Bertie'.

Bertie was busy too. The situation in France was changing hourly. Now it was Biffy's job to see what could be done about Bertie and his fugitive code-breakers.

> 23.6.40 *to Bertrand.* You and the officers of your staff as well as your Polish colleagues will be very welcome to come to us: apply to Lieutenant FLEMING or to WHINNIE at Bayonne and embark there.

> 25.6.40 *to Bertrand.* Please reply to my telegrams concerning your plans and those of your friends.

> 25.6.40 *from Bertrand.* Current plan is to continue to work under similar conditions.

How could this possibly be, given that the Germans were going to occupy the entire northern half of the country and the Atlantic coast and the new government being installed in the south was likely to be firmly under the German heel?

> 26.6.40 *from Bertrand.* For Dolinoff, in response to telegram No. 1: heartfelt thanks for your invitation; as to our Polish friends they were evacuated by plane before your telegram was received; so it is no longer possible to send them to you; as to the officers of the service, the command is opposed to all movement at the moment.

> 26.6.40 *to Bertrand.* Your telegram No. 4 of the 26th. My superior counts on you for the security of our work. Your telegram 2465. From what place do you expect to continue working. Denniston.

> 28.6.40 *from Bertrand.* For Dolinof. Are obliged to cease radio transmission by reason of Armistice conditions. We ask you to keep listening in each day in the same way as we hope to recommence soon clandestinely. You can count on me for security your work. Regards. Bertrand.[36]

In the midst of the chaos, on 19 June 1940, Henri Navarre had gone to Bordeaux – to where the French government had decamped – and ran into Rex. Navarre was in no doubt about what was good for Rex and good for France. Rex should be put as far away from the enemy as possible. Fortunately, Rex was the passport king. He had been thrown out of Spain for irregularities involving passports in 1920 and this experience had not in the least discouraged him from an energetic trade in false documents ever since.[37] So this occasion was not going to be a challenge. Navarre told Rex to report to the British – not at Bordeaux itself, as that was swamped with people seeking passage – but at Saint Jean de Luz further down the coast. Saint Jean de Luz was not much better, as thousands of displaced Polish soldiers were trying to get to Britain to regroup. The baronial Rex, accompanied by his wife, demanded a better place for her to wait, rather than for her to be jostled in the middle of the crowd of soldiers. The stressed British embarkation officer yelled at Rex. His attempt to queue-barge while waving some possibly-official-looking French order wasn't going to cut any English mustard. Rex stormed off saying, 'I would rather die here in France than live in England and be subjected to your insults.'[38]

A few days later, Rex was back in the unwilling hands of his controllers from the Deuxième Bureau, controllers who included Bertrand. In his suitcase Rex had confidential papers, codes from various countries, blank Dutch, Swedish and Danish passports, identity cards ... the whole gamut of counterfeiting and espionage. The bundle even contained German cipher bureau papers. Bertrand and his colleagues were horrified. Paris had fallen. If the Germans should search Rex's place in Paris ... If the Germans should find more than fake passports ... It didn't bear thinking about.

It might be all up for Rex; it certainly seemed to be all up for France. Like Poland, the country had been ripped in two by the invading power. A mirror, crack'd from side to side. The secret of X-Y-Z and that they had made great strides against Enigma was in the greatest danger. The Polish code-breakers had disappeared again. But Gustave Bertrand was working on a plan.

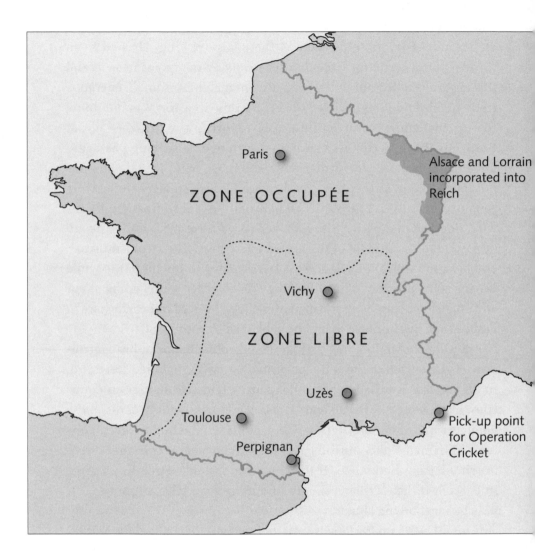

France 1940–42.

8

INTO THREE PARTS

Gallia est omnis divisa in partes tres.
[The totality of Gaul is split into three parts.]

Julius Caesar,
Commentariorum de Bello Gallico

While the body of France was being torn in half, and the immense French Army stood by powerless to prevent it, the future seemed clear enough to the Director of the Government Code & Cypher School. Once the rape of France was complete, Hitler would turn his guns on Britain. Plans were put in place for an emergency evacuation of Bletchley Park. Some documents would be taken for off-site storage in the vaults of Lloyds Bank in Merthyr Tydfil in Wales.[1] Others would have to be destroyed. Still others would go to Canada. Small sections of personnel would be dispersed and keep working in clandestine conditions.

Mercifully, the Director's staff were largely unaware of these fatalistic plans. In fact, the changed war conditions meant that the code-breakers were achieving results which had been unthinkable a year before. With the entry of Italy into the war on 10 June 1940, there was an opportunity for revival of Knox's manual Enigma code-breaking team. The Italians used the old-style Enigma machine without a plugboard, which was similar to that broken by Knox during the Spanish Civil War. In Hut 6, a temporary edifice put up to house code-breakers for whom there was no space in the pre-war buildings, the Luftwaffe's 'Red' Enigma key was broken on 22 May 1940. This was a massive breakthrough, not least because on 1 May, as foreseen, the Germans had abandoned the double encipherment of the indicator, thus rendering obsolete the Zygalski sheets method for finding the daily keys. 'Red' was broken despite this change. The code-breakers were using a new method.[2]

Enigma operators were air force men and soldiers and they were bored by signals work. When they were told that they had to choose three letters at random for a message's start position and a further three letters to send out the enciphered start position, they soon ran out of ideas. For some time, Bletchley Park had spotted that they were apt to use easily guessable combinations, like HIT and LER (if you are patriotic), or ISA and BEL (if you are romantic), or SQE and ISS (if you are just fed up, for which no explanation is suggested, except that Q was often an abbreviation of CH). Bletchley Park called these errors 'Cillis', while the Scarlet Pimpernels referred to the technique of testing for non-random start letters as the 'Method Kx'.[3] In the spring of 1940, the new technique was derived from another glimpse into the operator's mind. It was named 'Herivelismus' after its inventor, another young code-breaker from Cambridge called John Herivel. Herivel imagined the bored Enigma operator would not have a great deal of patience for randomising the positions of the rotors in his machine, so would lazily move the wheels a place or two in one direction or another from where they already were. So, given that you knew from the preamble where the rotors were for the three letters in the ground setting, it was a fair guess that the rotors' position for the indicator was not more than a few places away from that. These insights enabled the Bletchley team working in Hut 6 to find the daily key for 'Red' almost continuously for the remainder of the war.

Furthermore, the machine group was working on the Bombe, which had been delivered in March. It was having some success with naval Enigma messages, but the problem of too many false positives had limited its usefulness. Then, during the summer, one of the early recruits to Bletchley, a mathematician called Gordon Welchman, had a brilliant insight. It was a simple idea and based on simple logic. If the plug-board of the Enigma machine has a cable which plugs A to B, then that cable also plugs B to A. That logic could be translated into a simple adjustment to the Bombe machine, to ensure that the A wire in the B cable was electrically connected to the B wire in the A cable, and so on through all possible letter combinations. Gordon Welchman drew a diagram to show his idea to the incredulous Turing, with little diagonal lines to show the connections he proposed.

Welchman's addition was called a 'diagonal board'. When built, it was neither a board nor diagonal, but a skein of wires at the end of the cabling behind the machine. No matter, it did the job. By increasing the number of connections, Welchman had achieved two huge improvements to the performance of the Bombe. Not only did it stop less often – increasing the likelihood that a feasible start position it had found was the real one – but also it enabled more flexibility in designing 'menus' (the Bletchley jargon for wiring diagrams for the cables connecting up the reproduction Enigma rotors revolving on the front of the machine). In August 1940, the modified Bombe came into operation. It was called *Agnus Dei*, or Aggie for short, because it was going to take away the sins of the world, and with a bit of luck, grant peace.

After the fall of France, the Germans turned their attention to Britain. In early July, the code-breakers learned from decrypted messages that the Luftwaffe was planning to destroy the Royal Air Force completely in preparation for an invasion. Just like in France. For the next few months, the country would be subjected to attack from the air: bombings of airfields and aircraft factories; incendiaries dropped on civilian targets; dogfights and terror.

● ● ●

Colonel Louis Rivet noted in his war diary that he had, under the terms of the armistice, given orders for the official dissolution of Bertrand's department on 21 June 1940 and, two days later, the departure of the Polish code-breakers to Africa. On 25 June he reported that Pétain had addressed the French people. His diary entry concluded, 'Mourning of France … a day of infinite sadness'.

The previous day, a plane landed at Oran in Algeria and a small group of rather unmilitary personnel clambered out after an uncomfortable flight. This was only one day after the British telegram inviting the Polish code-breakers to Britain. The code-breakers themselves, bundled out of metropolitan France, may not have known that Bertrand (keeping tight control over his assets) had 'not received' the message until after the Poles had safely gone – 'safely' in the sense that he could continue to deploy them in his own personal war effort. Langer had his suspicions about Bertrand's statement. The evacuation of the Poles had been done in a hurry, with Bertrand claiming that he was fearful they would be discovered and that he was unable to contact Langer's Polish superiors.[4]

A week after the arrival of the Polish code-breakers in Oran, the British fleet appeared at Mers-el-Kébir, the port of Oran. The British were there not to enforce MI6's offer to rescue the Polish code-breakers, but to destroy the French Navy. If Admiral François Darlan did not agree to send the French ships to British ports or scuttle them, the risk of takeover by the Germans – and the threat that would pose to the country that claimed to rule the waves – would be intolerable. The French resisted; the British opened fire. The Polish code-breakers were still in the port on the morning of 3 July 1940; by some fluke they were put on a transport to Algiers only six hours before the shelling began. The established order, who was fighting whom and for what, was turning upside-down.

While Bletchley Park prepared for invasion and evacuation, France was undergoing a revolution. The emasculated, effete, discredited *ancien régime* called the Third Republic had been found wanting. What France needed was something new, something tough. Most importantly, for a nation carrying the tradition of Austerlitz and Jena and countless other victories, a military leader of unsullied reputation should stand as Head of State. Such a leader could be found in Marshal Pétain: erect, immovable and slightly deaf. The hero of Verdun, Pétain was the symbol of France. His nickname was *le drapeau* [the flag]. Pétain was not just the symbol of the future of France, he was France. In keeping with modern zeitgeist the new régime should be authoritarian and inspire the people with stirring slogans. What the Germans had failed to do in 1914, the new French government managed all on its own, abandoning liberty, equality and comradeship. From now on it was *travail, famille, patrie* on coins and official symbols.

The coming weeks were taken up in adjusting to the new Vichy régime. Fortunately the thirteen pages of armistice agreed between the Germans and the French had remarkably little detail on anything pertaining to the structure of the new French State. So it was in order for the Pétain government to set up something called the Bureau des Menées Antinationales (BMA), or the Anti-nationalist Activities Office. The BMA's job was, in theory, to inquire into and stamp out anti-patriotic behaviour; in practice, it provided a seedbed in which the acorn of a counter-intelligence service could grow anew.

By mid July 1940, the acorn had begun to germinate. Under the auspices of General Maxime Weygand – the aide-de-camp of Marshal Foch in the Great War, the liaison officer to Piłsudski in the Russo-Polish War of 1920, appointed Supreme Commander of the French Army during the Battle of France after it was too late to do anything and now Minister of Defence under Pétain – a new intelligence service was being formed secretly. The BMA would have a second division – MA2 – which would be the new designation of an old organisation, the Deuxième Bureau. Bertrand was back from Algeria, back in contact with the Vichy government, and almost back in business.[5] MA2 would have a code-breaking capability; it would be just like old times. But who, among those with anti-nationalist sentiments, would the service be watching?

The French had not been supposed to make a separate peace with Germany, at least not without the consent of their British ally. Perhaps the armistice did not violate that obligation. But the attempt by the French military authorities to sweep the Poles under the scope of its ceasefire terms was certainly an offence to Poland. Poland was going to continue fighting and on the BBC General Sikorski told Polish troops to have nothing to do with the capitulation. As far as Gwido Langer was concerned, the slippery machinations of Bertrand were at best opaque, but could be downright treacherous. Langer was trying to determine the right thing to do:

Although the French have entered into a truce with the Germans, tactically speaking the two are still at war with each other, therefore the French are not our enemies. How we are treated depends on our own authorities; thus far, we have not received an order ... A careless severance of relations ... [could] jeopardise the results of our work not just for us but also for Y.

What he needed was orders. Bertrand, piecing together his master plan for MA2, might be the answer, but until the Polish headquarters (setting up in the Hotel Rubens in London) could focus on this small team, already under a cloud of suspicion, located on territory of dubious loyalty, there was nothing they could do but wait.

> Whatever I want to do, I can never forget that we're on French territory, and it is the French that are in control ... We are sitting here doing nothing while others need us.[6]

Actually, there were some things to do in North Africa. Semi-detached from the war, the resort towns of the Mediterranean coast contrived to continue to provide a programme of entertainments and distractions for visitors just as before. Living there was cheap; food was good and plentiful, and the hotel accommodation, where the Poles were billeted, was all paid for. There were camel excursions to the desert, drinking in bars, visits to beaches and no work. Maybe it was not altogether bad, for most of them at least.[7]

For Henryk Zygalski, however, the experience of French North Africa had not begun well. On arrival in Algiers he began to feel feverish. His temperature went off the scale and immediately he was sent to the military hospital. It was pneumonia and complicated by an oozing abscess on his head. It would not be until 15 August 1940 that he was well enough to be discharged.[8] By then, as the Luftwaffe began its assault on Britain, a new war plan was forming.

● ● ●

One day in the hot summer of 1940, a gentleman in middle age, rather unfit, balding, and steaming slightly in a suit which was altogether unsuitable for the weather, could be found consulting estate agents.[9] The gentleman's name was Monsieur Barsac and together with his wife Mary (who was too elegant to indulge in steaming) he was looking for somewhere to live. After some weeks of searching, a suitable country villa – rather too large for a farmhouse, not quite imposing enough to amount to a château – was offered. It called itself, rather pretentiously, the Château des Fouzes, probably because outside its front door it boasted an elegant double staircase flanked by two towers. Behind this façade, it actually was a large farmhouse, unassuming and unremarkable. It also had some special advantages. M. Barsac, being a retiring and modest sort, wanted his new property to be some way off the road and he wanted it to be outside the centre of town. The Château des Fouzes was close enough to the road to see, across the parched lawn, who might be coming, yet far enough back for security. And it was a couple of kilometres or so from the nearest town, an attractive place called Uzès located in the department of the Gard, well within the south of France. In other words, the château was in the middle of nowhere. Mme Barsac agreed, the place was wholly suitable.

Funded by a special dispensation from General Weygand, the Château des Fouzes was acquired for the secret secret intelligence service by Bertrand in his latest alias as M. Barsac. This particular secret needed to be kept secret even from those who set the bounds of secrecy. Bertrand was still working for Rivet, who was working for France. France still needed an intelligence service, but who were the targets on whom intelligence was to be gathered? There was an armistice in place, but technically France was still at war with Germany. Although France was not technically at war with Britain, the bombardment of the fleet at Oran suggested otherwise. If that were not confusing enough, it might not be safe to assume that the interests of the Vichy government were the same as the interests of France. In the end, it was a question of whom you trusted.

On 23 September 1940, Rivet was summoned to Vichy for an interview with the new minister who had replaced Weygand in Vichy's volatile political mix. Charles Huntziger was one of the French generals who had signed the armistice on behalf of France and subsequently served as French representative to the German Armistice Commission.

Article 14 of the armistice required all French radio transmissions to cease. The clarificatory protocol added that the objective of this clause was to preclude activities which could operate to the detriment of the German war effort.[10] Now Huntziger was laying down the law to Rivet:

1. General situation. France conquered ... England little chance, compromise possible. Germany better chance.

2. No collaboration with [British] Intelligence Service given risk of reprisals ... Give nothing to the English.

3. Germans accuse us of allowing the English to use clandestine radio posts in France ... Seek out and close down ...[11]

Colonel Rivet commented in his diary, 'The general wants to play with a straight bat, without revealing his actual thinking.' Rivet was a master of code-reading. In deciphered form, he understood that Huntziger had authorised the establishment of a new *poste de commandement* in the château near Uzès. The out-station would be called PC Cadix, perhaps because the old *Via Domitiana* – the imperial highway from Rome to Cadiz – ran through Nîmes, the nearest town of any size. This part of France is crammed with Roman remains, but during wartime there were not going to be many tourists poking their noses around PC Cadix. Gustave Bertrand had his château, he also had his own car and chauffeur, Maurice, necessary to ferry him to and from Nîmes – where he and his wife actually planned to live – and there were two other cars and two vans for the rest of his team.[12] A team that would be composed of the Polish code-breakers currently kicking their heels in Algiers.

But it was still unclear what Bertrand's team would actually be doing – on whom they would be spying. Gwido Langer went to see the Polish consul in Algiers in early August to get his orders. His reception was unsympathetic. Langer himself was uncomfortable. Algiers was far too cushy for discipline and Bertrand's MA2 plan had divided the Polish team. With the seat of Polish government now established in London, it was not obvious why any of them should be working for Bertrand any more, under the terms of the armistice and the eyes of Vichy. Rejewski, Różycki and another code-breaker, Henryk Paszkowski, all wanted to get to Britain. Zygalski was in hospital. Others were content to go with Bertrand. Langer, at least, thought he knew Bertrand well enough, and concluded that the fight against Germany could be carried on under him. The time for debate was over, and good order and discipline should prevail.

Then Bertrand himself arrived in Algiers on 30 August 1940 and promptly began to dismantle the fragile unity which Langer had achieved. Against Langer's wishes, Bertrand asked every one of the Polish team individually if they wanted to return to France.[13] This was part of Bertrand's plan, divide and conquer, to establish himself as the chief and to trim down the size of the party. 'Plenty of buzz ensued within the team'. Even on the eve of departure there was still one dissident.[14] At last, on 26 September 1940, the whole group boarded a ship called the *Lamoricière*, bound for Marseilles.

Even that was not the end of it. On arrival, Bertrand had another go at cutting back the list of names to join his PC Cadix operation. The team was too large. Bertrand still had his Équipe D of seven Spanish code-breakers as well as fifteen French personnel, and unless he could reduce the numbers there were going to be fifteen Poles.[15] This time Langer put his foot down. On 8 October 1940 he obtained an order from General Juliusz Kleeberg, who was officially Polish military attaché at Vichy but in practice the acting commander-in-chief of the remnants of Polish forces still in France, to the effect that the movement of the intelligence group to PC Cadix was approved by the London government. Langer made all his group countersign it.[16] On 16 October, the Polish government in London sent out further instructions: the Polish team were to obtain intelligence on German, Italian and French forces and troop movements, orders of battle, and navy, army and air force dispositions. They would monitor German police networks, to find out what was happening in Poland. This was all to be done in secret as far as possible; the gathering of material on the French could be dropped if Bertrand was controlling them too closely.

● ● ●

During the autumn and winter of 1940, a new web was spun across Europe by the re-exiled Polish Intelligence Bureau. Outposts were set up in France, Lisbon, Berne, Stockholm, Jerusalem and many other cities. All strands led back to London, but the best place of all for gathering intelligence on Germany was France. Polish servicemen had mustered there in 1939 and many were ready to stay behind, notwithstanding the occupation of half the country. Ekspozytura F – Outpost F for France – was to be the most significant piece of the new fabric. It would be run from Marseilles by Major Wincenty Zarembski, cover-name Tudor. Various other branches of the network channelled their reports through Ekspozytura F, notably the sub-network in the Zone Occupée headed by Captain Roman Czerniawski (cover-name Armand), and the sub-network Ekspozytura AFR in French North Africa, headed by Major Mieczysław Słowikowski (cover-name Rygor).[17]

Into this complex knot of intelligence and spying one further strand was woven: Ekspozytura 300, run by Langer in his cover-name of Wicher, would report direct to London but liaise closely with Ekspozyturas F and AFR. As if things were not yet sufficiently confused, Ekspozytura 300 was to be funded and housed by their old ally Bertrand. Bertrand was to be allowed to imagine he also controlled it. Wicher, the cover-name for the now-defunct operation at Pyry, had now been adopted by Gwido Langer personally, while Ekspozytura 300 was known to Bertrand as Équipe Z.

Weaving seamlessly through the complexity of Vichy politics, the main difficulty faced by Bertrand was technical in nature. The intelligence officers of Ekspozytura 300 spent the month of October 1940 engaged in the war-winning activities of 'cutting down trees, chopping wood, peeling potatoes, preparing vegetables and, from time to time, plucking poultry'.[18] The fifteen woodcutters had, most of them, rather bad French and incomprehensible accents. Every single one had a fake name: Louis Lange (Langer), Mathew Muller (Ciężki), Antoine Balande (Palluth), Pierre Ranaud (Rejewski), Julien Roget (Różycki) and Henri Sergant (Zygalski), to name those we have met before.[19] It was primitive, too: 'We can't take a bath on site and the nearest toilet is 27km away'.[20] At least they were being paid by the French and – in view of the challenge with plumbing – someone did their laundry. But this was hardly the intellectual challenge the dramatis personae of Polish actors had signed on for.

Without listening equipment, they could not snoop. That was remediable, with the help of the BMA's handy budget. But much more significantly, they could not get the Enigma settings. They had carefully extricated one of the precious reconstituted Enigma machines from the débâcle which was the fall of France, but an Enigma machine will only decipher intercepted messages when you know how to set it up. There were no longer any Zygalski sheets – not that they would have been any use following the change in German operating procedures in May – and the other methods they had used during the Battle of France were haphazard. Furthermore, the radio networks which the Germans were using actively in the post-armistice period were different, so it would have been much harder to find settings than it had been in May and June. By contrast, the British at Bletchley had answers to these problems. If PC Cadix was going to be a success, it would be necessary to revive the old international co-operation between X, Y and Z.

On 9 October 1940, Colonel Rivet went to General Huntziger's office once again.[21] There was a thaw: the needs of PC Cadix could constitute an exception to the rule against dealings with MI6. The condition was that PC Cadix should also try to glean intelligence on the British themselves. The way was now open for Bertrand to try and re-establish contact with Biffy Dunderdale. Bertrand probably didn't know that Langer was also trying to reopen the same channel himself via the Polish government in London.[22]

The reaction in Britain to Bertrand's approach was nervous and confused:

C.S.S. [Chief of the Security Service], the F.O. [Foreign Office] and the Service Departments set store on the intelligence derived from cryptography in general, and in particular the E traffic, and are concerned to guard the security of this source …

The French and the Poles are quite aware of this, and in the last telegram from the French in July they undertook to safeguard us. This they have done in some unexplained manner. It is clear from our recent results that nothing has been divulged …

We must ask them:- Who are their masters? (i.e.) If they are officially paid by a Government which may join the Nazis at any time, it is too risky for us. (Or) If they are aiming for continuity so as to be ready for a French 'come back' …

45000 [Dunderdale] and his party are so pro-French that they may have difficulty in putting our point of view in this question of collaboration with a party, who cannot really help us at present, but whom we wish to retain as friends and future allies.[23]

Dunderdale was briefed accordingly. Meanwhile, Bertrand had prepared for the negotiations and had an unexpected gift, providing the British were willing to engage more concretely than just talking about friendship and a future alliance. Bertrand was offering intelligence on Italian naval movements, gleaned from an agent. Moreover, his interceptors had stumbled upon some Double Playfair messages his Z team had also begun to decoct.[24] Double Playfair was horribly difficult to decipher: it was a transposition cipher used by both the Luftwaffe and the German police. From the British point of view, having a flow of this material was a real temptation: all the more so since radio-interception coverage had been cut back after the fall of France.

Although attracted by Bertrand's offer, the British continued to debate anxiously what they could and could not do with him. Just where did his loyalties lie? Ultimately, like Gwido Langer, they needed to look into the whites of his eyes. A meeting in Lisbon might be arranged? Or Tangier?[25] 'I hope that Dunderdale will assure himself that Bertrand is really working in conditions of absolute security. I consider that he should not expect all the keys we have worked out since July … I consider that Dunderdale's mission will really consist in finding out why Bertrand wishes to reopen the co-operation and under what conditions.' Dunderdale's deputy wired back: 'Date between March 15th and March 20th only possible for Bertie [Bertrand] … He would be grateful if Doli [Dunderdale] could bring all keys E found since July, all indications on method employed to found them … All this because begin work now in complete security … Is Den [Denniston] interested for cypher machine of Swiss Army which is used for sending meteograms.'[26]

More temptation; the British succumbed. Dunderdale met with Bertrand – who had got himself across not-very-neutral Spain by train — in Lisbon in March 1941. He returned to Cadix with a portable transmitter for communicating with London and a spring in his step. X-Y-Z had been reborn.

• • •

When Julius Caesar described Gaul as partitioned into three, he had a somewhat different picture in mind to that of France in 1941. To begin with, his partition lines were not in the same place as the demarcation line between the Zone Libre and the Zone Occupée. And another thing: in Caesar's day, the third part of France was already part of the Roman Empire, and not part of France at all. In 1941, however, the Vichy government continued to rule the French Empire, whose main asset was in North Africa. The third area of focus for the nascent Polish intelligence network was going to be the third part of France and Ekspozytura 300 would provide the foundations for Ekspozytura AFR.

The fake French at the Château des Fouzes signed up to the new dispositions on 7 March 1941.[27] Maksymilian Ciężki would run signals intelligence for Ekspozytura AFR, the African show. Every two months a contingent of five Polish intelligence workers would come out to him for a tour, one dedicated to Russian material, one to German and two for sorting and distribution. Henri Braquenié, the one credible French cryptanalyst, would also be in Algiers, assigned to German traffic. They did not yet know it, but the Algerian outpost was going to carry out a crucial role in the gathering of intelligence for the Allies in one of the most critical campaigns of World War Two.

Major Słowikowski, cover-name Rygor, set up shop in Algiers shortly after Maksimilian Ciężki. Słowikowski arranged his first meeting with Ciężki in textbook spy school fashion. A dinner invitation was slid under the door of room no. 16 in the Hotel Arago. Ciężki arrived on time; indeed, from his perspective, Słowikowski was overdue. Messages from London had been backing up: there were demands for details of anti-aircraft defences; shipments of war materials to Germany; the Algerian railway network and more. Słowikowski pumped Ciężki for news of his old friend Langer: he used to be in radio intelligence, what's he up to now? There were no secrets worth finding in radio today, surely? Ciężki swiftly disabused his colleague. Since the time of the Russo-Polish War, signals and code-breaking had been the backbone of Polish intelligence. And they still were:

> Mathew [Ciężki] mentioned a case where a German radio message to their resident agent in Egypt was deciphered, ordering him to poison all the fresh water supplies in Alexandria with typhoid. London was immediately informed … [The telegrams] helped to arrest the German agent who could have dealt an enormous blow to the Allied forces in the Middle East.[28]

On deciphering the clutch of telegrams which Ciężki had brought, Słowikowski realised he had his work cut out. The next day Ciężki was back with more telegrams and more the day after. Now Polish HQ wanted maps and town plans for the North African ports; telephone directories; descriptions of ships requisitioned by the Vichy government; you name it. There was no other intelligence network in French North Africa, yet the Allies seemed to expect him to create one instantly out of hot, spice-scented air. For a magician like Gustave Bertrand, this, or at least the illusion of it, might have been possible. Słowikowski had to use more conventional means and, meanwhile, he had to keep his head down.

Thus it came to pass that a merchant of Polish extraction, going by the name of Dr Skowroński, became the co-owner of a barley meal factory, doling out porridge. As the rationing imposed by the Vichy régime was extended to French North Africa, the production of staple foods was a credible cover for Słowikowski, especially as his role was as capital-providing partner and he needed no technical knowledge about grains and gruel. It gave him an excuse for mingling among the upper échelons of the colonials, an opportunity for getting insight into the morale and inclinations of a divided country. Nobody need know that the so-called Dr Skowroński, settling in with his sultry-eyed wife Sophie and son George, was in fact a major in the Polish Army and the Chief of Allied Intelligence Services in French North Africa.

●　●　●

From the British perspective, it did not seem that there was much to learn from French military strategy in World War Two, unless you took the cynical view that there were several 'how not to' lessons. Nevertheless, the British had decided to follow one chapter from the French textbook to the very letter.

On 7 January 1941, a group of junior officers arrived at Bletchley Park. Two were from the army and two from the navy. Their mission was educational. They were there to find out whatever the code-breakers were willing to tell them. It was not that unusual for army and navy officers to visit the Park, to be blinded with a bit of science and in return to give back a hoorah speech and tell the chaps to keep up the good work. Nor was it unusual for new experts to arrive at Bletchley. The staff was growing, with over 500 people on the site now that GC&CS was proving its worth. Nevertheless, this quartet was out of the ordinary. They had strange accents and foreign uniforms. They were bemused to be offered sherry by Alastair Denniston, for that was not the usual tipple of their home country. The visitors were American.[29]

America was not at war and, despite Roosevelt's election success in November 1940, it would take an earth-shattering event going to the heart of American security to bring them into another European conflict. So the French strategy, which the British had embraced, was to begin with the sharing of information. A thin cord, but one that could be drawn on to pull in much more weighty ones. Just as the French had done in 1937–38, the British laid as bait their most vital secrets with the intention that once the Americans were hooked they would then be reeled in to a closer and wider military cooperation, beginning with supply and convoy protection in the Atlantic. The Americans were eager; the bait was gobbled.

Although the British had succeeded in obtaining an intelligence mission from the US, they were still wary of how much to reveal. The four visitors were shown more about organisation and unsolved problems than they were about the inner workings of Bombes and cryptological methods. But people who have made breakthroughs want to show off their achievements and such international opportunities are rare in the secret services. As with the initial X-Y-Z meetings, the important thing was that people who spoke the same language of cryptology were meeting each other and forming a mutual respect. The wheels were turning, X-Y-Z was evolving. The alliance against Enigma might, in time, add the next letter on. It was becoming X-Y-Z-A.

By early 1941, Alan Turing had become head of Hut 8, one of the unattractive temporary buildings which had been nailed together across the Park. Hut 8 was where the code-breakers were attacking Naval Enigma. Naval Enigma was a much tougher proposition than Army or Air Force Enigma and at the same time more critical for the British, who were fighting on alone. More difficult, because the German Navy did not use the three-letter indicator system for the start positions of rotors, let alone make the mistake of repeating the encipherment of it. Instead, they used a completely separate set of tables – in essence, a code book – common to ship and shore, which guided the cipher clerks as to how the Enigma was set up. If Bletchley Park had the code book, decryption methods being deployed against Army and Air Force Enigma would work; or, if they had plenty of deciphered messages from which to construct cribs, they could use Army and Air Force methods to reconstruct the code book. It was all very frustrating and only limited progress was being made on this critical problem. And it was critical, possibly the most critical of the war, because U-boats were attacking convoys at will, sinking merchant ships and stifling the country's oxygen supply.[30]

Another secret had to be shared, as another relationship was being forged at Bletchley Park. Working with Alan Turing on the Naval Enigma problem was a female code-breaker. Women were rare recruits to Bletchley and Knox had snapped up most of the promising young women to work with him in his 'research' section. There, using pencil and paper methods, they had notable success against versions of the Enigma machine with no plugboard. Gordon Welchman, however, had recruited one of his Cambridge students, Joan Clarke, to join Alan Turing's team. Bletchley Park didn't have code-breaker grades for women, so she had to be graded as a linguist, even though she spoke only English and Mathematics. But Joan was remarkably clever and she could relate to Alan Turing. Probably for the first time in his life, Alan Turing had found a woman he could talk to, and while they puzzled over the statistical approach he had adopted from Jerzy Różycki's clock method to find a way round the code book problem, Alan and Joan grew close. In the spring of 1941, Alan Turing popped the question. It was awkwardly done, but she said 'yes', she would become Alan's wife. There was muted jubilation in Hut 8: the two were obviously good for each other.

Except for the secret. In 1941, gay men could not afford to make much of their sexuality, for 'gross indecency' between men was a criminal offence and periodically the police would start a wave of prosecutions. Nobody at Bletchley knew about Alan Turing's secret, but in all honesty he could not fail to tell Joan. The day after his proposal, he made a clean breast of it. Perhaps it would be a *mariage blanc*? World War Two was creating some very strange relationships, but this one was not destined to last. The engagement was, after a short while, called off.

• • •

Girls were also thin on the ground at the Château des Fouzes. Opportunities for anything much more exciting than code-breaking were few. There were country walks in the nearby fields and vineyards, opportunities to go drinking in Uzès and occasional exeats on bicycles to the Roman antiquities. The code-breakers wore navy blue overalls and clogs supplied for free by the French. The shops in Uzès didn't have much to sell and the Poles didn't have much money, so they made do. As at the Château de Vignolles, dining was segregated by nation, and conditions were decidedly more cramped than they had been at the former centre for Gustave Bertrand's operations.[31]

One bright spot was that Bertrand had installed in the environs of the château a man called David as cook, as well his trusty chauffeur Maurice, who would use the car to get wine, brandy and other essentials for the team. As at the Château de Vignolles, the demand for booze was high. Sometimes it was quite fun. In the winter of 1941–42 there was the unusual event of a snowfall in Provence, allowing the code-breakers to see if they could climb a snow-laden palm tree. There was football. There were bullfights at Nîmes. And there were curious oversize terracotta jars in the grounds, which were tested to see if they would conceal a whole code-breaker. On one occasion, one of the Poles, having been admitted to Maurice's sanctum, had himself photographed standing prisoner-like behind the iron security bars of the basement windows. Bertrand did not see the funny side of that.

Also within the sanctum lived Maurice's daughter Monique with her pet rabbit. Kazimierz Gaca (the young officer who had buried the Enigma machines near Włodzimierz during the flight from Warsaw) may not have recognised it as a blessing when he suffered a ruptured appendix and had to be operated on. Nor that he had to convalesce without the benefit of antibiotics. Yet there was a positive to the situation. Monique may have been young but she was a sympathetic nurse, closer in age to Kazimierz than he was to most of the other code-breakers, and she was fun to have around. Monique was also small enough to fit into a terracotta jar without any difficulty and she soon found Kazimierz more interesting than the rabbit.

The Poles were also expected to do some code-breaking. To start with, Bertrand put the Poles on to the Swiss commercial and military ciphers. Nothing of the remotest interest emerged from the commercial material, but the military cipher had been done on an Enigma-like machine, which Marian Rejewski and his colleagues found fairly straightforward to reverse-engineer. It was on this device that the Swiss had enciphered their weather secrets, which Bertrand was dangling before the British. Edward Fokczyński, co-founder of the AVA factory, made a model of the machine out of cardboard, which Bertrand took with him to Lisbon to present to Biffy Dunderdale. It must have been an interesting handover: a fold-up cardboard mock-up of a Swiss enciphering machine and some old weather forecasts, for a powerful radio transceiver. Bertrand knew how to strike a bargain.

The Swiss material was probably a distraction. The actual enemies were Russia and Nazi Germany and German ciphers were what the Polish team focused on, now they could actually receive a good variety of signals. These included machine ciphers used by the Luftwaffe and hand ciphers used by the German police. Another cipher, cracked by Antoni Palluth, was being used by the Abwehr and its agents. In 1941, the code-breakers of Uzès read 4,158 German messages. 'The contents of the messages were interesting,' wrote Marian Rejewski:

their senders were German agents who, passing themselves off as ordinary tourists, observed the movements of ships in French and Algerian ports … This sort of activity in the unoccupied zone, in the light of the ceasefire agreement, was apparently illegal, and … the French police, tipped off by us in advance, organised a dragnet and caught them.[32]

The German activities in the Zone Libre were in contravention of the armistice. Equally illegal, technically, were the radio transmissions of Ekspozytura 300, since they were done with the blessing of the French. The radio-relay statistics were given by Langer in his annual report to Headquarters for the year 1941: 813 messages sent to Polish HQ, all relating to Ekspozytura AFR in Algiers; 666 sent to Algiers; 30 sent to Ekspozytura F and 361 sent to various Ekspozytura F agents. Over 1,100 of these, that is two thirds, were not known to Bertrand. Not just the content, but even the fact of the messages being sent. On top of this were over 2,000 messages exchanged with MI6.[33] The British concern about who were the ultimate masters of the operation was answered in this way. The Poles may have been housed and financed by the Vichy government, but they were able to operate with a large degree of independence.

● ● ●

For Henryk Zygalski and the small team who had gone to Algiers with Ciężki, the move to North Africa was a release. Zygalski, aka Henri Sergant, had not been happy with the arrangements at Cadix and only days after signing his (false) name to the orders naming him as a member of the first African party, he had petitioned General Kleeberg to be released from the strictures of covert intelligence and allowed to join a combat regiment. Whether Kleeberg replied is not recorded, but joining intelligence is a one-way journey. Those entrusted with the Enigma secret could not, ever, be permitted to go into combat zones where they could be captured and interrogated. Despite his misgivings and despite the memories of his unpleasant illness there in June, for Zygalski the tour of duty in Algiers was liberating. Free from the controls of Bertrand, the Poles could let their hair down. Soon there were girls, Ewa and Włada, with whom there were outings, beaches and parties. And, just before the end of the two-month tour, there was Simone ...[34] The romance of another Henri, the fake Henri Materon, aka Henryk Paszkowski, brought him the epithet 'Casanova' for his exploits, which was rather unfair as his liaison culminated in marriage to his girl, Janina.

Their French colleague, Henri Braquenié, found the antics of the team quite startling:

The only annoying thing about the Poles was how they drew attention to themselves abroad. When they went to the restaurant, they ordered extraordinary dishes. They were always doing things which drew attention to themselves. Not only in the restaurant ... For example, when at the beginning in Algeria we had this villa in the south of Algiers which was called 'Kouba', we took the tram which we nicknamed 'the cipher' ... at the end of the line, you took a bus which took us up to 'Kouba', and so, as they always talked in Polish or Spanish, on one occasion the conductor asked me 'Who are those blokes?' Turning away discreetly, I replied, 'Be quiet, that's the Italian Armistice Commission.'[35]

More serious was the Polish radio traffic going from Africa to London, which was re-enciphered at PC Cadix, and added to by messages Ekspozytura 300 was sending to London on its own account. This growing volume of beeps in the airwaves was becoming a matter of security. To encrypt their own material the Poles were using a machine of their own invention, the so-called Lacida or LCD, standing for its inventors Langer, Ciężki and Danilewicz (or sometimes LCP for Langer, Ciężki and Palluth). Like Enigma, the Lacida used a system of rotors to encrypt a message. One day in the summer, Marian Rejewski asked if he could see an encrypted report, and he and Henryk Zygalski had a go to see if they could break the cipher. It took them two hours. The reaction was predictable: Langer was by turns furious, outraged and alarmed, yet unwilling to shoot the messengers. All communications with London had to cease. Improvements in cipher security were ordered. With a bit of effort, Langer was calmed down. After all, his machine-breaking cryptanalysts were the best in the world, far better than anyone the Germans could pit against Lacida.

For his part, Bertrand knew nothing of Mieczysław Słowikowski and his operation or all these extra messages.[36] Nothing was quite what it seemed. The only thing that seemed real was that everyone was deceiving somebody else. Gustave Bertrand thought that his teams of Poles in PC Cadix and their outpost in Algeria were working for him. Maksymilian Ciężki was ostensibly working for Bertrand, though in fact he was working for Polish military intelligence, and the details needed to be kept from Bertrand. Słowikowski was under cover, keeping away from the Vichy officials, because he was working for the Poles, not the French. But Colonel Gano's new intelligence centre in London was, more or less, under the control of Dunderdale and it was fairly clear to Słowikowski that he was, indirectly, working for MI6.

As for Gustave Bertrand, nobody actually knew who he was working for. He wanted the Poles and the British to believe it was for the Allied cause, with liaison via Dunderdale. The Vichy régime generally did not know what it wanted, but from time to time it needed to put on a show of hostility to Britain, particularly when it came to colonial affairs. Since it was Vichy ministers who paid Bertrand's bills, he needed them to believe he was working for them. In fact nobody, not his superiors at Vichy, nor Gwido Langer, nor Biffy Dunderdale, knew very much about Gustave Bertrand at all.

● ● ●

Bertrand did not keep a regular schedule. He would disappear to Vichy. He had a flat on the south coast and he was living in Nîmes rather than at the château. Periodically, Bertrand would have Maurice drive him to the station, from where he would take a train north. On these occasions, he might be absent for several days.

When he travelled through France as Monsieur Barsac, Bertrand was, for these purposes, a parfumier's salesman, visiting Paris. A real parfumier friend furnished him with the what-have-you for a whiff of credibility. The fake perfume merchant's first actual task was to salvage the Enigma replicas from the Bélin factory. The engineering had been completed but there had been no opportunity to take delivery before the Germans invaded. So, using a variety of false names and *laissez-passer* documents, Bertrand would take the train across the demarcation line and secrete bits and pieces of precision engineering about his person for the return journey. There was, however, a more mysterious purpose to some of Bertrand's visits. At some point, while Bertrand was having a nice meal at Maxim's, Paris's famous restaurant (his excuse for this indulgence was that it was a good place to observe the 'gentlemen of the Wehrmacht'), he struck up an acquaintance with a German spy called Max. The purpose of these rendezvous was to furnish Bertrand with details of what the Germans were up to. For Max was well placed, working in the German Embassy in Paris. In his account, Bertrand says he never knew Max's other name, a claim that seems rather implausible, since Bertrand began a series of meetings with Max, many of which took place in Max's own office. Bertrand was probably being discreet and cooked up the meal at Maxim's as a convenient cover story. Among other favours, Max smoothed Bertrand's passage across the line, once even booking him (Enigma parts and all) into the compartment reserved for diplomats travelling between Paris and Vichy.[37]

The liaisons with Max were not just for the frisson of visits to the enemy's headquarters. The Service de Renseignements already had a mole in the German Embassy, called (or codenamed) Bodo, an Austrian spy landed by Rex in 1935 who had become part of the German Embassy establishment after the annexure of Austria.[38] Bodo, or Max (who may be one and the same), was able to provide an inside view not available from any other source, which was relayed straight back to London over the radio link provided by Dunderdale. London rated the information 'especially useful'.[39] Yet, Bertrand's behaviour was not unambiguously pro-British. On the wall at the château there were portraits of Pétain and Darlan, hardly necessary as a show in a farmhouse which was never – they fervently hoped – going to be visited by anyone checking on its occupants' political correctness. And Bertrand was still trying to make the X-Y-Z relationship a bargain rather than an alliance. In his eyes, the British should not have been given the Enigma for free, and they should continue to pay for it.

• • •

Bertrand the magician had made people appear. On his visits to the occupied North, he could also make people disappear. This was harder, even impossible, but doing the impossible is the stock-in-trade of magicians. Since the evacuation to Britain, Major Jan Żychoń had been running the Intelligence Department in General Sikorski's London-based General Staff.[40] It was with Żychoń that Gwido Langer communicated when direction from Headquarters was needed: 'Janio' was the principal contact. Also in London, in charge of Polish naval intelligence, was Brunon Jabloński, who also served as Żychoń's number two. Bertrand was to whisk the wives of these two Poles out from under the noses of the Germans in the Zone Occupée.

1º. Following the personal request of [Dunderdale], B. has done the impossible to extract Madame ZYCHON and her friend Madame JABLONSKA from the Zone Occupée. 2º. Madame Z refused to leave ... before being sure that her husband was in the Zone Libre. Madame J has arrived all right and asks for news and instructions from her husband. 3º. With extreme priority desire advice of Monsieur Z. on next steps for departure of his wife and response of Monsieur J.[41]

Disappearing acts were not easy and they were outside Bertie's area of expertise. He was also being asked to extricate Polish agents across Spain to Lisbon. Arranging some iffy paperwork, through sympathetic contacts in the Vichy régime, was usually not too hard: Bertie had been buying documentation for years. But setting up the transport and logistics was not his métier. Later on, Bertrand's powers of exfiltration would be put to a more serious test.

In the summer of 1941, though, the Vichy government was putting pressure on Bertrand that called upon all his fine qualities of psychology and diplomacy. He had to slip, eel-like, past the Germans, pacify the Poles and convince the British to keep faith. The Vichy régime itself was in disarray, needing to be alternately soothed and ignored. When the British attacked the French colonies – always the sensitive spot where Vichy pride was concerned – in Syria on 8 June 1941, that must surely be the end of Bertie's love affair with MI6? Not at all. A few days later Bertrand fired off a petulant telegram to Dunderdale with a litany of complaints, demanding the Enigma keys solved by the British since 23 May, and, in case Biffy was worried, underlining that the Bertrand organisation was out of range for the Gestapo and totally secure. The British prepared a disingenuous reply to Bertie's complaint: nothing since 23 May, the only method available was the Bombe. How much Bertie knew about British successes with the Bombes, which were just coming into their own, is unclear, but with hindsight it must have seemed a terrible mistake to have allowed him into the secret. If anyone with knowledge about successful techniques for breaking Enigma should be captured by the Germans ... the most comprehensive source of reliable intelligence could dry up overnight. Bertrand being at large in enemy territory could send a chill draught through the summer corridors of MI6.[42]

It is difficult to assess the motives of Bertrand, who always played his hand with subtlety and guile. Certainly he impressed his superior Louis Rivet, whose reports of Bertrand included comments such as 'fine qualities of psychology and diplomacy', 'constantly alert', 'hardworking and persistent', 'superior officer of integrity and exceptional worth', and so on.[43] For their part, the British were never sure whether there was something else. A telling remark comes from a certain Kim Philby, himself no stranger to deception, who reported to his control in Moscow that 'Dunderdale's direct contact is Commandant Bertrand, a fat unpleasant character, as silent as an oyster.'[44]

Across Europe, as in France, everyone was deceiving somebody else. The greatest deception of all had now been revealed for what it was: the pretence of amity between Nazi Germany and the USSR. Although Stalin refused to believe the evidence of German troops amassing on the Curzon Line, he could not ignore the invasion which began on Sunday 22 June 1941. Operation BARBAROSSA proved that the Molotov–Ribbentrop pact had, indeed, been nothing more than a cipher and now both of Kim Philby's paymasters were fighting the Germans. Germany and Russia – the two great enemies of Poland – were at each other's throats. Only time would tell how Poland herself would emerge from yet another superpower conflict being fought out on her own soil.

9

A MYSTERY INSIDE AN ENIGMA

I cannot forecast to you the action of Russia. It is a riddle wrapped in a mystery inside an enigma; but perhaps there is a key.

Winston S. Churchill
Broadcast, 1 October 1939

Among the Poles who had escaped to Britain from the fall of France in 1940 was a small team of code-breakers. Not everyone from the old Biuro Szyfrów had fallen into the clutches of Gustave Bertrand. Bertrand had been more interested in those from the parts of the bureau dealing with Enigma than those responsible for monitoring the USSR, so only a few Russian-specialists had ended up in his Équipe Z.

In August 1940, Colonel Kazimierz Banach of the Polish General Staff commissioned a paper on the capabilities of his own Russian-specialists. The stolid British became almost excited at the prospect of their very own Équipe Z.

2nd September, 1940. The organisation of an interception station for U.S.S.R. Military and Air information is most important ... We have 4 Polish W/T [wireless telegraphy] operators for reception purposes and 2 specialists for decoding.

5th. September, 1940. I cannot understand why we have not been told of them before. These and any other Polish operators with inter-ception experience ought to be made available to us at once ... It is questionable whether the decoding expert mentioned would be of any use to us, but we certainly ought to see him.

5th October, 1940. We have now had an opportunity of seeing what the Polish party have done, and feel that use could be made of them in interception of Russian work …

23rd. November, 1940. If they could furnish us with their cypher knowledge in exchange for which we could furnish ours … As we intercept no military material we can send the Poles copies of naval intercepts …

4th. December, 1940. The Polish D.M.I. [Director of Military Intelligence] agrees to allow Dower House to be used for:- (a) W/T Interception of Russian (b) Cryptography by Poles (c) Billeting accommodation for intercept operators and cryptographers …[1]

The Dower House in question was in Stanmore, on the north-western outskirts of London, a place which was to become the nerve centre of Polish activities contributing radio-related intelligence and engineering skill to the Allied war effort.

The Poles say they have available about 8 trained operators, and they are quite willing to be guided and instructed and put these operators at our disposal but as an organised Polish body working under our instructions, wherever we may desire … A.4. [Dunderdale] 16.5.41.

Commander Travis [Number 2 at Bletchley Park] It seems curious that we should turn down this Polish offer completely when U.S.S.R may be involved in hostilities at any moment … SM [Stuart Menzies] 20/5.[2]

The British authorities did not turn down the offer and soon a satisfying relationship developed between Bletchley Park and the Polish Russian unit at Stanmore, led by Czesław Kuraś, who had originally been recruited by the Signals Corps in Poland in 1923. Kuraś had been reactivated from the reserves on the eve of the war and evacuated to Britain in 1940.[3]

Sir Stewart Menzies, now head of MI6, was right to expect hostilities beween German and Russia at any time. Enigma decrypts coming from Bletchley Park indicated that German forces were massing along the

Curzon Line in Poland, the demarcation agreed between Molotov and Ribbentrop two years before.[4] Now, it seemed, Czesław Kuraś's country was going to be the scene of further conflict and devastation. Never had the need for an understanding of what both Germany and Russia were doing been greater. Only Joseph Stalin seemed to be in denial. No preparations were being made to meet the assault. The Downing Street diarist John Colville recorded Churchill's thoughts on Saturday 21 June 1941, the day before the Germans launched their attack.

> The P.M. says a German attack on Russia is certain and Russia will assuredly be defeated. He thinks that Hitler is counting on enlisting capitalist and right-wing sympathies in this country and the U.S. The P.M. says he is wrong: he will go all out to help Russia ... After dinner, [he said] that he had only one single purpose – the destruction of Hitler – and his life was much simplified thereby. If Hitler invaded Hell he would at least make a favourable reference to the Devil![5]

Churchill's simplified view might be fine for British foreign policy. The USSR was a long way away and Britain was not under Russian occupation. From a Polish perspective, the political line to take was not so straightforward. There was, however, one immediate consequence of BARBAROSSA, Hitler's offensive in the East. The monitoring of Russian encrypted radio traffic had to come to a halt. According to a footnote in the official *History of British Intelligence in the Second World War*:

> All work on Russian codes and cyphers was stopped from 22 June 1941, the day on which Germany attacked Russia, except that, to meet the need for daily appreciations of the weather on the eastern front, the Russian meteorological cypher was read again for a period beginning in October 1942.[6]

That, indeed, was the official story.

• • •

General Władysław Sikorski had foreseen the realignment of politics which would be imposed if Germany were to attack the USSR. It
would be a rash person who questioned Sikorski's patriotism, but the
fact is that he was born and educated in what was (before the Great
War) Austrian-controlled Poland. Sentiments tended to follow pre-
independence lines: if you came from Warsaw or eastern Poland, it was
self-evident that the Germans were less ghastly than the Russians, and
if you came from the German or Austrian partitions, the Russians were
clearly the lesser evil. For Sikorski, a deal with the Russians against
Nazi Germany – whose evil march swiftly pushed the Russians right
out beyond the 1939 borders of Poland – was a pragmatic thing to do.
Diplomatic relations should be restored and Polish soldiers held as
prisoners of war in Russia since 1939 should be re-constituted as a new
Polish Army under General Władysław Anders and set to fight against
the Germans. Moreover, such a deal would be welcomed by the British.
Without agreeing to a Polish-Soviet pact, Poland's only government
might collapse into irrelevance.

Still, a remarkable exercise of leadership was needed to convince the
fractious, multi-party government-in-exile that it was safe and sensible to treat with the Russians, particularly if the question of Poland's
eastern border was not part of the deal. By 30 July 1941, the majority of
the Polish Governing Council were won over. The intractables resigned
and Sikorski signed the pact. The Downing Street insider, John Colville,
wrote in his diary:

> Was present at the signing of the Russo-Polish treaty ... against a
> background of spotlights and a foreground of cameramen by the
> P.M., Eden [British Foreign Secretary], Sikorski and Maisky [USSR
> Ambassador to Britain], while a bust of the Younger Pitt looked down,
> rather disapprovingly I thought. Although this treaty abrogates the
> Soviet-German treaty of 1939, and leaves the frontier question unset-
> tled, it has caused a lot of Polish heart-burning, including, I believe,
> the resignation of the President. To a Pole, a Russian has no advan-
> tages over a German – and history makes this very understandable.

Now that, officially, Britain, the USSR and, apparently, Poland, were all on the same side, what was going to become of the Polish station at Stanmore, which was only just getting into gear? Russia was still a riddle, a mystery, an enigma. An ally of convenience. So the theory that the British cryptanalytic struggle must come to an end now that the USSR and Britain were on the same side was exactly that – a theory. Certainly, the official file of the GC&CS has nothing more in it after 2 September 1941. And yet, 'In the autumn of [1941] the English stopped their USSR-directed interception, and put its entire burden on our cell in Stanmore.'[7] The Stanmore code-breakers – the old ally which had been invaded in 1939 by the new one – were going to continue listening to the secret thoughts of their unpredictable, perfidious neighbour. And they were going to share those thoughts with the British, who would maintain the glossy appearance of having discontinued such underhand practices.

• • •

The Eastern Front was also being watched at PC Cadix. Bletchley was breaking into Enigma messages using the 'Method Kx' and forwarding the settings to Bertrand. One area of study agreed for the Poles of Ekspozytura 300 was 'German Police'. In the Nazi state the police had many roles. As the panzers dieselled irresistibly eastwards, there was 'clearing up' to be done in the rear. This task fell to the SS Police Division, whose signals were being followed by the code-breakers of Uzès, but not at Bletchley Park. In the absence of Major Ciężki in North Africa, it fell to Wiktor Michałowski to prepare the digests of the intercepts for Dunderdale, and via him, to John Tiltman at Bletchley Park. The dispassionate military drafting style could not disguise what was happening in western Ukraine:

SS Kavbrigade: 27.8.41. stationed at STARE DORCJO, 2.9.41 DOBRUJSK. General task, the cleaning up of the PRYPEC MARSHES and Forests along the DOBRUJSK-MOHYLOW highway ... the 2nd. Regt. on 21.8.41 after a bloody battle captured TUROW 40km. east of DAWIDGRODKA, levelling this town as well as other places to the ground like Kollektivmasnahme [collective reprisal] ... Up to 3.8.41. the Kavbrigade liquidated 3,274 partisans and Jews.

The next day's digest reported on the activities of an SS brigade in Belarus, some miles east of Pinsk:

The following items figure in the list of results achieved by the above unit:

26.8. – 46 prisoners, capture of 2 guns, shooting of 82 Jews.

30.8. – after the clearing up of the region ZYTOMIERE – 99 prisoners i shooting of 16 Jews.

The Pol.Reg.Sued shot on 23.8. – 367 Jews, and on 26.8 – 69 Jews. It reports the complete destruction of the 3rd guerrilla battalion, as well as the wiping out of half of the 9th battalion.

The Staff Company HSS Upf. Sued. shot on 26.8. – 546 Jews.

The 320th batallion after having cleared up the region of KAMIENIEC PODOLSKI, where together with the Einsatzgruppe der Stabskompanie at the time of Sonderaktion, on 27.8. they have shot 4.200 Jews ...[8]

Sometimes the intelligence generated by PC Cadix was of more immediate tactical significance. Britain and Poland were fighting Germany in Africa and substantial intelligence on the war in the desert was being supplied through the X-Y-Z channel. Lieutenant-General Erwin Rommel had arrived in Libya at the head of the German Afrika Korps in February 1941 and the Germans had been pushing on steadily ever since. Tobruk was besieged, with the Polish Independent Carpathian Brigade locked up there alongside the Australian 9th Division. The obstinate resistance of these troops at Tobruk deprived Rommel of a supply port close to his operations. Bertrand had news for the British: to help with Rommel's supply problems, 400 new trucks were being urgently shipped from France to Bizerte.

Although PC Cadix was working flat out, Bertrand's demands were unpredictable and always super-urgent. Tasks had to be dropped half-way through to give priority to Bertrand, despite the resulting negative impact on efficiency.[9] After the German attack on the USSR, the volume of material being intercepted had gone up, creating 'a gigantic amount of work,' said Gwido Langer.[10] The code-breakers were at their duties round the clock. To be sure, there was less potato-peeling, but other chores such as wood-chopping and electrical work still had to be shared out among the team as no outside help could prudently be engaged.

And that was not all of it. With the establishment of the new Polish intelligence organisation headed by Mieczysław Słowikowski, cover-name Rygor, in North Africa, the volume and importance of the messages being transmitted via Ciężki in Algiers and the radio-relay team at PC Cadix had also grown. These covered coastal and air defences across French North Africa, ship movements and the dependency of the colonies on American supplies of fuel. The Vichy régime was getting ever closer to alliance with the Germans. Permission was given for Luftwaffe aircraft to land at Oran, in French territory. Moreover, despite the appointment of a special oversight commission, American fuel was being sent on to the Axis forces in Libya. Nobody else was supplying the Allies with this quality of intelligence so vital to Allied interests in the North African desert.

● ● ●

The volatile Vichy régime was trying to adapt to the new world order, as German successes to the East and South added to their dominance. Yet Vichy had no solid support among the French population and lacked self-confidence. Symptomatic of its rotten structure was its persistent creation of new organs to spy on itself. When Admiral François Darlan took over the helm of the Vichy government he had instigated a confidential surveillance mission, which reported that the French Army and Air Force intelligence services were still working against Germany and Italy and passing details to the British. Darlan reacted by setting up a new coordination body, the Centre d'Information Gouvernemental, whose job was to keep people like Louis Rivet and his subordinates in check.

Thus, Bertrand reported to the British in October 1941 that he had been told by Vichy to cease relations with the British, and there was a report that December on the activities of the British MI6 in France and its colonies, noting that the British were using stay-behind Polish agents.[11] Rivet fended off these intrusions with some suitably dressed-up half-information from Bertrand about machine encryption and super-encipherment, accompanied with examples to show that British material was at least being tracked.[12] It was indeed being tracked, by another organ of the Vichy establishment, the Groupement des Contrôles Radioéléctriques, which had been set up to snuff out illicit Resistance radio broadcasts but was in fact working under Bertrand's direction.[13] Not everyone in Vichy France was doing as they were told.

Vichy rule was also changing l'Afrique Française du Nord. French North Africa was no longer the devil-may-care place of beaches and parties. Coal was in short supply. As the French government grew closer to the Nazis, *travail, famille, patrie* slogans appeared every-where. Listening to the BBC was forbidden. Anti-semitic rants in the press increased in volume and darkened in tone. Pro-Gaullist move-ments were hounded by the official authorities. The train timetable had to be changed because of the coal shortage and spot checks on travellers were stepped up. The attempt to close down Gaullist senti-ment had the opposite effect, but still, many colonists supported the proud authoritarianism of Pétain, without necessarily agreeing to sup-port the Germans. Even the anti-Vichy resisters were divided between royalists and republicans. The only thing that everyone agreed on was the villainy of the British, but beyond that nobody knew what anyone really thought.

While the need for secrecy in this troubled territory intensified, the volume, importance and visibility of what the Poles were doing there was rising. Maksymilian Ciężki reported to Słowikowski that his French liaison officer, whom Ciężki thought of as his minder, was (prompted by Bertrand) asking questions about the reasons behind the growth in volume of radio traffic.[14] Ciężki had responded with a feeble excuse about an internal reorganisation, but this would not hold up for much longer. Ciężki said his room had been searched. He'd been keep-ing Słowikowski's materials in his own safe, in a building controlled by the French. It was messy, and increasingly dangerous.[15] Something needed to change.

• • •

On 7 December 1941, everything did change. Everything. The attack on Pearl Harbor (and on some British shipping near Indonesia) took everyone by surprise. Suddenly, Japan was at war with America and Britain. Germany declared war on America. If the war between Germany and the USSR had unsettled the relations of the Allies, the entry of America into the war was going to be an earthquake by comparison. President Franklin D. Roosevelt called it a day of infamy. Prime Minister Winston S. Churchill said, 'to have the United States at our side was to me the greatest joy … we had won after all!'[16] In this new construct, Poland, Britain's first ally – for a year, Britain's only ally – was receding from sight.

For Słowikowski it was fitting to reach out, Z to A, to contact the Americans in Algiers. He did not go in through the front door; it was better to lay some bait. So his first step was to use a contact to leak that the Polish forces might have some sort of secret intelligence operation. And then he watched for the reaction. The Americans were intrigued, and once the depth and quality of what the Poles knew – and the depth of their own innocent ignorance – became apparent, a permanent relationship was proposed. During the coming months, that relationship would grow into the most important intelligence liaison for the North African theatre.

Meanwhile, though, Słowikowski had to solve the radio traffic problem and the Americans could help. They agreed that their diplomatic bag could be used to send Słowikowski's non-urgent despatches. There was still a need for a direct radio link to London, cutting the outpost of Ekspozytura 300 out of the loop so as to dampen the French suspicions. Stanisław Gano, head of intelligence in London, could not send anyone to North Africa;[17] the problem was worsened because one of the Poles, Ryszard Krajewski, had suffered a breakdown and was in hospital in Algiers. Ciężki would have to manage regardless. But Krajewski's illness gave Langer a good reason to pull the wool further over the eyes of Bertrand, keeping the radio-relay operation in place for a while longer.[18] As things turned out, Ciężki's tour of duty in Algiers was going to be extended until the summer and only then would Ekspozytura 300 cease to have responsibility for keeping Słowikowski in touch with London.[19]

Meanwhile the group who had been supporting Ciężki in Africa were being sent back to France. Krajewski was still in hospital. So, on 6 January 1942, along with the suspicious Capitaine Lane (who may have been the person who searched Ciężki's room), four Poles once more boarded the Marseilles steamer *Lamoricière* at Algiers. The Polish code-breakers embarking on the voyage were: Paszkowski, known as Casanova; Różycki of the original Enigma team from Poznań; Smoleński, whose photography at the Château des Fouzes had drawn upon him the wrath of Bertrand, and Graliński, who at 47 was one of the oldest of the Ekspozytura 300 staff and the only expert on Russian ciphers in Africa.

● ● ●

The *Lamoricière* was a passenger ship of 1,450 tons, originally built in the Swan Hunter yard in Newcastle in 1921. On the day of departure her coal was bad and the weather was very bad. She struggled to make headway. The Captain announced that their arrival in Marseilles would be delayed. He changed course in response a distress call from the cargo ship *Jumièges*, but in the heavy seas he could not find her and discovered his own ship was taking on water. The pumps could not cope and the rising water level threatened to swamp the engines.[20] The captain called for volunteers to form a chain of buckets and Paszkowski and Smoleński stood for six hours in the freezing water handing up dripping containers. By 8 a.m. on 9 January 1942 the captain knew the game was up. The ship had a heavy, uncontrollable list. Passengers and crew were ordered to grab lifebelts and go to their abandon-ship stations. Another ship, the *Gueydon*, was standing off, but the seas were too high for a coordinated rescue and the *Lamoricière* was about to go. The boats on one side could not be launched; boats on the other were quickly swamped.

Without discussing it, each one of us started to plan their own jumps into the sea. Ralewski [Graliński] left us just before 12 and went to the front of the ship. Around 12.10, after a short conversation with me, Rouget [Różycki] followed him. Smolny [Smoleński] and I were left in the bar. Around 12.20 the waves consumed the bridge just outside the bar and water started pouring into the bar. We left it then in an attempt to reach the rear of the ship. When we got there, Ralewski and Rouget were nowhere to be seen. Next thing I see is Smolny taking off his camera and coat ... At 12.27 (the time shown by the watch on my arm) I jumped into the sea ...[21]

Henryk Paszkowski, the author of this account, was the only code-breaker to survive the shipwreck. He managed to survive half an hour in the water and swim to the waiting *Gueydon*. His bride Janina was lucky to have been left behind in Algeria. She would see her husband again, but Barbara Różycka's 2½-year-old son would never know his father. Capitaine Milliasseau honourably went down with his ship, but over half his crew managed to save themselves while leaving more than four out of five of the passengers to drown.

Słowikowski had been worried about Maksymilian Ciężki. He thought Ciężki was getting paranoid and it didn't help that the major had been left to run the Ekspozytura AFR radio operation almost solo.[22] Then came the news. There were scenes, almost a riot, outside the shipping office on the Boulevard Carnot. Only 50 out of the 272 passengers on board had been saved and the others had become victims of the coal crisis in Algeria. Ciężki was crushed.

The shocked group at the Château des Fouzes were plunged into despondency when – the day after the disaster – the news reached them. Bertrand appeared to offer his personal condolences and Paszkowksi himself arrived after a few more days. It was going to be difficult to adjust to the loss and the workload had not let up at all. Janina Paszkowska was an obvious choice to help with the staff numbers, and with effect from 23 February 1942 she was hired as a cipher clerk with the splendid cover-name 'la comtesse Makarewicz'. Another Polish alumnus of the Biuro Szyfrów called Tadeusz Suszczewski had turned up, attending a hydraulic engineering course in Grenoble. Henryk Zygalski made a couple of trips there and by the end of May Suszczewski had also been recruited (with the much more dreary cover-name 'Dubois'), to replace Graliński on decoding the Russian intercepts.[23]

The arrival of Suszczewski brought a new pastime, namely frog-hunting:

After arriving by car or bicycle at an area of ponds and meadows, we would select a suitable muddy pool where we heard the loudest croaking, and spread a large red cloth on the grass. Evidently this colour is very alluring to frogs, because after a few minutes several of them would appear on the cloth, and then more and more would hop aboard.

The frogs soon found their way to the pot, a welcome supplement to the wartime diet.[24]

In Algiers, where the diet was porridge, Słowikowski's radio problem was taking its time to find a solution. A two-way wireless was smuggled from London via the American consulate, but the real issue was finding someone to operate it. There was no progress until March, when one of Słowikowski's French national agents, who was a radio technician by profession, agreed to take on the job. Słowikowski set up his cover using the best deception technique in the book: to hide the wireless in plain sight. A radio repair shop was established in suitable premises in the Arab quarter and amongst the second-hand junk ostensibly for sale was a disembowelled radiogram containing the fully operational device. The aerial would be rigged only when needed for transmissions. Nothing could look more innocent. Establishing reliable communications was harder and it was only on 18 July 1942 (and after a visit from Bertrand) that Ciężki could finally go back to join his remaining pre-war colleagues in France.[25]

Meanwhile the intelligence continued to flow to London and, via headquarters and Biffy Dunderdale, to MI6. The unpleasant details of what the German 'police' were doing included particulars of 'evacuation' trains (971 Jews left Bremen for Poland in January 1942) and a demand for figures (such as the number of furs seized from Jews in Poland). Between May 1941 and June 1942, Dunderdale's people signed for over 1,400 despatches and other materials handed over by the Polish General Staff, ranging through messages intercepted by

Ekspozytura 300, aid for Słowikowski's operation, supplies delivered to the Germans in French North Africa, French collaboration with the Germans, Russian messages, cash transfers for the French and African outposts and messages from Bertrand himself.[26]

● ● ●

Bletchley Park was busy. By 1942, Alan Turing's work on Enigma was largely complete, with Bombes being built by the score and – unknown to Bertrand – the settings on a dozen or more networks being churned out daily in factory-style production. The staff who had had to endure freezing wooden huts were being transferred to new, brick-built edifices of stupendous ugliness which were now lining one side of the once glamorous Victorian lake. Americans had arrived to strengthen the forces working against Naval Enigma. Now Turing was being given a new role, helping the Americans in the war against the U-boats.

The problem of Naval Enigma was central to the Battle of the Atlantic. The race was to find the U-boats and re-route the convoys before the U-boats found the merchant ships. It was a game of cat and mouse and the German Navy was very good at it. Not only were they able to read the coded messages of the British Merchant Navy and, for most of 1942 and the early part of 1943, the Royal Navy as well, the U-boats had developed tactics for punishing convoys and evading their escorts. On 1 February 1942, they had also introduced a new Enigma machine, the M4, with four rather than three rotors. The U-boats had eight, rather than five, possible rotors to choose from, and their 'indicator' procedure did not depend on the vulnerable choose-it-yourself approach of the Wehrmacht and Luftwaffe. Altogether, the U-boat system was more solid, more reliable, less breakable than Army and Air Force Enigma and without breaks, Bletchley Park couldn't get cribs and without cribs, they couldn't use the Bombes. Worse still, once the four-rotor machine came into operation, a three-rotor Bombe was of very limited use unless you were able to set aside twenty-six Bombes to run a single problem.

All this made the task of Naval Enigma very tough. At the same time it was Churchill's number one priority. The country would starve, let alone be able to continue to fight, if the lifeline across the Atlantic were severed. Huge efforts were piled into the challenge. Alan Turing solved the indicator system early in the war, but it required 'pinches' (captures of the 'confidential books', the all-important ciphering instructions containing the daily Enigma settings) before Bletchley Park could break in, solve messages and create cribs to keep their methods alive.

On 30 October 1942, the U-boat *U-559* was patrolling in the eastern Mediterranean when she was spotted by an aircraft. In company with several other ships, HMS *Petard* intercepted the boat and subjected her to a merciless depth-charge onslaught lasting ten hours. After all her desperate evasive efforts, the air in the U-boat was foul and the charge on her batteries was low. To escape, to refresh and to recharge all pointed to a run on the surface under cover of darkness. *U-559* surfaced gingerly and tried to sneak away. Unfortunately for her, she was picked up instantly on radar and the battle recommenced. There was nothing for it but to scuttle and the crew abandoned ship. But something went wrong; in fact two things went wrong. The scuttling charges didn't send *U-559* instantly to the bottom of the sea and the orders to destroy the 'confidential books' had not been carried out.

Lieutenant-Commander Mark Thornton, the captain of *Petard*, ordered a boarding party across and they raided the captain's tiny cabin. There they found a strange machine which looked a bit like a typewriter, a collection of cog-wheels with the letters of the alphabet around them and the much-prized confidential books. These were handed out to the Royal Navy crew manning the whale boat above and then the boarding party went back for another look. Suddenly the U-boat took a gulp and began to founder. The scuttling charges had made enough of a hole after all. She went suddenly, too fast for Lieutenant Anthony Fasson and Able Seaman Colin Grazier to escape. But a piece of pink blotting paper printed with water-soluble ink was already in the whaler. Still dry, the pink paper reached Bletchley Park on 24 November 1942 and it was the way in, via the short-signal weather code, to unravel the four-rotor Enigma. Fasson and Grazier were posthumously awarded the George Cross.

The four-rotor machine would also need a new engineering solution, and while the British worked on one possibility, Alan Turing was sent to America to advise their engineers on another. The American naval Bombe was an astonishing advance in technology. While it used the logical design of the Turing–Welchman Bombe, its hardware solution was revolutionary. If a three-rotor Bombe of the 1940 model took ten minutes to complete its run, a four-rotor Bombe built on the same principles would take twenty-six times as long: four and a half hours. The fast rotor needed to go much faster for the machine to do its job. This was within the tolerance of electromechanical parts, but problems happened when the machine reached a possible solution and its moving parts were supposed to stop. Whizzing around at over 1,000 rpm, the fast rotor had so much momentum that it was never going to stop in the time available. So the Americans – to be specific, Joe Desch, an engineer working at the National Cash Register corporation – were going to use electronics to 'memorise' the overshot stop position. Alan Turing went to visit Joe Desch and discuss his prototype. It was the first use of electronic technology in a code-breaking machine and may have been the first step on the road to post-war electronic computing machines. Y and A were taking intelligence co-operation into a completely new dimension.

• • •

On 15 June 1942, Słowikowski, as the false Dr Skowroński, went to the American Consulate in Algiers to collect some cash and despatches which had arrived from London. Along with the despatches was a gentleman who introduced himself as Colonel Solborg, who brought greetings from Stanisław, thus establishing his connection with Stanisław Gano, the head of military intelligence in the Polish General Staff and the immediate boss of Mieczysław Słowikowski and his colleagues in France. Colonel Robert Solborg was not fake. He was a genuine Polish-speaking American whose job was to help President Roosevelt work out what was what in French North Africa.

The two of them began with the map on the wall. Look, said Słowikowski, surely there is more we can do. The Mediterranean is naturally composed of two basins. In the East the Germans have naval and aerial control and have the British pinned down in defence of the Suez Canal. West of Malta there is no effective obstacle to convoys and the place is open to an invading force. So the Allies can occupy North Africa and use it as a jumping-off point to harry the Italians. Look how close Tunisia is to Italy! And if you play the scenario the other way, just look what a danger a German occupation of French North Africa would pose. Not just to Suez, but, by providing additional U-boat bases, to convoys across the South Atlantic. The strategic picture would be completely altered. And what do the intelligence reports suggest? Well, it's evident that the Germans are thinking about taking control of the region.

Słowikowski reported back to Stanisław on his meeting with Solborg. Central office did not deign to reply. Perhaps they knew that the Americans and the British thought Solborg a little too unreliable to involve in their network. For one thing, he was known to German intelligence. Worse, the guesswork in front of the map was far too close to the mark. Unknown to Słowikowski, it was the Allies, not the Germans, who were making plans. Winston Churchill had first thought of an American occupation of French North Africa the previous year, before the Americans were even in the war. Now, in mid 1942, those plans were given the go-ahead: the soldiers were to be trained to clamber down the sides of ships; the tanks were in production; the fleet was to be made ready. The operation was codenamed TORCH, and the intelligence from Słowikowski, in response to the endless questionnaires from London, was furnishing the details to ensure the action did not become a bloodbath on the beaches of Vichy-controlled French North Africa.

● ● ●

In France, Bertrand had been grumbling on and off to the British about sharing of Enigma settings. 'Is it really true that you have no results on the E. machine or just that it is too tedious to send them to us?' he asked on 6 December 1941. The complaint was repeated in March 1942: 'it is impossible to accept that your A-team is getting no results... [to receive the E settings] would enable me to bring round to your cause certain of your former friends who seem to me to be inclining more towards you.' Bletchley Park explained to 'C', the head of MI6, that they were sending Bertrand some minor Enigma settings 'about twice a week'. In fact, nothing at all had been sent for over three months. The drip-feed was re-established, with sixteen settings, relating to the Luftwaffe, the Wehrmacht on the Eastern Front and the SS, sent between March and July. But for the British the security questions had not gone away. What they were sending was a tiny fraction of the GC&CS achievement. In February 1942, the British had found the settings for sixteen networks and decoded 41 per cent of the messages received. During the month of June, 261 lots of settings were found, using 11,833 hours of time on the Turing–Welchman Bombes. The sheer scale of the British operation made Bertie's little outfit seem too small to bother with.[27]

The balance between the two intelligence centres was made more even after 10 September 1942. On that day, Bertrand messaged London happily that he had just received three Enigma machines. No, Bertie had not been out on to the battlefield and captured this priceless kit; these machines were the ones he had ordered in May 1940 and Bertrand had now smuggled back enough parts to reassemble a fighting force of Enigmas. The first Polish-model replica Enigma machine had been demonstrated to Louis Rivet and his new commanding officer, General Roux, on 22 July 1942. Now, in September, Bertie explained to London that he had a ready-made solution to the challenge of secure communications. 'Agreed in principle,' responded an incredulous MI6, having consulted Bletchley, 'but are your machines equipped with a *Stecker* [plugboard]?' Indeed they were, and X and Z began to liaise with Y using the enemy's machine. Henri Braquenié relished the irony of the situation. His messages to and from London were now being super-enciphered on a reconstituted Enigma machine and so he signed off his messages 'Heil Hitler'. He knew the Germans wouldn't be able to get anything out of the messages even if they could work out the Franco-British key, since the entire text was nothing but gobbledegook, even in the original: the plain text was decrypted German Enigma keys, and there was no way to make any sense of this incoherent jumble of stuff.[28]

During Bertrand's border-crossing trips to pick up Enigma parts, PC Cadix had been supervised by his wife Marie, called 'Mary' by everyone after she had been rechristened in the early days by the monoglot English. Mary was 'respected and obeyed' by all, probably because her firm grip was mellowed by a sense of humour, good looks and charm. Everyone wanted to please Mary. In songs (Ciężki and, in the days before the *Lamoricière* incident, Różycki, had good voices and were often called upon) she was called *'notre chère princesse'.*[29] Mary was the glue that bound the men of PC Cadix into coherence.

Behind the veneer of domesticity, the atmosphere at PC Cadix had not much improved during Maksymilian Ciężki's absence, at least as far as the Polish group were concerned. There had been, for instance, a run-in between Gwido Langer and Bertrand about decrypted material which Langer sent to his superiors in London, but which Bertrand wanted to sell to the Swiss. Bertrand had already put in place a broking scheme about other messages and that was far more inflammatory. This scheme was called Liaison 414 and the occasion for an even bigger dust-up.[30]

Liaison 414 was the fruit of listening in on an agent working for the German counter-intelligence organisation called the Abwehr. Over 150 telegrams emanating from this source had been intercepted and decrypted during the course of 1942. Unusually, they were in French, and they related to Russian affairs. Bertrand's ploy had been to sell the intelligence, via Vichy, to the USSR.[31] Like Vichy itself, Moscow found the subject of who was spying on it, and how, and what they wanted to know, to be of irresistible fascination. As John Colville noted, however, anything helpful for the Russians was likely to be regarded at the least with distaste, and probably as toxic, by the Poles.

There was also a simmering disagreement between the Poles and Bertrand over North Africa and the future of the Ekspozytura 300 team. The Polish intelligence workers had been in the open prison of the Château des Fouzes for nearly two years, but the dynamic of the war was changing. Wiktor Michałowski noted how the French had the jitters and their tension was rubbing off on his own compatriots at the Château des Fouzes.[32] It was bearable, but it seemed a long time since those light-hearted days of chasing one another around the grounds and hiding in earthenware jars. Other Polish agents who had stayed behind in France had been feeling the pressure more directly.

In August 1942, there had been arrests and the erasure of networks. Conditions were getting harder for anyone with Resistance sympathies and it was harder still for foreigners. Just what was going to happen next was difficult to predict. Even Gustave Bertrand was finding it difficult to anticipate the future and to remain afloat in the slippery, poisonous bowl of Vichysoisse politics.

● ● ●

In July 1942, Colonel Louis Rivet was summoned to see Prime Minister Pierre Laval, head of the Vichy government, to receive an instruction.[33] Rivet's anti-German activities were to cease. Laval also told Rivet that his government had agreed with the Germans on 'joint policing' in the Zone Libre. A creeping takeover of the Zone Libre by the Germans had begun.

Rivet was called to another meeting on 29 August 1942.[34] This time there was an almighty row about arrests, intelligence and loyalties, and another reconstruction of the Vichy government's intelligence services. The Bureau des Menées Antinationales was abolished. Bertrand's secret code-breaking section, MA2, must surely perish with it. Rivet was replaced, effective 1 September 1942. New organs, under firmer control by Laval, were to take over intelligence work. Astonishingly, in their ignorance of what it did, Bertrand's outfit was allowed to survive, renamed as 'Section ET' and continuing as before. Laval's grip was not as complete as he imagined.[35] Moreover, the wily Admiral François Darlan, Laval's predecessor as Prime Minister (seen by the Germans as less biddable than Laval), had plans of his own. Although Rivet thought Darlan was difficult to read and was playing both sides, Rivet accepted a role working for Darlan.[36]

Bertrand, like Darlan, was trying to see what was happening on both sides of the line that divided France. It was an open secret that the Allies were planning an intervention, either in North Africa or in the south of France. The fog surrounding the invasion meant that the target was unknown until the very last minute. What was more certain was how the Germans would react to an invasion. As the south of France had to be on the Allied list of possible targets, sooner or later, and likely sooner, the Germans would take over the Zone Libre; a prospect that everyone was talking about.[37]

On 3 September 1942, Bertrand went to Paris for another chat with Max, his spy in the German Embassy. He learned that the Germans would automatically take over the Zone Libre, even if the Allied target was North Africa. Two divisions had been assembled near Dijon and these would co-ordinate with the Italians moving from the south-east. London was notified. In turn, Bertrand was given a code-phrase and some advice. The code: if he received a message saying, '*La récolte est bonne*' [the harvest is good] then an invasion – of somewhere – was imminent. The advice: get the Polish team evacuated to Algiers now. If that proved to be unachievable, the British would mount a seaborne rescue in one of three named places, with Bertrand and his wife to follow by air pick-up.[38]

● ● ●

Dilly Knox, the man who taught Alan Turing about code-breaking and the person who so nearly jeopardised the transfer of Enigma secrets in those long-ago meetings with the Poles, had been working on a very special Enigma problem. In the autumn of 1941, Knox began working on one of the 'outlying German Enigmas' which defied regular lines of attack.[39] This was the machine used by Abwehr agents and it was completely different from the army/air force machine and different again from that used by the U-boats. With a combination of insight and serendipity, which so often provides breakthroughs in cipher problems, Knox had reverse-engineered the machine. It had no plug-board, but four rotors, and the rotors had multiple 'turnover' notches which would engage the next wheel. Gloriously, Knox showed that the turnover pattern meant that rather frequently all four rotors could turn over together, thus preserving the entire wiring sequence of the machine for successive enciphered letters. Where this happened either side of the four-letter indicator sequence – a phenomenon Knox called a 'lobster', for reasons long lost to history – it gave him the way in he needed. The women at Bletchley Park recruited by Knox were sent on a lobster hunt, which trapped enough information to work out the wiring of the rotors and their turnover patterns. One rotor had eleven notches, another fifteen, another seventeen. By the end of 1941, the Abwehr Enigma was wide open and generating a new species of intelligence called 'ISK', standing for Intelligence Services Knox (or possibly 'Illicit' Services Knox, in view of the fact that some Abwehr operatives had been in Britain before they were rounded up).

By 1942, as far as the British were concerned there were no effective Abwehr operatives left in Britain, but the story was different elsewhere. ISK was beginning to get some useful material from their activities in continental Europe. There were Abwehr spies along the north coast of Africa, whose secret findings were all about the fog of war and no secret at all:

Madrid to Tangier. 29 September at 1350 hrs 7 Escort boats left from BASTA. When passed and to where? [messaged Control to an Abwehr watcher]

Tangier to Madrid. From 13 to 17 hours thick fog and rain [replied the agent the next day]. Absolutely no visibility.

Tangier to Madrid. V894, whose reports almost always mix fantasy and truth, signals that on 4 November in BASTA 50 heavy American bombers arrived, and in the night of 4 to 5 November 12 units of the American fleet with troops.[40]

The intelligence gleaned from Knox's pencil-and-paper methods was helping to build a picture of what the Germans knew – and, just as important, what they did not know – about the plans for Operation TORCH. And there was one fact which, crucially, they did not know.

Monitoring the shipping commentary was not the headline success of ISK in the autumn of 1942. Ahead of TORCH, the Allies were implementing Operation OVERTHROW. Operation OVERTHROW involved more Abwehr spies, old-fashioned spies who watch things and report to their superiors. In the case of OVERTHROW, the spies were working for Nazi Germany and they were reporting in alarmed tones on the build-up of strength in Britain. Troops were being trained for mountain and arctic warfare and aggregations of units were massing in the south-east. The inference was clear: an imminent invasion of Norway and probably a cross-channel invasion of France. Stalin was going to get his Second Front now. And it was tosh, all falsehood, served up with a garnish of real facts, by the 'London Controlling Section' responsible for deception. The spies in question were run by London, not Berlin. Not only that, but the tosh was being swallowed. ISK decrypts followed the Germans as they digested the stories they were being fed, and the British authorities knew that the Germans didn't have a clue what was actually going to happen.

● ● ●

Colonel Paul Paillole had taken control of one of the new intelligence organisations set up by Laval in August 1942.[41] Some of the intelligence he was reading was very strange: 200 blank identity cards had been signed out by the police ministry and handed to the Gestapo; twenty-three car registration numbers had been reserved by a certain Captain Desloges; the same officer had requisitioned the Château de Charbonnières near Lyon; and the threads all led back to Desloge's commanding officer, General Delmotte, *chef de cabinet* of the Vichy Secretary of State for War. Paillole requested a meeting with the general to find out what was going on. Delmotte admitted frankly that the Abwehr wanted to track down radio transmissions coming from the Zone Libre. The Germans had not only intercepted transmissions; they had deciphered them and they knew there were cells in the region, working for the British undercover. The nests of anti-Nazi activity had to be stamped out. Contrary to the stipulations of the armistice, 'joint policing' in the Zone Libre meant that the Germans had been given permission to operate mobile radio direction-finding vans. The Château de Charbonnières was their headquarters, the operatives had fake French identities and the new branch of German counter-intelligence was called the Funkabwehr.[42]

The net began to close more tightly around the Poles left behind in France. Radio transmitters were captured in October at Caluire and Rochetaillée. And the same happened, with the arrest of British and

French operators, at Feyzin. All three places were close to the château HQ of the Funkabwehr. On 23 October 1942, the Funkabwehr ventured further afield to Châtelguyon, not far from Vichy, where they made another kill: a team of Poles belonging to Ekspozytura F was arrested.

Gwido Langer requested guidance from London. Should he stay, bearing in mind that protecting the Poles of Équipe Z was unlikely to be a priority for the French if and when the Germans took over completely? The answer came on 28 October 1942. Only if the French put up a fight should he stay. Maybe a few radio operators could stay, but it was time for the rest of Équipe Z to prepare for disbandment and escape. The arrangements would be made by Dunderdale and relayed via Bertrand.[43]

Then there was another row between Langer and Bertrand, the biggest dust-up yet. In accordance with his directions from London, Langer intended that the evacuation would be to Algiers. Bertrand said no: that was too dangerous. Langer, primed with secret intelligence unknown to Bertrand, dug in his heels. But Bertrand said his own sources in Vichy confirmed his view. That settled it. And in reality, if Bertrand said no, Langer could do nothing whatever about it.

It was bad enough having rows with people supposed to be on your own side. The real enemy were about to make it a great deal worse.

On 25 September 1942, Bertrand had visited Nîmes. There he learned that the Funkabwehr had established itself in a new location, this time much closer to home, at Montpellier, about 70km to the south-west of Uzès. Twelve local registration numbers had been provided for their interception vans. Within three weeks, a detachment had set up in Pont-Saint-Esprit, 40km north-east of Uzès, in the opposite direction. Soon after, one of the vans was spotted on the road leading north-west out of Uzès to Alès. The Funkabwehr were triangulating on PC Cadix.

From time to time, the power in the building would falter, co-inciding with the timing of transmissions, probably to see whether they ceased when the lights went out. The Funkabwehr were homing in.

Gustave Bertrand had been seeing the omens for some time. St Odile, the patron saint of Alsace, had apparently seen it for herself as long ago as AD 890, and her prophecy had been handed down the generations: terrible violence would be inflicted on the world by *Germania*, with its apex of success in the sixth month of the second year of the war, which was about now if you started the clock in May 1940. And then there had been the birds. A Hitchcockian gathering of nightingales congregated on the telegraph wires around the Château des Fouzes in mid October. The rumours about a total occupation of France reached fever pitch in November. And now the special coded message came to Bertie from London. *La récolte est bonne.* It was time for Bertrand, Langer and their team of code-crackers to pack up and go.[44]

There was only one thing that had to happen before they could go. Bertrand actually had to read the message. And he couldn't read the message, because he was away on one of his trips.

Henryk Zygalski with Ewa (right) and another girlfriend on the beach at Algiers. (Anna Zygalska-Cannon)

Camel rides for code-breakers in the desert. (Anna Zygalska-Cannon)

Jerzy Różycki with Włada, one of Zygalski's girlfriends. (Anna Zygalska-Cannon)

The Château des Fouzes. A contemporary picture taken by one of the Ekspozytura 300 members. (Anna Zygalska-Cannon)

Premier league. Code-breakers turned footballers at PC Cadix. (Anna Zygalska-Cannon)

En route, 17 June 1941. Henryk Zygalski (*above*), Captain Lane, the Poles' French liaison officer, and Kazimierz Gaca (*below*), on the way back from North Africa. Lane perished the following year in the *Lamoricière* shipwreck. (Anna Zygalska-Cannon)

Festival. Gustave Bertrand (7) looks round as someone cracks a joke. The others are Langer (1), Gaca (2), Paszkowski (3), Monique (4), Marie Bertrand (5), Sylwester Palluth (6), Antoni Palluth (8) and the wives of David and Maurice (*). (Anna Zygalska-Cannon)

Cadix 1942. Marian Rejewski relaxes with a book. (Anna Zygalska-Cannon)

Disaster at sea. The *Lamoricière* (centre) listed and sinking, while the *Gueydon* stands off to rescue survivors. (Reproduced with kind permission of French Lines)

Code-breaker cousins. On the wall behind Antoni and Sylwester Palluth at PC Cadix is a chart of military operations in North Africa. (Anna Zygalska-Cannon)

Moment of passion. Henryk and Janina Paszkowska. (Anna Zygalska-Cannon)

From top left: The art of concealment. Bertrand comfortable on top of a terracotta jar, sharing a joke with Marie; Gaca almost in a jar, with Paszkowski alongside; Monique fits in one easily; finally a code-breaker manages to get right inside. (Anna Zygalska-Cannon)

Wanted list. Pre-war mugshots of the code-breakers featured, alongside alleged criminals, in annexes to the 'Wanted' lists circulated by the German Security Police in France in 1943. (Archives départementales d'Indre-et-Loire (Tours. France), Cote 17 ZA 6)

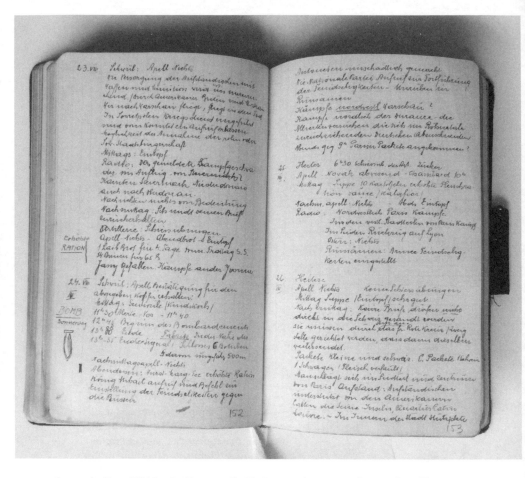

Langer's diary. Writing in German, Gwido Langer documented every day of his captivity, and his falling weight. (The Józef Piłsudski Institute, 238–246 King Street, London)

A home to return to. After the German Army had crushed the Warsaw Uprising in 1944, it was ordered to raze the city. (Author's collection)

Left: Peacetime. The emaciated Langer and Ciężki after they reached Britain in 1945. (Barbara Ciężka)

Below: Capable of originality. Henryk Zygalski managed to overcome the prejudices of post-war Britain to make a career as a lecturer in mathematics. (Anna Zygalska-Cannon)

10

HIDE AND SEEK

Comptez sur mon entier dévouement jusqu'au bout – même en jouant cache-cache avec la Gestapo.
[Rely on my total dedication right to the end – even in playing hide-and-seek with the Gestapo.]

Gustave Bertrand
Message from Bolek to Janio (Żychoń), 8 April 1943[1]

On 6 November 1942, Bertrand was relaxing in his bath. His reverie was unpleasantly interrupted by a noise like a derailed 4-6-4 steam locomotive thundering along the corridor. The train erupted into the bathroom in the form of Monsieur Beaujolais. The form of M. Beaujolais was, alas, not equal to the task of running, or the sight of Bertrand in the bath. In any event, Bertrand considered that a man in M. Beaujolais' condition should be offered a glass of rum to settle him.[2]

Gwido Langer was nicknamed 'Beaujolais' by Gustave Bertrand for his fondness for wine. But this was not the time for a joke. Langer's irruption into Bertrand's bathroom reverie was because he had seen one of the Funkabwehr Chevrolet vans coming down the road, with its broad circular roof-mounted aerial shining in the sun. It was driving in the direction of the Château des Fouzes, heading straight for the château and all its incriminating equipment, papers and people. Bertrand and his team at PC Cadix knew all about these vehicles. They knew all about their activities. And they knew exactly who were their occupants. Gustave Bertrand and his team had not just been tracked by the Funkabwehr, they had been following the Funkabwehr themselves and decoding the Funkabwehr's secret communications for weeks. And that meant they knew that the luck of Ekspozytura 300 had just run out.

● ● ●

The night before, Bertrand had returned from his trip and Langer presented him with the *Récolte est bonne* message from London. He didn't want to act on it immediately, apart from telling Rivet. Langer demurred. Bertrand accused his Polish colleague of wanting to 'bugger off'.[3] Bertrand was implying that Langer was betraying him, leaving him in the lurch. How could it have come to this? Bertrand knew that the risk of betrayal was the risk of capture and a risk to the Enigma secret. He knew that to evacuate the code-breakers was his duty. Yet, for Bertrand the man, to do so would be to eviscerate his own organisation. For over three years Bertrand's reputation had grown and grown, as a result of his feeding extraordinary morsels of delicate information obtained from inexplicable sources to the British, the French General Staff and to Vichy. This information was mostly obtained through the labours of his Équipe Z and the X-Y-Z symbiosis. Bertrand had to resolve this conflict within himself, a way to pilot the Poles to a safe haven without casting himself adrift.

Bertrand and Langer had already had one row about whether it was safe to go to Africa and now Bertrand was finding excuses for delay. First, Bertrand got on the transmitter and suggested to Dunderdale that he should to go to Paris and see what the Germans were up to from his source Max. Fortunately, the British quashed the idea without right of appeal: *La récolte est très bonne et il n'est plus le temps de voyager.* [The harvest is very good and it is no longer the time for travelling.] The British added that there was less than a week before the Germans would make their move.[4]

That they should visit Nice was something two conflicted intelligence leaders could agree on. Bertrand thought the main purpose of the trip was to conceal two suitcases full of documents and some equipment somewhere about his mother's house in Nice. Langer and Palluth had other ideas. They intended to see 'Mak', the cover-name of Lieutenant Colonel Marian Romeyko, who, under the cover of being a farmer, was running Ekspozytura F2 of Polish military intelligence. The Polish F2 network had just taken over from Ekspozytura F, which had been eviscerated by the efforts of the Funkabwehr and its collaborators in the Vichy police. From the Polish perspective, Mak was now running the service that might be able to arrange the exfiltration of Ekspozytura 300's team of over a dozen code-breakers. For two years, Ekspozytura F had been finding ways for trapped Polish servicemen and others to cross the Pyrenees so they could rejoin the fight. All of this had been well concealed from Bertrand, who was quite astonished to be taken to the secret address in Nice: a secret kept so well that even Bertrand himself had no idea that the organisation existed, let alone its address. But all was not well with the Polish underground. There had been too many arrests. For Poles wanting a ticket for the underground, there was currently no service and no date set for resumption.[5]

• • •

It was shortly after their return from Nice that the radio van of the Funkabwehr came within 200m of the Château des Fouzes. A bunch of policemen jumped out. Their direction-finding could not have been particularly sharp, as the men went into the neighbouring house, giving Langer and the dripping Bertrand time to order the concealment of everything. Someone kept watch on the road, where the police had moved on to the next building. Équipe Z switched off all their radios and pulled down the antennas. Equipment was being bundled away, but the police had given up on the second building and the château was next. The château was set well back from the road, surrounded by gardens and a few trees. The police pointed the circular pelengator on the top of their van towards the gates of the building. Nothing. All they could see was the bored 'gardener', one of the code-breakers in fatigues scratching weeds out of the gravel. The place looked quiet in the autumn sunshine; the suspicious transmissions had stopped; it was time for a coffee. The men got back into their van and drove off.[6]

This was too close a call. Bertrand got in touch with Colonel Rivet, urgently asking for directions. Rivet was no longer in charge, but his former number two, Émile Delor, was, and came to the château, arriving just before midnight. Bertrand and Langer agreed: the operation should be shut down and the château evacuated. Another auto-da-fé of documents followed and more equipment was hidden. On the following day, the third exodus of the Polish code-breakers began.[7] The only issues to decide were where they could go and how they could get there.

• • •

Over a hundred ships left Chesapeake Bay in late 1942, stuffed with under-trained American troops heading for an uncertain reception in French North Africa. The U-boats were not yet beaten. At this time, the balance of power in the Atlantic was in favour of the submarines and their torpedoes. Fortunately for the transports, the U-boats had identified other prey. A merchant convoy was inching its way towards Europe from its rendezvous at Freetown, Sierra Leone, and that was too tempting a target. Twelve ships from the commercial convoy were lost, but the troops glided by unseen.[8]

As the ships steamed through the Straits of Gibraltar, German intelligence still had no idea what the target was going to be. No one predicted landings at Oran or Algiers. Tactical surprise was complete. On Sunday 8 November 1942, the troops landed and the Americans had now obtained their foothold on the continent of Africa.

The best thing for Équipe Z was to repeat what they'd done in 1940 and clear out to French North Africa. The Spanish team – Bertrand's Équipe D – had already been allowed to go. With Darlan, as well as the Americans, in North Africa, Rivet was himself was going to board a flight to Algiers. Rivet had been asked about the Équipe Z team at Uzès, but Rivet had replied *Les officiers d'abord!* [officers first]. Despite the risk to the Enigma secret, with the Germans about to swarm over PC Cadix and the rest of the South, the Polish team had been left to their own fate.

Gwido Langer later noted acidly that, 'this was the act of a gentleman who promised us many a time that he'd look after us, that we would never end up in the hands of the Germans'. The gentleman had been relying on Admiral Darlan, but Darlan's attitude was far from clear. To

Langer's disgust, 'it later transpired that not all the seats on the planes were taken.'[9]

Within days, the opportunistic Darlan was treating with the Americans, whose grip on the continent was rapidly assured. Back in metropolitan France, on 11 November 1942, German and Italian forces took over the former Zone Libre.

Bertrand thought that with the African and Polish underground options unavailable, he might instead be able to sort something out directly with the British. In the days after the occupation, despite the challenges of communication, a frenzy of messages passed between Polish HQ in London, Dunderdale, Bertrand, and the Poles trapped in France. Not just messages: Langer was sent 800,000 francs (nearly £4,500 at 1942 values) in cash.[10] Biffy Dunderdale ruled out a mass evacuation by air; there were just too many Poles. What remained was the sea route or the land routes via neutral Switzerland and not-quite-so-neutral Spain. The Swiss route was unattractive, as the Swiss would probably intern the Poles. And their version of internment would be much stricter than anything the Poles had experienced in Romania. Biffy Dunderdale didn't like the Spanish idea. So the sea route it would be. The date set for the voyage was 4 December.

Eventually, the details were sent across by the British. The evacuation was called Operation CRICKET and it would take place at 2 a.m. on the night of 2–3 December. The pickup point would be a few kilometres south of Théoule-sur-Mer, in the Italian-occupied zone, where Gustave Bertrand had an apartment and Équipe Z had reassembled. 'Signal from the land: letter H. Signal from the ship: letter U. Password from the ship: *'Où est le poisson?'* [Where's the fish?] Response: *'Dans la friture.'* [In the fryer.]

But the remaining underground Poles based with Mak in Nice were nervous. The Italians had the rendezvous under observation. Operation CRICKET was postponed.

They tried again. On 11 December 1942, Polish HQ sent Langer another message:

Operation CRICKET will take place in 10 days … I will not send parcels relating to Operation CRICKET. You will receive them at a post box in

Lyon. I will let you know when they are dropped off. They will contain money, 4 radio sets, a camera and photographic materials, cigarettes that put you to sleep, Monaco certificates and a bit of food for you.

Later it was confirmed that CRICKET would go ahead on Christmas Day at 9 p.m. But then, in London, the significance of the surveillance by the Italians sank in. It was too dangerous. Operation CRICKET was called off.[11]

Meanwhile, the Polish code-breakers were living in various hotels and rented villas on the Côte d'Azur. Mimicking the lifestyle of rich expatriates swanning along the promenade, with a genteel aperitif, enjoying the sunshine and gazing hopefully at the sea. This picture of paradise was somewhat marred by the Organizzazione per la Vigilanza e la Repressione dell'Antifascismo (OVRA) – the Italian cousin of the Gestapo – strutting around, the food shortage, the winter weather and the dangers of slipping a pro-Ally sentiment into a strangely accented remark. Still, the Poles managed to get out and about. Walks, English lessons, concerts, church, and the occasional outing. On 24 December 1942, a seasonal celebration, at which Langer and Ciężki became impressively drunk, before midnight mass at Notre-Dame-des-Fleurs. A remembrance mass, on the anniversary, for the victims of the *Lamoricière* sinking. Bertrand noted sarcastically how the funds of the Polish intelligence service were being put to use.[12]

The gaiety of the Riviera was an illusion. The inescapable truth was that the illicit Polish team of code-breakers was stuck in occupied France. By the time Operation CRICKET had been called off, the head of the new Ekspozytura F2 had been arrested by the Abwehr and the OVRA. Along with him went nine more Poles from the fledgling Ekspozytura F2 and a hundred others. It was the biggest round-up yet and it took place the weekend before Bertrand's message to Dunderdale about the inviability of CRICKET. The Germans were leaving no one any place to hide. No wonder Langer and Ciężki had got soused on Christmas Eve.

Worse was to come. Two weeks later it was the turn of the Gestapo to tighten the screws. This time the target was the old French Service de Renseignements. For months the Germans had harboured suspicions about the pro-Ally tendencies of French intelligence: in October,

Admiral Canaris, the chief of the Abwehr, had made it known to the French that he knew the service was providing cover for pro-Allied activities in the Zone Libre.[13] Now the Germans had control, they could act. Under an order from the Führer, roundups began at 5 a.m., 8 January 1943. Over one hundred officers and other personnel serving in the French Army, Air Force and Navy were arrested. Now the guts had been ripped out of the French Deuxième Bureau as well as the Polish intelligence networks. With nothing left of the old organisations, there was nowhere reliable for either Bertrand or Langer to turn.

• • •

While Langer and Cieżki were seeing out the old year, Polish HQ in London sent a message to its regional centre in Berne. Berne was acting as the hub for communications with Poles in France, including Mak and his immediate group. 'In France, one Lieutenant Henryk Paszkowski has been working with Radio Intelligence inter alia as cipher specialist. We must evacuate him to Switzerland together with his wife who is 8 months pregnant.'[14] It was hopeless, though, with no one to put the idea into action. Bertrand had not yet given up; he was still sending telegrams to Dunderdale. In one, he explained that the Swiss route was impossible. Perhaps, though, the road to Spain was still open, despite Dunderdale's reservations.

Leaving via Spain would not be easy. First, the team had to get across German-occupied France, notwithstanding their fake identities and unconvincing accents. The mountain paths were physically demanding and the reception given by the Spanish unpredictable. It would also be expensive. But, said Bertrand, evacuation via Spain stood 'a good chance' of succeeding. The team would be divided into small groups and delivered up to the British or American legations in Pamplona or Barcelona. Please could Dunderdale prepare the ground and take things on from there?

Bertrand's second telegram was more general:

1. I must warn you that the Gestapo and French police are to carry out a major round-up between the 12th and the 15th across the

entire former Zone Libre, to arrest everyone in their sights: foreigners, Jews, Gaullists, officers, etc. 2. Next the demarcation line is to be brought down. 3. Lastly, the coast and borders will constitute a forbidden zone ...[15]

It was not prudent to delay. The next day, 9 January 1943, Bertrand's number two, Captain Honoré Louis, sent word to Langer that the time had come to move. The first group, comprising Langer, Ciężki, Rejewski, Zygalski, Fokczyński, Gaca and the Paszkowskis (including the enormously pregnant Janina), would depart for Toulouse on 11 January. On the day of departure, Langer and Ciężki got soused again. It was an emotional occasion, being a farewell to Bertrand, who had been their 'patron' since the evacuation from Poland over three years before and Langer's liaison officer for over ten years.

A hangover does not make affairs look good, even in Toulouse. Langer later recalled, 'we were put up in an attic of a very old building which was in a terrible state. It was guilty of the proverbial "French cleanliness".' Rejewski and Zygalski did not fare much better, their accommodation described as another 'attic' by Rejewski and a 'hovel' by Langer.[16] There was no food. The evacuation plan, as explained by the agent in Toulouse, was a fantasy: they would go to Perpignan and then walk the 30km or so from there into Spain. How was Janina Paszkowska supposed to manage this? The proposal was another symptom of the disorder of the French secret service. Langer was beginning to realise, as were the others, that the smooth-running machines of the old Deuxième Bureau had utterly broken up. The French people they were dealing with had no connections and were improvising disorder out of chaos. Paszkowska began the minor contractions which sometimes accompany the last days of pregnancy. An ambulance was called and she was given some sort of sedative. Langer ordered the Paszkowskis to stay behind in Toulouse.

After a miserable night in Toulouse, Langer got into a car very early together with Ciężki and Fokczyński for the drive to Perpignan. The driver, the first of many dubious characters they were to meet who were cashing in on the border-crossing trade, gave bland reassurances about the walk into Spain. They'd set off right after breakfast. If they

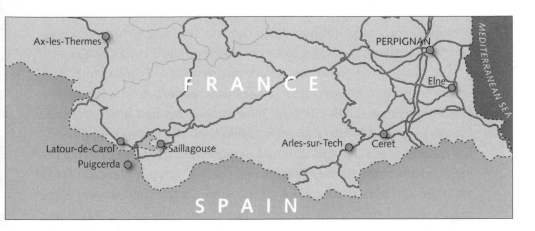

The eastern border of France with Spain.

got tired – Langer was 47 years old, and weighing 80kg he did not look like much of a gymnast; Ciężki was 43 and a chainsmoker with a history of lung trouble – they could do it in two stages.

The driver's description of the walk was wholly incredible and nobody was surprised when it turned out not to be true. At Perpignan, there was at least a breakfast, but no early departure. They were told to wait in the café. After a while, they were introduced to a Monsieur Perez, then taken to an apartment, then introduced to the 'vice-chief of the organisation', then the chief, and then they were told to await the arrival of Gaca, Rejewski and Zygalski, and it was evident that nothing was going according to plan. On the next day, instead of Rejewski and Zygalski, Gaca had the Paszkowskis with him. There was a row: 'you cannot play with human life,' said Langer. 'I think I have a say in the matter of my own life,' said Paszkowska.

None of the Poles had much say in the next plan. According to this, they would take a bus to the village of Arles-sur-Tech, which is about 20km from Perpignan but only 5km from the border. Then they would walk about 1.5km, get on another bus to the border village of Prats-de-Mollo, then cross the mountains on foot. It was a plan that made no sense for Janina Paszkowska. Still, at 8 a.m. on Friday 15 January, Langer, Ciężki and Fokczyński, together with the Paszkowskis, got on the bus to Arles-sur-Tech, accompanied by the fixer M. Perez. At Ceret, mid-way to Arles, there was a routine ID check. The Paszkowskis, with their evident encumbrance, could not have been more innocent-looking and Perez vouched for them. So far so good. Next along on the bus was Langer.

'Are you French?' said the officer suspiciously. 'From Lyon?' The officer wanted to know where Langer was headed, noting his accent was not Lyonnais. 'Off the bus.' Now suspicions had been aroused, Ciężki, Gaca and Fokczyński were ordered off the bus too. This peculiar quartet ostensibly had different occupations and were carrying ID cards issued from all over France, but the IDs were in identical form and they all seemed to be going to the same place. All four were frog-marched to the police station. Heads down, the Paszkowskis stayed put and the bus went onward to Arles-sur-Tech. At least two of them might make it.[17]

● ● ●

Communicating with home was always tough for the code-breakers in exile. If the family was in Russian-occupied Poland, it was basically impossible. If the family was in the German-occupied half, Polish servicemen in France could transfer postcards in envelopes to friends in Romania or Hungary who would forward them on as if the Poles were actually in those countries.[18] Later in the war, more subterfuge was needed. Sometimes sending an obscure, bland message to a friend or a distant relative who lived a long way from the immediate family might transmit the subtext 'I'm still alive' loudly enough to be passed on to those who most needed to know.

In Warsaw, Jadwiga Palluth had not been able to shake off the attentions of the Gestapo despite her adroit handling of the crisis with the illicit radio equipment in her flat. 'Turn out your bag, please, madam,' said the officer, on one of the Gestapo's uninvited visits. Out from her bag tumbled a letter which was not addressed to Jadwiga Palluth. Fortunately the Gestapo did not recognise the clue, but it was a close call.

Some time later, another letter had arrived, this one summoning her to a meeting at a certain address on the Aleja Szucha. This kind of missive seemed innocuous but these letters were notorious and the implications unpleasant. The venue was the Gestapo headquarters and there were two choices. You could go to the meeting and you would either be sent to a camp or you would be shot. Or you could not go to the meeting and you would be shot. People who went to these meetings didn't come back, but the only chance of survival came from going to the meeting. Mrs Palluth went to the meeting.

As always, the conversation was in steely German. But this one was not going on in Mrs Palluth's hallway and she was not in charge this time. So, this time, the conversation was very much more direct.

'You still say you do not know where your husband is. It is very simple. You have two options. Either you tell me, or I will shoot you and the children. You have two minutes to decide which it is.'

But the Gestapo officer had not come across someone like Mrs Palluth before. She didn't quake or shake; she looked the officer in the eye and came straight back. She didn't need two minutes. 'Listen to me, Herr Oberst. I am the mother of two boys. As a mother, I choose the option to tell you where he is. But as I do not know where he is, I choose the option that you shoot us.'

The colonel was dumbstruck. Nobody had ever chosen the 'you shoot us' option before. Maybe, in truth, she did not know where her husband was. But if that was the case, Palluth might try to get in contact with his family; maybe further surveillance might be a better policy than reprisal. Whatever went on in the colonel's head is unknown, but Mrs Palluth was released.

Mrs Palluth may have survived her visit to the Aleja Szucha, but that was not the same as being free. She was being closely monitored. For their next move, the Germans tried something more subtle. One visitor was a Mr Pilarski, who had previously worked in radio intelligence in the pre-war Polish General Staff. Having made himself at home in a visit to Mrs Palluth, Mr Pilarski tried his gamble. 'I knew Antek very well, I just wondered how he is getting on?' The smell of rat was overpowering. Antoni Palluth allowed only a tiny inner circle of friends to use the diminutive of his first name and Jadwiga knew exactly who was in that circle. Pilarski most certainly was not. 'Haven't heard a thing. What do you know?' Pilarski wasn't invited back again and Jadwiga learned from the underground that Pilarski had a certain notoriety as an Abwehr agent.[19]

In February 1943, Antoni Palluth sent another letter. This one wasn't addressed to Poland; he was trying to contact Gustave Bertrand. He had been told to stay behind in occupied France, to help the new Ekspozytura F2 establish its wireless communications, but things had not gone well. *'Je suis malade après avoir mangé des haricots verts. Prière prevenir Helène et George. Lenoir.'* [I am unwell after eating green beans. Please let Helene and George know. Lenoir.] What this meant was that Palluth had also fallen into the hands of the Germans. Across the note was a diagonal line, the colour of permanganate; clearly Palluth's captors had been on the lookout for a hidden message in invisible ink.[20]

● ● ●

The second evacuation team, comprising only Rejewski and Zygalski now, was supposed to follow Gaca and the Paszkowskis to Perpignan. Two days after the arrest of Langer and his group, they learned the disheartening news. Clearly the evacuation plan was off. The pair of Poles left in Toulouse found somewhere better to stay than their filthy attic. The only thing they could do to fill their time was use their cash supply to sample the local restaurants: the Tocque Blanche, the Bonas and the de la Paix. They liked the Bonas. But they'd also heard that the Paszkowskis had decided against the border crossing and were free in Perpignan. Zygalski and Rejewski went to visit them. Janina was in hospital, nursing a newborn son. The code-breakers stayed with one of the dubious contacts – Rejewski called him a smuggler – but it was better than the attic in Toulouse.

Perpignan, however, was not all unbounded joy. A female money-changer ran off with Rejewski's cash and the pair of code-breakers spent a fruitless day chasing after her. None of this was going to help them get out of France; they would have to go back to Toulouse if anything positive was going to happen. The idea of returning to the attic was less than appealing; this time they'd do things differently. A pleasant night at the Hotel Terminus in Narbonne, to break their journey, a room at the Hotel Raymond IV in Toulouse. (The nice irony that the Germans had requisitioned much of the Raymond IV was not lost on them, nor on the porter, who was watching everything on behalf of the Resistance.) Dinner at the Bonas. Lunch, the next day, at the Bonas, then the cinema. A new attempt at crossing the border was scheduled for that evening.[21]

In the winter darkness, the two took the train from Toulouse to the village of Ax-les-Thermes, 10km from the border with Andorra in the Pyrenees. The hotel at Ax was a far cry from the elegance of the Terminus at Narbonne. The place was obviously a wormery of the underground, where the number one occupation was trafficking of people and contraband across the border. They decided to stay holed up in the hotel for the day, until it was time to catch the train for the short journey to the border at Latour-de-Carol.[22] Yet an anticipated guide was not on the train and at Latour they were the only two people to get off the train. Their feeling of exposure went skywards when the gendarmes asked for their (forged) ID cards and asked pressing questions about their presence in the forbidden border zone in midwinter. Next it was the turn of some German guards. The two Poles were spies, out of uniform, in a foreign country under enemy occupation. By all reasonable reckoning they could expect to be taken away and shot.

Border patrol in France was a cushy posting if you could get it. Life in France was what all the Wehrmacht aspired to. After all, which was more palatable, that or the Russian front? What a question. France had cheap, fabulous food, booze, tobacco, girls, soft beds and you-name-it. At Stalingrad, General von Paulus's army was surrounded and his last airfield, his last means of supply, had been captured by the Soviets on 24 January 1943, the day the code-breakers were in Perpignan admiring the latest recruit to the Paszkowski family. For the rank-and-file German soldier, there was no sense whatsoever in making a fuss. Keep focused on the main chance, do enough to show the brass that you took your soldiering seriously and do nothing to draw attention to yourself.

Perhaps Rejewski and Zygalski had deceptive skills of the highest order, or maybe it was that the winter mountain air reminded their German inquisitors about the risks of too great a display of zeal. The pair of fake tourists were allowed off to explore and to go back to a hotel at Latour-de-Carol for dinner. Zygalski soon realised that Latour was another nest of snakes, as his suitcase, cash and other belongings were missing. It was too late to fret. The guide who had missed the train turned up: he had got hold of a bike and cycled from Ax-les-Thermes. After dinner, they all said goodbye to France and headed back out, into the dark and into the snow.

● ● ●

Saturday 27 February 1943 was a bad day for the world of code-breaking. Since around the time of his breakthrough on the Abwehr machine, Dilly Knox had been taking increasingly long bouts of sick leave. He had been diagnosed with cancer early in the war and his illness was apparent to all by 1941, though the cause and prognosis were known to few. On that February day in 1943, the man who had broken the Spanish, Italian and Abwehr Enigmas died and with Knox's death the classical era of code-breaking came to a close.

On the same day, another drama with dark significance for code-breaking was being played out in the mountains of south-western France. Louis Guillaume Rudolf Stallmann, aka Rex and now conveniently known as Rodolphe Lemoine, was about as retired as he was ever going to be. In 1943, he was over 70 years old, but 'retirement' did not come naturally to the old card-sharper who had long settled into the respectable trade of trafficking in code books and dodgy passports. Since the contretemps on the dockside during the chaos of 1940 had obliged him to remain in France, it had behoved Rex to take a more discreet lifestyle.[23]

Rex was always difficult to handle. You could accuse Rex of many things, but not of undying patriotism. Throughout the Vichy period, it was unclear, in particular to Paul Paillole, one of Louis Rivet's staff, whose side Rex was really on. Paillole had met Rex on several occasions in connection with the informant inside the German Embassy in Paris, and Paillole knew that the Nazi authorities had long expressed interest in the so-called Rodolphe Lemoine. The Germans had kept a file on Rex since 1920; there had been unflattering press coverage of 'Lemoine' in the *Volkische Beobachter* in 1939 and the Germans had even arrested him on a trip to Berlin in 1938. That incident had put the wind up the French, who had only been partly reassured when

Rex laughed it off by saying that he had offered his services to the Germans as a double agent.[24]

The fact was that the Germans were still trying to recruit Rex and early in 1942 had sent an intermediary to sound him out. Paillole's antennae picked up on that soon enough and Rex was despatched to live in obscurity, confining himself to pastimes appropriate for a respectable, retired spy.

> In the calm and invigorating air of the high Cerdagne, Lemoine's health began to improve little by little. He played away rainy days in games of *belote* with the local country types, arranged several lucrative crossings into the [Spanish] enclave of Llivia, kept himself and his friends supplied in the black market, played *pétanque* with the police, took walks with his wife and his little dog, greeted all the way as a notable.[25]

To retire Rex to the clean mountain air of the high Cerdagne – in the eastern Pyrenees – may have been an error. The residence chosen for Rex to regenerate his health and practise his lob at *pétanque* was in the the village of Saillagouse, situated about halfway between the crossing points of Latour-de-Carol and Prats-de-Mollo, and not far from either of them. Since 1941, Saillagouse had become 'the turntable of clandestine passages to Spain ... the chief of police Bottet was the king-pin ... Discreetly recommended to Bottet, [Lemoine] gauged the advantages of the region and the possibilities of trafficking of all descriptions across the border.' Rex had not, in fact, retired at all.

Indeed no. There were cards still in play. On 31 October 1942, Gustave Bertrand wanted to know if the British were interested in buying an Italian code book that 'someone' was offering for sale. Rex had got access to the Italian *Code Impero*, and was trying to find a buyer. The British weren't playing, but the Abwehr were, so it seemed. Who knows whether the Germans wanted to spy on their allies? But the intrigue and deception around the code book were what made life worth living for Rex. Rex had been approached by an old colleague, known to be a German collaborator, in June 1942. This was an invitation to play for the House and the House always wins. Rex was back at the table and the *Code Impero* was a chip to be wagered. So when the Germans occupied the Zone Libre, he was not minded to disappear to French North Africa in accordance with Paul Paillole's instructions. Rex was staying and watching what was going on.[26]

One matter going on was that a case officer had been assigned by the Abwehr to look into the *'affaire Lemoine'*. This was Hauptmann Georg Wiegand, who had been studying Rex's files for months. When the Germans occupied Paris in 1940, they had been able to add substantially to their collection of material. Documents had not been destroyed by the departing French. Even better for Wiegand, on 19 June 1940 the Germans had found an entire train-load of materials parked in a siding at La Charité-sur-Loire, comprising the secret archive of the French General Staff. This contained not only copies of the Allied codes but a vast trove of material, including several files documenting the exploits of France's very own Rodolphe Lemoine. Hauptmann Wiegand was very keen to have an encounter with Monsieur Lemoine.

There was also a joker in the pack. The Abwehr was not the only agency interested in the mysterious ex-Baron. The Nazi agencies, always at war with each other, were competing for this particular trophy. If Rex did not play his hand right, he could end up in the hands of the Gestapo, which would be a much less enjoyable game than playing with the Abwehr. He knew an arrest was imminent, but should he stay, or should he go? The Spanish border was close to hand, but the *Code Impero* gamble was not yet played out.

Thus, on 27 February 1943, as Dilly Knox breathed his last in his woodland home in Berkshire, it was with some relief that Rex greeted Wiegand, who had come to Saillagouse to arrest him. 'I wasn't expecting you until tomorrow,' said Rex, with the sangfroid which he customarily inflicted on his card-playing victims.[27] Wiegand's orders were to take the Lemoines to Paris. The Abwehr had plans for Rex.

● ● ●

After a night in custody, Langer, Ciężki, Gaca and Fokczyński were hauled before the prosecutor and charged with attempting to cross the border with false documents and attempting to take foreign currency out of the country. The standard sentence for illegal border crossing was one month and that is what they got. Despite assurances from Captain Louis, nobody seemed to have been told in advance about this group of evacuees. Either Louis was untrustworthy or the system was even more disorganised than they thought. Langer and the other three soon found themselves in another bus heading for the prison at Perpignan.

On their release in February, they had no idea what their next move would be, except that they were sure they wanted no more dealings with the unreliable Monsieur Perez or his associates. Lacking an alternative, they went back to their old flat, where they discovered that the Paszkowskis, so far from being safe in Spain, were still being accommodated along with their baby by none other than Perez. There was nothing to do, nowhere to go, except while away the days eating lunch. Gustave Bertrand says that Langer and Ciężki 'distinguished themselves' in the bars of Perpignan.[28] As Bertrand had vanished in January, his reportage may be suspect, or at best second-hand, as the only remaining link between him and the ex-prisoners was Captain Louis. Langer didn't much care for Louis, who was, wrote the leader of the Poles, 'disliked by everyone, an awful type'.[29] One assumes that Captain Louis was not invited to participate in lunch.

A week after their release from prison, they were arrested again as they arrived home from another lunch. They were put in a windowless cell and told they were on their way to a concentration camp. After two nights, the door banged open, and, miraculously, they were released again, though obliged to report daily to the police station. Two days later there was a police round-up and once again the four found themselves in custody. This time there was a Commissioner from Vichy who was extremely sceptical, taking the view that all Poles in France were members of the Resistance. Even so, sympathetic and helpful people were all around: the lawyer who had been looking after their case since their first arrest six weeks before; several of the regular police; survivors of the old networks of French intelligence. The Commissioner was, reluctantly, convinced about the four Poles. They were free once more.

● ● ●

A third contingent of Polish code-breakers, led by Wiktor Michałowski, left Cannes the week after the Langer group. On reaching Toulouse, they learned of Langer's arrest and Bertrand sent orders for them to return to Cannes. Their turn came around again two days after Zygalski and Rejewski had set off across the mountains. All the remaining code-breakers – Michałowski, Szachno, Suszczewski and the two Palluth cousins – were to make up the second group, except that Antoni Palluth was pulled out to set up the Ekspozytura F2 radio network. The other four were to follow the route pioneered by Rejewski and Zygalski: train to Ax-les-Thermes, then on to Latour-de-Carol for the mountain crossing. Michałowski didn't like it. Captain Louis and the remnants of the French intelligence were far too trusting of the low-life people traffickers; the organisation was haphazard; everywhere was crawling with Germans. There was a Polish lieutenant at Ax who seemed far too close to one of the French fixers, who, it seemed, had a nice trading relationship with the people traffickers. Everyone in the chain was on the make. On arrival at Latour, the smuggler from the Spanish side was introduced to the four. Brazenly, in front of their French liaison, he demanded a supplement of $50 on top of what he'd already been paid. Reluctantly Michałowski handed over $25, with the rest to follow on safe delivery. No go, said the guide, full whack now or no service.[30]

Michałowski paid. The temperature fell to -15°C and the snow was deep. At the crucial point on the border the guide drew a revolver, ordered the four Poles to hand over all their valuables and abandoned them to their fate.

● ● ●

One thing was clear for Langer and his group: after three arrests, one prison term and two hair's breadth reprieves the time was long overdue to make a concerted effort to leave France. Despite his unconvincing record, only Perez was still offering options and solutions. Perez's number one choice was a trafficker called Gomez, who was quoting around ten times the going rate for regular evacuees.[31] Perez, of course, knew that these would-be evacuees were anything but regular: these ex-convicts could be milked for every sou they possessed and it was clear that outsiders were providing an endless source of funds. Perez may have thought that this was just a financial matter and may even have been wholly straight with his charges, but one of the friendly policemen warned Langer that dealing with Gomez was another matter.[32]

Langer needed Bertrand to come and sort out the muddle, but Bertrand had disappeared. Captain Louis unexpectedly turned up in Perpignan one day, just as Langer and his colleagues were coming back from their daily reporting at the police station. Louis evidently did not expect to see them and certainly had not prepared to be met with a broadside of questions about the failed evacuation attempt in January, the crumbling French underground and the shady Gomez. Louis agreed to get fresh fake ID cards for the group, to meet Perez and to square things with Bertrand. Langer's mistrust of Louis must have shown in the conversation. 'Why doesn't Bolek [Bertrand] come here at least once?' he asked. Louis dissolved in a fountain of emotional blackmail, tears, incoherence. Nothing more was seen of Captain Louis, the ID cards did not materialise, nor did Bertrand, and Langer was left in the hands of the untrustworthy Toulouse team who had taken care of the Rejewski and Michałowski groups.

On 10 March 1943, a Toulouse contact came with cash, but it was 80,000 francs short of what Gomez had demanded. Now there was a stand-off: Langer voiced his opinion of Gomez, Perez said there was no evacuation without the cash. Then they spoke to a sympathetic inspector of police who had helped them after their recent arrests, who said he could provide a different, trustworthy guide across the border. Perez could see his milking machine was about to fall to pieces. The next day, the price had fallen to 35,000 francs for the four. They would leave on the night train for a village on the coast only 5km from the border and the guide would take them on from there.

They were all set to go, enduring the anxious wait for the train, when the form of Perez appeared with the unwelcome news that Gomez was going to escort them after all.

The group gave Gomez the slip and the new guide seemed to know his stuff. His agents were on the train and one of them sounded a discreet alarm as soon as the four Poles came aboard. The Gestapo were conducting a search, something which the agent had never seen before. The Poles stepped into the next carriage, then Ciężki nudged Langer. The Gestapo had followed them – time to get off.

On the platform was one of Gomez's associates. It was back to square one. The agent from Toulouse came round the next morning. Langer said they would go by taxi instead of the train. The agent had a couple of French evacuees to add to the party as well, a businessman and a chemist, who had each paid 100,000 francs. For security, Langer was to sign a 20-franc banknote and rip it in half. On safe arrival in Spain, Langer would give his half to the guide, who would get paid when it was delivered up to Gustave Bertrand. Now, at last, something well organised was going to happen.

The agent came back as arranged, but now there were half-a-dozen changes of plan. The ever-present Gomez was back in the frame. Langer was in no mood to comply with any of this and was unpersuaded by the argument that Gomez's contacts with the Gestapo allowed for their smoother transfer through the closed border zone. The two Frenchmen were the only guarantee that the thing was not a set-up. Perez gave way.

As dusk fell, the four Poles tramped out towards the periphery of the town. The car and the two Frenchmen were there. They got in, and the car went off. At the village of Elne, as planned, they got out. Gomez was waiting. Gomez bade them an insincere farewell and passed them over to the guide who was to take them to the next village, where the relay would be taken up by another guide to show them across the mountains. They traipsed through the snow, glad to be rid of the egregious Gomez.

After an hour's walking the group heard the noise of motorcycle engines. At the same time, a group of men in Gestapo uniforms leaped out of the bushes and blocked their way, shooting to make their point. The group were surrounded, unarmed, incapacitated, there was no hope of escape – except for the guide, who mysteriously melted away into the landscape. The Poles were taken to the village of Argeles-sur-Mer, where all their belongings were seized, searched and interrogated, and their security – the torn-in-half 20-franc note – was taken along with their other cash. It was pointless to try to dissemble, because the ID cards which they now had were in their real names. For Langer, Ciężki, Gaca and Fokczyński, it was the end of World War Two.

● ● ●

Maksymilian Ciężki had done his best to destroy every iota of documentation about his pre-war work before evacuating Poland in 1939. He was not alone. Colonel Stefan Mayer, head of the Second Department of the General Staff, had done likewise, checking that his subordinates had also burned their papers. So had Major Jan Żychoń, when he was head of Intelligence Station III at Bydgoszcz. The Abwehr had expected to find nothing, especially as Żychoń had left his business card on his empty desk, in his empty office, to welcome them.[33]

So it was with open-mouthed amazement that the Abwehr discovered an entire room near Warsaw full of secret documents. 'Six trucks had to be fetched to transport the secret material from Fort Legionów and take it to the appropriate departments. The analysis resulted in the detection and arrest of more than one hundred persons who had worked for the Polish secret service.'[34] Fort Legionów was the Polish military archives centre, to which standing orders decreed that copies of all paperwork be supplied. The Polish Army had, by its own efficiency, defeated its own secrecy.

There was nothing too obvious in the haul about Enigma decryption, but the materials which the Nazis had found contained enough evidence to suggest something had been going on. There were deciphered copies of messages sent from a German cruiser in Spanish waters during the Spanish Civil War. There was a cipher centre called 'Wicher' located at Pyry, which the Germans searched. There were staff lists of the Biuro Szyfrów which indicated that two young civilians, mathematics students from Poznań, were being paid disproportionately large salaries, which implied that they were doing something remarkably useful.[35]

German detectives began work to unravel a part of the mystery. Gwido Langer's office manager in Warsaw was Zofia Pawłowicz. Her two brothers had senior positions in the army and distinguished service records, and she herself had worked for the Biuro Szyfrów since 1924. Pawłowicz knew everything that had been going on. Every document which passed under her boss's nose had been through her own hands. She had not been evacuated with the others, but until the German offensive against the USSR she had been in south-eastern Poland on the Soviet side of the demarcation line. With the Germans in control everywhere, she had then come back to Warsaw, taking an anonymous job in a café.

Then someone denounced her and she was taken to the building in the Aleja Szucha where Jadwiga Palluth had been threatened, but in Pawłowicz's case she was put in the 'tram' for softening up. The tram was a narrow room with benches arranged like a streetcar; prisoners were forbidden to communicate and forced to endure loud martial music, possibly to drown out the sounds of interrogations going on nearby. When it was Pawłowicz's turn to be questioned, they took her upstairs. The room was nicely furnished and the interrogators were from the Abwehr and not the usual Gestapo thugs.

At first, they were very courteous and assured me that they wanted only to confirm known facts and to elucidate some less important details. They knew that for many years I had been an employee at the General Staff. Surely I would not be so unreasonable as to deny obvious facts. Otherwise they would be 'forced' to leave me to spend even longer in the hands of the Gestapo. I must have played my role well – the role of a not-too-bright but also not-too-dull grey office clerk, one of the hundred or more who had worked for the Polish General Staff and War Ministry.[36]

The grey clerk quickly realised that her interrogators were not cipher experts and she did her best to bore them with the details of office procedures. The dread subject of Enigma was avoided. But for Zofia Pawłowicz the end of her interrogation did not spell freedom. She had to do time in solitary confinement in the Pawiak prison before the Abwehr lost interest in her some time later.

It was not a coincidence that both Mrs Palluth and Mrs Pawłowicz had been dragged in for questioning. As the fortunes of war turned, the German authorities began to worry again about the security of Enigma: 1943 saw a reopening of the attempt to get to the bottom of what the Poles had known and how secure the Enigma machine might be. General Erich Fellgiebel, the German Army's Chief Signals Officer (and later one of the conspirators in the 'July plot' to assassinate Hitler), ordered a further effort.[37] The pieces were beginning to come together. Other interrogations had revealed that the Czechs had had some pre-war success against German hand ciphers and they had been cooperating with the French. Maybe the Wicher Poles had gone to France? The search of the Deuxième Bureau in Paris had not helped much, because the cryptographic service records had been spirited away. But what they could do is keep a good lookout for the men whose names had showed up in the files at Fort Legionów.

The Zentralfahndungsstelle, a branch of the German security police based in Paris, issued a Wanted List every month, with at least two updates in between. On the Wanted List of 1 March 1943 appeared some seven new Polish names, all emanating from *Feldpostnummer* 20803-89092/42g, where the 'g' stood for *geheim* [secret]. The seven were Ciężki, Graliński, Michałowski, Palluth, Rejewski, Różicki and Zygalski. The deaths of Graliński and Różicki in the *Lamoricière* disaster had not yet registered. Nor had the arrests of Ciężki and Palluth. But the net was closing in. Several of the code-breakers, including Palluth, Rejewski, Różicki and Zygalski, had their mugshots circulated by the Zentralfahndungsstelle in *Meldeblatt* [Information Sheet] number 130.[38] It was only a matter of time before the people holding Ciężki and Palluth did their cross-checks.

German bureaucracy is renowned for its thoroughness, but under the Nazi régime many agencies competed to achieve success against recidivists, foreigners, non-Aryans and whoever else might be in their distorted sights. So cooperation was rare and Fellgiebel's plan ambled along slowly. Rex, in his guise as Rodolphe Lemoine (alias Stallmann Rudolf alias von Koenig), had been on the Wanted List longer than the Poles and it took until many months after his arrest in February 1943 for the list to catch up with the fact that he had been found. Perhaps, instead of chasing after the elusive Poles, there might be something useful to be gleaned from Rex.

On 20 March 1943, Rex, the king of spies, was under interrogation in his comfortable apartment at the Hôtel Continental in Paris.[39] The Abwehr was still hoping to turn Rex; their technique was quite different from the intimidations of the tramcar in Warsaw. Having seen how the cards had fallen, Rex was not going to resist. Hauptmann Georg Wiegand picked up his notebook and began to listen to the most incredible spy story of World War Two.

11

THE LAST PLAY

[A confused noise within.]
'Farewell, brother!'
'We split, we split, we split!'
ANTONIO: Let's all sink wi' the king.

William Shakespeare
The Tempest, Act 1, scene 1

Marian Rejewski and Henryk Zygalski crunched through the snow. The going was difficult in the dark, but after an interminable march the two friends were relieved to hear their guide tell them that they were now across the border. Their welcome to Spain was a demand for more cash, or else they would be abandoned right there, in the dark, on the mountains, directionless and in the middle of nowhere. They had no choice. They gave up what little they still had: a watch and Zygalski's camera. Then they were shown the way down the hill. Eventually they lighted upon signs of civilisation – to be exact, the Spanish police. Their first night in Spain was spent in the cells of the Puigcerda village jail.

Wiktor Michałowski's party met a similar fate.[1] After being robbed, they too stumbled downhill and, like the two code-breakers who had taken the same road before them, soon found themselves arrested and sent off to the police station at Guardiola, a few miles south of the border. The day after, they were moved to Barcelona, and from there to a prison where they were kept in solitary confinement. It seemed that the war was now over for all the code-breakers of Ekspozytura 300.

Gwido Langer kept a diary which starts on 15 January 1943, the date of his first arrest in Ceret in the south of France.[2] It may be that the first few pages were written up some time after the events. It's written in German, probably because he was writing it under the noses of his captors, and for the same reason it has very little in it beyond a record of the weather, the sparse food, and occasional petty excitements of prison such as the arrival of a food parcel. Gwido Langer also recorded his weight: it was 80kg when he was first arrested.

Following their arrest at Elne, Gwido Langer, Maksymilian Ciężki and Edward Fokczyński, were taken to Compiègne. There they were held in a camp, Frontstalag Number 122, which was for 'civilian intern-ees' such as supporters of Charles de Gaulle. There they discovered Antoni Palluth, who was awaiting deportation to Germany. On 28 April 1943, Palluth and Fokczyński were sent off to work in Germany. Two weeks later, Kazimierz Gaca – who had belatedly been brought to Compiègne as well – followed them. Meanwhile, Langer and Ciężki were left behind in France.[3]

Compiègne was no holiday camp. Food was scarce. Shootings were not. Dogs were set on the prisoners. During an escape attempt by some inmates in early April, six prisoners were executed. Communication with outsiders was difficult and only likely to put the Gestapo on the trail of those whom the prisoners were trying to contact. But the departures of Palluth and then Gaca provided some opportunities to get back in touch with Bertrand, and Langer was able to re-establish links with the Polish Ekspozytura F2 network. Some food and clothing parcels began to get through. The only good thing, apart from the par-cels, was that they were imprisioned with the civilian recidivists: so far, it appeared, nobody knew who they were. At least, not yet.

● ● ●

In the well-fed surroundings of the Hotel Continental, Rex began to sell to the Abwehr the story of his life. Indeed, his life was at stake, but it was Hans-Thilo Schmidt who was the mark in the last, the most deadly, of the games played by the baron of the casinos.

By 20 March 1943, the details had all come out: how Schmidt had approached the French; the initial suspicions that Schmidt was a plant by German intelligence; the first meeting at Verviers. Then the photography (not omitting the detail of the bathroom); the 10,000 Reichsmarks paid to Schmidt; the correspondence in invisible ink; the locations of the following meetings; the flow of secret documents; the soap-factory cover plan. The attention of the interrogators was on what Hans-Thilo's brother had negligently divulged, the secret War Ministry materials which revealed high German strategy.[4]

Over the coming weeks, Rex spilled more beans. One by one, Rex's contacts were rounded up. Among the victims was the French mole in the German Embassy. Hans-Thilo Schmidt's proximity to the Enigma secret could not be ignored. The enquiry was widening. The German factory which manufactured Enigma machines was required to provide details of their dealings with Hans-Thilo Schmidt.[5] On 23 March 1943, Hans-Thilo was arrested. On 10 April, his brother General Rudolf Schmidt was relieved of his command on the Eastern Front.

The interrogation of Rex and the wide-ranging inquisition concerning Schmidt was not the only threat to the Enigma secret. The German Supreme Command Cipher Division had a new commanding officer, Major-General Wilhelm Gimmler. A new man at the top, a new investigation into the security of Enigma. Sooner or later, the threads must surely come together and the German bureaucrats catch up with their prisoners.

● ● ●

On 2 July 1943, a telegram from Słowikowski reached Polish intelligence headquarters in London. 'SECRET. From Algiers. From Rivet – The following officers from the cryptology cell have been arrested in Spain: Maj. Michałowski, Capt. Palluth, Lt. Rejewski, Lt. Szachno, Lt. Suszczewski and Lt. Sylwester. Four of them, including Maj. Michałowski, are in Las Misiones prison in Barcelona, two in Lerida. Rivet asks if those officers could continue to work with the French in North Africa, instead of being withdrawn to England. RYGOR.'[6]

The information in the telegram wasn't completely accurate, but it was certainly good news. On 27 July, the prisoners were bundled off to Madrid, then to Portugal and then on to an overcrowded trawler called the *Scottish* which took them to Gibraltar. They had been in prison for almost six months. On 2 August, a transport plane took them, not to Rivet in North Africa, but to Hendon in North London, where they arrived the following morning.[7] The bewildered group of released Poles – Rejewski, Zygalski, Michałowski, Szachno and Sylwester Palluth (but not his cousin Antoni) – were under the orders of the Polish Army. There was a debriefing. It still had to be decided what their role should be. Indeed, the role of Poland in the war was becoming a difficult question for the Allies.

Following their victory at Stalingrad, the Red Army began to roll back the Wehrmacht. Consequently, the Polish government-in-exile had been looking for assurance about their post-war eastern border. Relations between the Poles and the Soviets had been dealt a near-fatal blow by the announcement by German radio in April 1943 that the bodies of 3,000 Polish officers had been discovered in a huge ditch at a place called Katyn. In defiance of the wishes of the British, whose diplomacy was designed to appease Stalin at any cost, the Polish government-in-exile demanded an investigation into the find, which – as the Germans had expected – showed that the Poles had been executed by their Russian captors. Only the towering authority of Sikorski could hold the shaky Russo-Polish alliance together. But on 4 July 1943, only days before the code-breakers themselves reached Gibraltar, Sikorski's plane crashed on take-off there. For Poland, for the code-breakers, Russia was less of an ally than an enemy and certainly a force to be watched with the utmost care.

The London to Bletchley railway line runs alongside the Grand Union canal for much of its length, passing the town of Hemel Hempstead, on the outskirts of which sits the village of Boxmoor. Unlike Hemel, Boxmoor has a station on the line and it is less than a mile – if a stiff uphill walk – from the station to a large house in comparatively rural surroundings, in a place too small to have a name, but nonetheless called Felden. Its isolation, hilltop setting and railway link made Felden the perfect place for foreign spies to keep an eye on an ally of dubious intentions. The house was called 'The Arches' and it was requisitioned by the British in May 1943 because the radio reception at Stanmore was inadequate for long-distance communication and interception. On 22 June 1943, the Polish Radio Intelligence Company commanded by

Captain Kazimierz Zieliński moved into the house, in whose grounds there were now 8m radio masts and associated outbuildings. It was a bit like Bletchley Park, just on a smaller scale.[8]

A few weeks later, on the orders of Jan Żychoń, a meeting took place between Biffy Dunderdale and Major Władysław Gaweł, the officer in charge of Polish signals intelligence in London. Item 4 on the agenda was the group of code-breakers formerly belonging to Ekspozytura 300. Dunderdale was told the team would be assigned to the Radio Intelligence Company at Felden. 'We may use some of them to improve Russian cryptology.' Dunderdale was delighted. 'He said he was especially interested in intelligence focused on Russia, since the Radio Intelligence Company at Felden was the only source of information about Russia for them.'[9] Here, in a large suburban house, on the fringes of the peacetime commuter belt, the fugitives from Ekspozytura 300 would be put to work for the rest of the war.

● ● ●

Gustave Bertrand had been practising his magical tricks. He could make people disappear; his latest act was to disappear himself. There was a hint to Gwido Langer that Bertrand had looked in on the prison in Perpignan where Langer was locked up with Ciężki, Fokcyński and Gaca, but they hadn't seen him then or since. After that, he had made something appear: half a 20-franc note bearing the signature of Gwido Langer. The second part of the payment to the courier who was to deliver the four Poles to safety was due to be settled only when Bertrand had both halves of the note. One half had been seized by the Gestapo when Langer was arrested. Now Bertrand had both halves of the note and he had paid off those who had led the Poles into ambush. Langer never forgave Bertrand for this. To Langer, it was a betrayal and the 20-franc note was proof positive that, having pulled off his disappearing act, Bertrand was being played by the Germans, if not actively working for them.[10]

The business of the note was proof of something, certainly. It did not take a torn 20-franc note to provide evidence that shady characters like Gomez and his associates had done some deal with the Gestapo. But the farrago with the note did not prove that Bertrand was working for the Nazis. In a telegram to Stanisław Gano in London, Bertrand apologised for not helping more with the evacuation: his country had been 'conquered and sold to the enemy.'[11] And, unknown to Langer, there was an explanation for Bertrand's disappearance. He was working underground.

The Kléber network wasn't a traditional spy network at all. It was a complete bureaucracy replicating as much of the structure of the pre-war Service de Renseignements as was feasible in the circumstances of conquest and sale. 'It was a vast organisation covering numerous networks and sub-networks.' Its crucial role was to keep the French underground – the Forces Françaises de l'Intérieur – connected with senior anti-Vichy officers in North Africa and (via Dunderdale) their Allies in London, and to keep both those constituencies abreast of developments in France. As the Allies lumbered towards the inevitable invasion of France, Kléber and its subdivisions would furnish them with the order-of-battle and other details about the defending Wehrmacht, as well as provide coordination with the Resistance. The heart of Kléber was its radio organisation. At the head of Kléber was a French officer who was expert in radio intelligence. His name, sometimes, was Gustave Bertrand.[12]

● ● ●

On 9 September 1943, Gwido Langer (weight now 66kg) recorded in his diary that he and Ciężki were being transferred from the prison camp at Compiègne to the Schloss Eisenberg in the Sudetenland. Internierungslage IV was no more an ordinary camp for prisoners of war than Compiègne. It was an internment centre for 'prominent personalities'. Among the approximately 138 luminaries held at Eisenberg in early 1944 were General René Altmayer of the French Army; Michel Clemenceau, son of the Great War era French premier, and Pierre de Gaulle, brother of the Free French general. Clemenceau was in room 46, where Langer and Ciężki were placed. Unfortunately, such august company did not presage an uplift in the conditions. Langer's weight continued to fall. By 15 January 1944 he was at 58kg, a 27 per cent drop in weight. He had all the appearance of a living skeleton. At least, though, letters had begun to arrive from Poland and Red Cross parcels were now allowed. Slowly, Langer's weight began to creep back up. On 27 January, he got his first letter from Janka his wife.

Now it was Ciężki's health that was the worry. Langer records that:

> people were getting very sick due to malnutrition, and if the food parcels had not come in February the whole camp would have turned into a cemetery. It was difficult to walk even to the second floor. Major Ciężki was unwell too. That year Dr Clarte [another inmate in the same cell] told me he didn't think Ciężki would make it. The doctor thought Ciężki would die of tuberculosis.'

Ciężki wrote home from the Schloss Eisenberg that, at '51 kilograms, I now belong to the featherweight category'.[13]

● ● ●

Georges Baudin was always thinking about radio. Radio communications were a lifeline in the upside-down world where his home country was occupied by one group of foreigners and the hope of freedom lay in the hands of another group of foreigners. So it was a major concern of his that the amount of equipment at his disposal was constantly diminishing. Every time there was a raid, precious equipment was captured or destroyed. Fortunately, the intelligence service had arranged for a drop-off of some replacements and information on the pick-up was to be given in Paris.

Baudin's rendezvous with the intelligence service was at the church of the Sacré-Coeur at Montmartre on 3 January 1944, and the procedure was a textbook example of tradecraft. Baudin did not know his contact, so they would meet by the statue of St Antony of Padua. The contact would have a copy of the paper *Signal* in his left hand. Baudin would say '*Salve*' and the countersign was 'Amen'. Yet when the day came, no one carrying *Signal* was anywhere to be found. Another man had come in and made a show of praying, but nowhere near the statue. Baudin and the other man were evidently both waiting and after a while it dawned on Baudin that they were waiting for each other.

'*Salve*,' said Baudin tentatively.

'*Est-ce bien vous qui venez de Clermont-Ferrand?*' said the other man.

By this point, Baudin ought to have twigged that something was amiss. Instead, he arranged to meet two days later in the same place. On that occasion, despite the time appointed being the early hour of 8 a.m., the church was positively teeming with the pious. One kept his hat on. One guarded the door. The other two took pews before and behind our man, each poking a revolver into his ribs. Baudin was soon on his way to 101, Avenue Henri-Martin, and he had only himself to blame.[14]

101 Avenue Henri-Martin was a branch office of the Abwehr, whose chief had sallow skin, an unwelcoming expression and appalling taste in clothes. He was Christian Masuy (real name Georges Delfanne) and he specialised in water torture. Masuy's victims were repeatedly immersed in a bath, filled with 'cold water, blood, clumps of hair, and excrement.'[15]

Georges Baudin did not wish to take a Masuy bath. Having had his pockets emptied and his fake ID examined, he decided to confess his true identity. He was, in truth, the Commandant Gustave Bertrand, of the French secret intelligence service. It was not much of a surprise, for Masuy and his boss were already acquainted with Commandant Gustave Bertrand.

Back in the spring of 1940, Louis Rivet and his regiment of intelligence officers had been carefully watching the German Embassy in Brussels. The embassy was the place from which the Abwehr conducted operations. The director was an officer called Hermann Brandl, cover-name Otto, and his chief agent was someone called Delfanne, alias Masuy. When the war overtook the game of the spies, Otto was ordered out of no-longer-neutral Belgium. He could not go to Germany by the direct route because that lay straight through the combat zone. Their only option was to take a train, through France, and trust in their diplomatic status to give them safe passage.[16]

When the train pulled into the station at Lille it was searched, as everyone had expected. Inspector Robert Blémant was vulgar and contemptuous, and, unfortunately for Otto, he was also diligent, anti-Nazi and not impressed by official bits of paper. In Inspector Blémant's view, Germans should just be locked up, particularly as everyone knew

Otto was a spy working for the Abwehr and the claim to diplomatic immunity was a veneer of falsehood. Despite the complaints of the ambassador himself, Otto was taken off the train and marched off the offices of the *Surveillance du Territoire*, France's MI5.[17] Otto began to talk his way out, telling the French about German radio operators working under cover in France. It wouldn't matter, since the Germans were coming anyway and saving his own skin was the priority. Otto's first disclosure was of a 70-year-old man with a transmitter and a much younger Javanese wife, whose expensive needs could only be satisfied from a reliable spying income.[18]

An emergency call went out to Gustave Bertrand to investigate the ageing spy, his transmitter, and the Javanese wife, and true to duty Bertrand leaped into a car and drove the 250km to Lille. The man confessed and was taken from his Javanese wife. Otto told Bertrand what he needed to know about the transmitter and the technical instructions found with it.

Meanwhile, the French high command had got wind of the case of Agent Otto. It was now a matter of honour: Otto had to be released. Blémant was wild with fury. Paul Paillole, Blémant's minder from French counter-intelligence, agreed, honour be damned. So Blémant put together a plan. The train would be allowed to proceed on its journey, but Blémant would remain aboard and cause an accident. Then Otto could be taken off and disposed of quietly. Everyone would be satisfied.

There was only one flaw in Blémant's plan and that was that he told people about it. Otto certainly knew that his life was in peril. And orders were orders and these orders had come from General Gamelin – the French commander-in-chief – himself. Paillole could not allow the general's instructions to be disregarded in so transparent a way. Someone, though, needed to take Otto to the station and send the train on its way. Clearly Blémant was not the person for that task, which fell to the one French officer on the scene who had not been involved in the illegal detention or assassination plans. That officer was Captain Gustave Bertrand.

So it was Bertrand who brought the good news and escorted Hermann Brandl to the railway station on 14 May 1940. It seemed, to Otto, that the officers from French counter-intelligence had been trying to get him to switch sides and Otto's parting shot to Bertrand was, possibly, a conspiratorial remark: 'Perhaps, one day, we'll see each other again.' Within weeks, much to the chagrin of Paillole, Otto was established in Paris as head of the French branch of the Abwehr, running an extortion racket called the 'Bureaux Otto' and acquiring notoriety and cash with equal speed.

But that march to the railway station in 1940 saved Gustave Bertrand when, indeed, the two spies met again. The French files were in German hands, and Brandl knew that Bertrand was part of Rivet's organisation; he knew that Bertrand was in touch with MI6. And in Bertrand, Brandl hoped to find the ultimate double agent. A double agent trusted by all, but working for the Abwehr. Bertrand was confronted with the truth: we know all about your pre-war story and the informant you had in Berlin. The Abwehr, it seemed, knew all about Hans-Thilo Schmidt.

Bertrand knew that dissembling and deception would be hard, but he could foresee the areas of interest as they were just the ones he would have asked about himself: the structure of the Resistance's organisation in France; the relationship of the Resistance with Algiers and London; the names and funding and codes and modes of communication. And then came the big question. Would Bertrand take the torture chamber downstairs, or turn and work for the Abwehr?

For Bertrand that was no choice at all. He could effortlessly get through the questioning by feeding the Abwehr with harmless technical detail about radios and interception. There was, however, still one further interrogation to endure, from Otto's boss, Colonel Rudolf, in the Hotel Continental, where Rex had already dished up the juicy story of Schmidt. The encounter with Rudolf proved to be nothing more than an exchange of bland niceties about the peril of the Russians and then Gustave Bertrand, the head of the Kléber network in metropolitan France, found himself signed up as the highest-ranking French agent of German counter-intelligence.

● ● ●

After their debriefing, the Polish code-breakers who had escaped from Spain endured four weeks of bureaucracy. There were upsides –

back-pay for the period from February, fresh uniforms, a boozy night – and plenty of meetings as well as a brief posting to Kinghorn. Located on the northern side of the Firth of Forth, guarding the approach to the marine base at Rosyth, the village of Kinghorn was home to a radio interception station and a company of Polish ex-patriate servicemen. Then there were a few weeks' holiday for the German-ciphers experts: Henryk Zygalski went back to Edinburgh, where there were some old friends, including Włada, one of his girlfriends from the old days in Algiers. By mid-September it was back to work, in the new place at Felden. Zygalski and Rejewski were billeted in a nearby house, where they were delighted to see the lawn next door was sprouting mushrooms that were sadly ignored by the house's owner. A debate on the wisdom of eating toadstools ensued; the crazy Poles were allowed into the neighbour's garden to take the harvest. The next day, much to the amazement of their British neighbour, they seemed to be alive and to have gone to work as usual.[19]

At Felden the exiled code-breakers settled in to new jobs with a new boss, and, after mid October, they were given formal commissions into the Polish Army as second lieutenants. Gone was the eccentric Bertrand and the ambiguous agenda which might have been serving Vichy. Now it was Polish Army routine. Except that the Polish intelligence service in exile was, if not entirely under British control, certainly under its influence. For the time being there was a diet of German police messages, similar fare to the poisonous SS material they had been looking at in France the year before. 'The German 5-letter [code-group] telegrams that are currently intercepted … in Felden (Captain Zieliński) are, according to Commander D, very valuable.'[20] Bletchley Park was not breaking this material, in part because the British did not have resources devoted to interception of the traffic in the first place. Nevertheless, for Bletchley Park, 'police traffic is steadily gaining in operational importance,' and the Poles were filling a gap in the picture. Via the ubiquitous Biffy Dunderdale came a message of thanks from Hut 6 filtering its way to Rejewski, of whose identity Bletchley Park remained utterly unaware.[21]

• • •

On Tuesday 7 March 1944, Langer's diary recorded:

> Cloudy ... No assembly. Dreamed of Janka and Ilanka [Langer's wife and daughter]. When will I have news of them. Lunch: soup, goulash and potatoes ... After 2.30 I was taken to an office (private) where there was a commission. General inquiry about found documents. Later I sent C. Took ± 3 hours.

The Schloss Eisenberg was offering new experiences to its unhappy inmates. Langer's 'commission' consisted of two cipher experts and a third man who was from one of Nazi Germany's many security services, Langer guessed the Gestapo. The cipher experts belonged to Inspektorat 7/VI, the German Army's signals intelligence service, and their names were Dr Hans Pietsch and Dr Walter Fricke.[22]

Dr Pietsch had been studying the security of Enigma for years and he knew exactly how vulnerable the system was. To be precise, the Germans had at first adopted a thoroughly insecure procedure for enciphering the 'indicator' on a message twice. The decrypts which had been found in Warsaw, and all the other evidence they had, pointed clearly to the Poles having exploited this weakness. The security officer started by telling Langer, not asking him, 'you were working in the intelligence service.' Langer observed, 'He was looking at me in such a way as to make me think he must have known something.'[23]

It was another typical interrogation, another chance to turn an agent. With Russians clawing back their territory and Americans, British, Canadians, French and Poles grinding bloodily away at the Gustav Line in Italy, Germany needed to seize every chance to turn around her fortunes. The immediate question was whether Langer would see sense, put his Aryan ancestry and German language skills to proper use, and come and work for the Fatherland.

> It wasn't said explicitly, because as the captain was saying that he had already been in the process of recruiting others, I interrupted him immediately and said that one can die only once and [referring

to a notorious Austrian spy of World War I] that I wouldn't become a 'Redl'.[24]

So that wasn't going to go very far. The officer handed over to Dr Pietsch. Pietsch's interrogation of Langer launched into technicalities.

When I was asked if we'd been breaking and reading any machine ciphers during the war I said that it became impossible after the Germans introduced the changes to the machines in 1939. Because I was speaking to cryptography experts and I wasn't as familiar with the matter as Major Ciężki, in order to increase the likelihood of my interrogators believing my story I asked the commission to interview Major Ciężki himself … The reason they knew we had been reading their messages before the war was that somewhere in Warsaw they had found some messages we read from during the Spanish War … They also knew about Pyry.

The security service officer could not have cared less about the historical niceties of some obscure cipher process in use five years ago or more; the interview was over.

So then it was Ciężki's turn. It may have seemed somewhat unfair to shift the interrogation to him, but the likelihood of discovery of the pre-war achievements had been foreseen by both Ciężki and his boss. So Ciężki, the cryptography expert, racked with tubercular disease, confirmed that the Poles had cracked the system before 1939 and how. Alas, the Germans had changed the machine and the procedure, and after that the Poles had been locked out. Indeed, an abrupt cessation of results is what the remnants of the paper record had shown, so Pietsch and Fricke were vindicated. After all, Inspektorat 7/VI had done the research back in 1939 which led to the change of indicator procedure and that had stopped the rot. Enigma was safe. And so were Langer and Ciężki.

● ● ●

One summer day in 1944, while V-1 pilotless bombs were raining down on London and the Poles were safely out of range in their hideout on the hill at Felden, the telephone rang. Polish HQ wanting an update, perhaps. Marian Rejewski answered and nearly jumped out of his skin when he recognised the ebullient voice on the other end. It was not Polish HQ; instead, it was the most bizarre update imaginable. For the voice belonged to Bertrand, and he was in town. The last Rejewski had heard of Bertrand was during the period of *cache-cache* with the Gestapo eighteen months before.[25]

Gustave Bertrand had pulled off one last conjuring trick. Now reincarnated as Lieutenant Colonel Michel Gaudefroy, he was in Britain and in some manner working for General de Gaulle's Free French. Bertrand's rebirth was, naturally, a cause for celebration. He came out to Felden, and there was a grand dinner, *arrosé de nuits-saint-georges 1914*, at the White Horse Inn in Boxmoor, where the survivors of Équipe Z relived their escape stories and reminisced about life at PC Bruno and PC Cadix.[26]

Bertrand's own escape story was, possibly, the most remarkable of all. In January, Bertrand had agreed to act as Germany's spy. The list of betrayals required of him was long: Bertrand was to hand over the cash, code books, names and addresses of officers of the Kléber network, and the locations of radio emplacements; to get from London details of which German ciphers were being read and of the forthcoming Allied invasion; to help infiltrate a German agent into Britain; to make contact with members of the network so they could be rounded up in France and Algeria; to deliver up the network's radio equipment; and, finally, to hand over the files containing notes on interrogations of German agents arrested by the French. Bertrand agreed to everything. Somewhat jaded after a long night of torture and interrogations, Masuy was satisfied. Bertrand was free to go.

Then I made haste to retrieve my things and to give all suitable warnings. I next enciphered a telegram for London in order to cancel the rendezvous [arranged in his previous message sent under Masuy's control] and to sort everything out. Finally, in the night, we left Vichy for Brioude, in order to withdraw a cipher and the [French] Intelligence Service funds (one million) from the Credit Lyonnais in order to send them on to my second-in-command, Captain Lochard. Then to Nîmes and the open arms of a refuge.[27]

Thus, once again, Bertrand conjured his own disappearance.

A serious question emerges against the background of Bertrand's story. We do not know for certain what he told Masuy, who was executed on 1 October 1947 following a post-war trial.[28] Did Gustave Bertrand buy his escape, by revealing some of the secrets he knew, or was he a master of guile? The British said of him that even Alastair Denniston was 'no match for this experienced Frenchman'.[29] The most informative judgement comes from the Germans themselves. Captain Wiegand – the interrogator of Rex – said, after the war, 'I had the impression that Captain Bertrand had played a comedy and had had the intention to take flight when the time came.' Bertrand had returned after one trip to Vichy and won the trust of Masuy; when he slipped away on the next occasion, Masuy and his operatives knew they had been played.[30]

The fact is that Bertrand had been working for the enemy of his Vichy employers for a long time. The enemy in question was the greatest threat the French government could face: the Forces Françaises Combattantes, also known as the 'Free French', led by Vichy's bitterest foe, General Charles de Gaulle. Since December 1942, when the emptiness and bankruptcy of the Vichy régime became apparent with its inability to prevent the occupation of the Zone Libre, Bertrand had realised where his loyalties should lie. Starting with the transfer to London of information on the Funkabwehr and their mobile radio detection vans, Bertrand had been growing closer to de Gaulle's alternative administration-in-waiting.[31] An airlift, to pick up Bertrand and his wife on 3 June 1944, had only been possible because he was known to be working on the right side. From 1 August 1944, Gustave Bertrand, now a lieutenant colonel, took over as chief of a new Deuxième Bureau, the intelligence division serving de Gaulle's FFC.[32]

● ● ●

Antoni Palluth, Edward Fokczyński and Kazimierz Gaca were not interrogated by Inspektorat 7/VI or anyone else. They found themselves introduced into the slave-labour system at Sachsenhausen concentration camp. There, they were put to work in the factory making Heinkel bombers for the Luftwaffe. Before long, Antoni Palluth found himself involved in a resistance group of Poles, and, since he was one of the more senior inmates (aged 43), a qualified engineer and a German speaker, he was soon in a position where it was possible to influence what was going on. In time, Palluth managed to subvert the quality-control system, arranging for the official checking stamps to be applied to aircraft wings with deliberately weakened ribs and other sabotaged parts. Under Palluth's management, the Heinkel factory was working for the Allies.[33]

In one important respect, imprisonment at Sachsenhausen was better than life at Uzès. You could send stylised letters home. Indirectly, as usual, Antoni Palluth began to re-establish communication with his young family back in Warsaw. In return, the Palluths sent Antoni a bar of soap, something rare and prized in Sachsenhausen. Inside the soap was a picture of his sons, Jerzy (thirteen) and Andrzej (ten).[34] Life outside was going on; the Nazi régime would not last forever.

• • •

The toehold established by the expeditionary force in Normandy in June 1944 spelt the beginning of the end of the war in Western Europe. For Marian Rejewski, it was the beginning of a problem. To be more precise, it was the absence of a problem: the absence of any interesting cryptological problems to work on. Three weeks after the landings, Dunderdale let it be known that the Allies no longer had any need for the intercepts of German police messages which, the previous year, had been so useful.[35] Eight weeks later, the German police changed their encipherment system. Rejewski was locked out and even his intellect was outmatched. There was nothing he could do. He was bored and he was very fed up.

If the British would only share their current know-how, maybe the Poles could get back on top of the German ciphers. Rejewski picked up his pen and composed a proposal for his superiors in London.

Before the war, there was a Polish-British-French cooperation in the field of ciphers, in the course of which, it should be emphasised, that the side which gave, and gave generously, was exclusively Polish. It would be advisable to remind the British now of their debt of gratitude which they have towards the Polish Cipher Bureau, and that without the help of the Poles they would have been unable to read even one German telegram cipher during the Norwegian or French campaigns or subsequently ...

It would seem the point to specify once again what the Polish cryptographers expect and demand of their British colleagues. In the first place, they should be asked to return the German Enigma machine that had been given to them ... Next, they should be prevailed upon to share the experience they have gained in the field of German ciphers these last five years. The best way would be via direct contacts between the Polish and British cryptographers concerned. And finally, an attempt should be made to persuade them to supply their intercepted material ...[36]

Rejewski's long, closely argued paper was sent off on 1 October 1944. Polish Headquarters was sympathetic and asked Dunderdale to see what he could do.[37]

It's not recorded how the British replied, but it is possible to imagine how unrealistic Rejewski's request may have seemed at Bletchley Park. Enigma code-breaking had changed dramatically since the X-Y-Z cooperation during the Norwegian and French campaigns. The modern Turing–Welchman Bombes were operating in hundreds and were managed in the style of a factory. Whereas PC Bruno had processed 8,440 messages of all types over a period of six months in 1940, by 1942, Bletchley Park was dealing with an average of 1,995 Enigma messages a day. And that was just Army and Air Force, i.e. not counting police, railways, or the all-important Naval Enigma, or indeed any other type of cipher.[38] The familiar structure of the old Government Code & Cypher School, whose representatives Rejewski had met in 1939 and 1940, was gone forever. Dilly Knox had died in 1943. Alastair Denniston was no longer in charge at Bletchley, having been moved over to focus on diplomatic ciphers. Alan Turing was now working at a separate establishment at Hanslope Park on voice encipherment. Nobody who knew him was at Bletchley to vouch for Rejewski. In this massive system, this tiny group of Polish experts was simply irrelevant.

Yet there was plenty for Rejewski to do other than focus on Enigma. Ever since the Ekspozytura 300 Poles had turned up in Spain, the Polish General Staff in London had wanted to turn their attention to the USSR. In March 1944, the Polish General Staff held a cryptology conference, which was all about Russia.[39] In this context it made sense to redeploy Marian Rejewski and Henryk Zygalski, who, together with Sylwester Palluth, had formerly been known as 'team N' – specialising in Niemcy, or Germany – to 'team R' – directed at Rosja, or the USSR. Team N was closed down in November 1944 and from that point the reports Dunderdale received were all about what the Russians were doing.[40] And there was more. Starting from nuts and bolts (among other stationery supplies for Felden, the Poles needed maps of Russia and a Russian typeface typewriter), the March conference had concluded that a step-up in interception and decryption activity in the Middle East was needed. Czesław Kuraś, who had led the anti-Soviet decryption effort in Britain since 1940, was now in the Middle East and needed reinforcement. 'Kuraś is to keep this mission top secret ... Kuraś's task: set up the interception station ... choose and initially select candidates as cryptologists.'[41]

Everything was directed at the Russian threat and all the work was being done in close liaison with Biffy Dunderdale. Major Wiktor Michałowski, veteran of Ekspozytura 300, was also sent to run the operation based in Cairo and it seems that Henryk Zygalski was also placed there for a while. The British also had a Special Communications Unit there. The unit was part of MI6's network of communications facilities that were primarily engaged in direction-finding and interception, but it also performed mysterious work to convert typewriters into cipher machines. One visitor became intrigued in their project; he was Polish, and he was, apparently, Henryk Zygalski.[42]

● ● ●

As the food parcels arrived at the Schloss Eisenberg, Maksymilian Ciężki regretted his previous remark about his weight. 'You need to know that I find it very difficult to eat the food items you send me, knowing how crucial they are for you and the children.' He was wrong.

Maksymilian Ciężki was on the Wanted List of the German security services, and, like her friend Jadwiga Palluth, Bolesława Ciężka had experienced an encounter with the Gestapo. On 5 June 1942, her sons Zbigniew and Henryk had been arrested while visiting friends. Bolesława tried to bribe or bail them out with her jewellery. The jewellery was taken, but only Henryk, aged 13, was released. Zbigniew was 16 and old enough to go to Auschwitz. He could receive parcels there, for a while. By 1944, the last parcel had been returned by the postal service. There was no prisoner named Zbigniew Ciężki at Auschwitz, not any more. His fate was the same as his older brother Zdzisław, who was arrested and in 1944 shot by the Nazis for sabotage. Stuck in Eisenberg, Ciężki knew nothing of this. Of his three sons, only Henryk was still alive, and desperate to join in the fighting in Warsaw.[43]

In the city, where the Germans still clung on, Jerzy Palluth and his mother received a visitor who wanted to interview them. It was October 1944 and the occasion was a visit from an officer of the Home Army, the underground force which had stolen and captured and manufactured its own weapons and improvised its way into the history books. The Polish resistance army had attempted to recapture Warsaw from the Wehrmacht but was in desperate straits. After an unimaginable two months since the uprising began, the Home Army was still holding out, despite having no appreciable assistance from outside and absolutely none from the Soviets on the other side of the river. Jadwiga Palluth was not an easy person in an interview, as the Gestapo had previously discovered. The Home Army officer was approaching Mrs Palluth in order to recruit young Jerzy. At this stage in the combat, the Home Army was out of ammunition and out of personnel and almost out of hope. To join up was a 99 per cent guarantee of a death sentence. As he was only just 14, Jerzy knew she would say no, as mothers are supposed to do. 'Your decision,' said Mrs Palluth. Jerzy joined up.[44]

The Home Army surrendered on 3 October 1944.

The Poles left in Warsaw were marched off to captivity: to Germany if they were wearing the armband of the Home Army, or to a camp at Pruszków, on the outskirts of Warsaw, if they were not. Jerzy's spell in the Home Army had been too short for him to be in the armband group, so with his mother, brother, a small packet of letters from his father Antoni, a minute dog and nothing else whatsoever, the camp at Pruszków was their destination. From there the Poles were herded on to trains by German soldiers. They had no idea where they were headed. Irena Rejewska and her two children also found themselves at Pruszków.[45] The trains, they discovered, were to transport Poles to Germany to work. The Home Army of Warsaw had been disarmed and the Russians were nowhere to be seen.

According to Arthur Bliss Lane, appointed as America's ambassador to Poland in 1944, the inaction by the Red Army during the uprising was a calculated act, to discredit the Polish government-in-exile and, more importantly, to ensure that the Home Army was eviscerated by the Germans so that no effective armed resistance would remain behind after the Germans had been thrown out. The Red Army moved into Warsaw in January 1945, more than three months after the Home Army's surrender. Meanwhile the Germans, left in occupation, had razed Warsaw to the ground. Every last vestige of a city that had previously been known as the 'Paris of the North' was destroyed. The stage was set for subjugation of the 'liberated' state.

● ● ●

The Cold War began with the Polish monitoring of Russian communications in 1944. After the ghastly discovery of the Katyn massacre in 1943, the USSR had broken off diplomatic relations with the Polish government-in-exile for the terrible crime of telling the truth about Russia. The Russian threat to Poland became daily more real, as the Soviet Army pushed the Wehrmacht back and itself moved once again into Polish territory. The war on the Eastern Front brought the question of Poland's borders – or, to be more accurate, the USSR's expansionist ambitions – back on to the conference table. Winston Churchill moved matches on a table in Tehran to show how lines could be redrawn on maps. Poland was going to move westward, regardless of what actual Poles might think about their homes, families, or control by the Soviets. The eastern border was going to be along the Curzon Line, because the British had invented it and nobody was in a position to stop it.

The Poles at Felden were providing the core of the material relied on by the Polish General Staff and Biffy Dunderdale to try to explain to the politicians – not just of the government-in-exile but also the British and the Americans – what Stalin was really doing. Getting hold of high-quality intercepts of Russian traffic was difficult, but with the liberation of France a new possibility of doing so had opened up and the right person to help with this was conveniently to hand. That person was 'Colonel Gaudefroy', formerly Commandant Bertrand, restored in his role as kingpin in the renewed alliance of X, Y, Z and A. He would provide what was needed. There were discussions between X and Z about what the French should monitor and which type of message yielded useful material and, soon enough, the French began to supply Felden with their Russian material.[46]

Dunderdale had set up a 'Special Liaison Controllerate' which was providing reports tagged 'SBH' to the CIA's predecessor, the Office of Strategic Services in Washington. 'SB' stood for 'Secret Broadway', with 'Broadway' meaning the headquarters of MI6 in London. The content gleaned from the airwaves provided colour on the Russians' operational problems, military establishment, personnel, and more. It complemented broader intelligence from material from broadcasts, newspapers and other sources about the state of affairs in the USSR and the NKVD and its methods.[47] It was the culmination of the X-Y-Z-A liaison; but it would take more than the content of SBH reports to convince Y and A to save Poland from the Soviets.

Already there had been plenty of intelligence about Poland, which did not make comforting reading, if anyone had been reading it.

March 3rd [1945]: The bloody Soviet occupation is surpassing the German one in bestiality. There are arrests in every village, murders, raping of girls and pillaging.

March 23rd: The Office of Security … is rounding up former soldiers of the Home Army … they seized about 40 persons in Dobre (50kms. ENE of Warsaw) and vicinity, who were then transported to the camp near Rembertow (outside of Warsaw). The Office of Security is announcing, mendaciously, that arrested Volksdeutsche are in this camp.

May 12th: Round-ups and raids on the population are increasing, while terror and destruction of everything Polish are also growing strength.

May 25th: In the Wodynie district, the corpses of 75 people were discovered while barracks, previously occupied by Soviet forces and the NKVD, were being pulled down. Some of the bodies have been recognised – they were those of the arrested members of the former Home Army from the neighbourhood.[48]

While such intercepts kept the Poles occupied at Felden, more important, from the perspective of the former team-mates of Équipe Z, was the question of their belongings – both technical and personal – which had been abandoned on the evacuation of the Château des Fouzes. Gustave Bertrand, now shuttling between Britain and France, promised to bring it all over.[49] Some archive material was delivered in March, but still the Poles wanted their reverse-engineered Enigma machine and their suitcases full of personal items. So, in April, Marian Rejewski and Henryk Zygalski went to France. Bertrand met them in Paris and handed over the official documents, the Enigma machine and three chests of personal belongings.[50] The rest of it was in Cannes:

When Bertrand found out about our intention to travel to Cannes, he became extremely embarrassed and had to admit that he had not paid the rent on the room that was being used to store our cases and that we could therefore have problems in retrieving them. He also warned us that the man had taken advantage of our trust in him and plundered the cases. He was right, because the woman whose house the room was in, after a great deal of persuasion finally gave us the keys to the room. A terrible mess greeted us, cases were slashed, the locks had been forced open, and beyond doubt several items had been stolen and the woollen items had been attacked by moths.[51]

But Bertrand had been a wonderful host, equipping the duo with a car and smoothing their way through the bureaucracy and paranoia of a country disentangling itself from occupation, self-destructive home rule, and a criss-cross of alien armies. To be sure, there was design as well as goodwill in Bertrand's bonhomie. Bertrand was planning to rebuild the glorious Équipe Z and he wanted as many of the old team on board as he could get.

• • •

On 30 April 1945, Adolf Hitler killed himself in his bunker in Berlin. A week later, Gwido Langer and Maksymilian Ciężki were told to get on a train.[52] Fighting was still going on close by; the Red Army was approaching. The train pulled out moments before the Soviets took control of the station. The journey seemed to go on forever. Once again it was a slow flight from a war zone, with secrets that must be kept from the enemy. At Karlsbad (Karlovy Vary), however, Langer and Ciężki found the American First Infantry Division. The two Poles were safe.

After a brief (and not entirely harmonious) reunion with Bertrand in Paris, Langer and Ciężki were on their way to London. The war was over. The Nazis were finished. The fact that a Polish team had played its part throughout the war and helped to make major inroads into Enigma-encoded communications was a secret that had been kept safe from the German authorities. They had made a contribution to the Allied victory over Germany and it had been a major one. All that remained to be done was to live happily ever after.

BALTIC SEA

USSR

● Vilnius

● Bydgoszcz

Poznań ●

● Warsaw

USSR

CZECHOSLOVAKIA

● Lviv

USSR

POLAND AFTER 1945

Poland before 1939

Poland after 1945

ROMANIA

EPILOGUE

POLES APART

Peace, perfect peace, with loved ones far away?

Hymns Ancient & Modern, No. 537

On Tuesday 27 February 1945, it was the turn of Winston Spencer Churchill to get to his feet in the House of Commons. He had just returned from Yalta, where, along with the dying Franklin Delano Roosevelt, he had ceded control over tracts of Europe to Iosif Vissarionovich Dzhugashvili, also known as Uncle Joe Stalin, the architect of the nastiest terror, not even excepting that of Nazi Germany, ever seen in Europe. 'I did not listen,' wrote John Colville – Churchill's secretary at Downing Street – in his chronicle. 'He is trying to persuade himself that all is well, but in his heart I think he is worried about Poland and not convinced of the strength of our moral position.'[1]

Over 50,000 Polish servicemen were in Britain at the end of World War Two and another 80,000 in various forces across Europe and the Middle East but outside Poland. Airily Churchill offered 'citizenship and freedom of the British Empire' to those who considered they could not go home.[2]

Among the Polish servicemen in Britain were nine cryptologists who were serving at a secret establishment near Hemel Hempstead. On 25 September 1945, they were detailed to attend a Polish school for intelligence officers. Included in the group of nine were Marian Rejewski, Henryk Zygalski, Stanisław Szachno and Sylwester Palluth of the old Ekspozytura 300.[3] The code-breakers were to become merged into the official army structure, except that the army was no longer going to exist.

Also among the Polish servicemen in Britain were Gwido Langer and Maksymilian Ciężki, who arrived from Paris at the end of May more dead than alive after their ordeal at the Schloss Eisenberg. Langer and Ciężki immediately petitioned the head of Polish intelligence in London, Stanisław Gano, for arrears of salary.[4] Their reception was frosty. Gano had been persuaded that the failure of the escape plans in early 1943 and the capture of Langer, Ciężki, Palluth, Gaca and Fokczyński had been down to 'hesitation, lack of initiative, almost cowardice' on the part of Gwido Langer. This poisonous account was hearsay and not based on hard evidence. In the second half of 1945 and again in 1946 Langer devoted weeks to writing up his own account of it all and remained convinced for the rest of his life that Gustave Bertrand had betrayed the team before covering up his own duplicity.

On 6 July 1945, the British government – in interregnum following the general election of the previous day – recognised the Soviet-controlled provisional government of Poland. The government-in-exile, to which Gano owed fealty, instantly became unofficial and irrelevant. By 15 March 1946, the Second Department of the Polish General Staff, which had fed priceless information to Britain and America for years during the conflict, had been disbanded. The remaining Russia-watchers at Felden were closed down a few weeks later.

In early 1946, the idea of a 'Polish Resettlement Corps' was proposed by the new Labour government. It was an arrangement to keep Polish servicemen under military discipline and with continuing pay, while they were retrained and ultimately released into regular civilian jobs. Rejewski and the other cryptanalysts were not going to be intelligence officers after all. In fact, there had been no work for them to do since October 1945. A vague idea surfaced that they might be re-employed as cryptologists, doing what they did best, working directly for the 'clients' (a reference to Dunderdale and his masters).[5] But as Bletchley Park itself was downsizing, this was never more than a pipe-dream.

Langer and Ciężki found themselves in the Polish Resettlement Corps and based in Kinross, in Scotland. The reception given by the Scots to the Polish forces stationed amongst them was warm and welcoming. The *Kinross-shire Advertiser* reported eagerly on entertainment provided by YMCA ladies to Polish soldiers on 17 January 1945, followed the next day by a Grand Concert in memory of General Sikorski. This was attended by a large audience, even though the temperature was -15°C. In early 1946, there were still dances and entertainments for children where Polish soldiers shared their chocolate rations.[6] As a lieutenant colonel, Langer went to live in the Kirkland Hotel in the town. He needed what little Kinross could offer in the way of creature comforts. Ciężki noted, in a letter home, how 'Gwido ... has grown old so much.'

In March 1946, Maksymilian Ciężki had some positive news. Stanisław Gano had not been entirely hostile. Ciężki was awarded the Polish Golden Cross of Merit with Swords.[7] The Polish Army had found Ciężki a job, as head of the Signals Learning Centre at the Turfhills Camp in Kinross, helping with the effort to retrain the troops. Better still, his son Henryk made contact. Henryk had enlisted, underage, in General Anders's army, after getting all the way to Italy after the Warsaw Uprising. The Red Cross had put the two in touch and Henryk would be coming to England later in the year.[8]

By the spring of 1946, the public mood with respect to the Polish Resettlement Corps was beginning to sour. Britain was bankrupt and the days when Polish fighter pilots had saved the country had been conveniently forgotten. The Polish Army was not represented in the Victory Parade in London which took place on 8 June 1946. Three days afterwards, the Kinross Town Council voted to issue Notices to Quit to Poles living in council houses. Polish soldiers on loan from the Polish Resettlement Corps produced more coal by hand than British miners could with a mechanical cutter and they were taking the jobs of demobilised British servicemen. The Poles should just go home.

The War Office was wringing its hands: 'we are ... faced with the problem of resettling either in the United Kingdom or by emigration overseas, this large mass of some 17,000 officers ... these officers are the intelligentsia of Poland.'[9]

But when it came to the practicalities, they were as you might expect from an army:[10]

1.   The benefits for officers whose commissions are terminated ... will be as in the following paragraphs.

2.   Cash grant of 56 days' pay and allowances in lieu of leave ...

3.   Issue of Civilian Clothing ... The scale of issue to a military officer will be as follows provided the officer has completed six months' service on full pay with the Polish Armed Forces under British Command and has not previously received from either Polish Military, Naval or Civil Sources a civilian outfit or a grant towards the cost of civilian clothes.

Jacket	1	} or suit as available
Trousers	1	
Cap or hat	1	
Shirt	1	
Collars	2	
Tie	1	
Studs	2	
Cuff links, pairs	1	

Langer and Ciężki might debate whether they had served under British Command; it is not recorded if they were issued with cufflinks or, if so, with what rapture they received them.

Ciężki's reunion with his son Henryk should have been a time for celebration. Maksymilian had also been searching vainly for his older sons, Zdzisław and Zbigniew, and Henryk should have news of them. He did. But his mother had placed Henryk under the strictest duty of silence. On no account was anyone other than Bolesława to break the news of their deaths to Maksymilian. And aged only 17, Henryk found this as tough an assignment as anything he'd faced. Avoiding the subject of his brothers, the two discussed Maksymilian's plan to return home. But by Christmas 1946, Maksymilian Ciężki had come to recognise that to go back to Poland was out of the question. There was no prospect of a job in the armed forces of a Communist country with a CV like his.

What was happening at home, once known only to a few, was now general knowledge and unpleasantly clear. If you were associated with the pre-war and wartime forces of Poland, you were at risk – none more so than those who had been involved in gathering intelligence on the ill deeds of Poland's neighbours. There was no place to hide in the new version of Poland, which had been reshaped to Stalin's design. General Anders – who, after all, had been imprisoned in the USSR until Stalin allowed Polish prisoners of war to reform as an army under him – was stripped of his Polish citizenship in 1946, along with seventy-five other senior officers located overseas.[11] That was a plain text message clear enough to read. For a former code-breaker to live in Poland and give any hint of what he had been doing, namely spying on Stalin, now the patron of Poland, might well be terminal and the code-breaker's family was likely to be persecuted or executed.

Not wanting to talk about his role in intelligence work, Maksymilian Ciężki could not explain to his son why he was staying in Scotland. The secrets went in both directions; the gulf between father and son was appallingly wide.

• • •

Marian Rejewski, on the other hand, wanted to go home. He was the least likely of the Polish code-breakers to take up a life of lies, raw courage and guile. But Poland was where Irena and the two children were, as well as a chance to pick up the shreds of his academic career. To go back, he would have to carry out the greatest undercover operation of his life. He would grey out his CV and disappear.

Henryk Zygalski had been friends with Marian Rejewski since they attended the Poznań course on cryptology together seventeen years before. They had so much shared experience, much of it life-threatening: the train out of Warsaw in 1939; robbery in the Pyrenees; imprisonment in Spain .... And they had shared too moments of exhilaration, such as the Enigma breakthroughs and evading the Gestapo. Grey, post-war, rationed Britain was no place to stay. Zygalski understood that. But to return to Poland was madness. Words were exchanged. For Rejewski, family was back home and he would go. For Zygalski, home was where the heart was and the heart was firmly in Britain.

In early 1944, Henryk Zygalski had met a girl in Boxmoor. Like Henryk, Bertha Blofield was musical and they'd been to a symphony orchestra concert together in Watford at the end of January. Within two weeks, Henryk had started taking English lessons. By May, Henryk was out cycling with Bertha through the woods of Ashridge, not far from the workplace at Felden. In July, they were dining together at the White Horse at Boxmoor, with 'exquisite wine and Drambuie'. Bertha was not just the lastest on the long list of Zygalski's fun flirtations. With her he was serious.[12]

Henryk Zygalski was faced with a puzzle, one far harder than the Enigma. His desire to make a life with Bertha was overpowering. But Bertha was married, to a serving RAF officer. Marian Rejewski couldn't see how to solve that puzzle either, so the debate about returning home developed a sharper, more personal edge.

> What a big piece of news – Rejewski going back [wrote Bertha to Henryk on 5 October 1946]. Major [Michałowski] said he knew the Russian instructions for dealing with espionage agents when they could get hold of them.

> Of course, M. does not know there is any cloud between you and R. [she continued, on the 10th] – unless you told him. I let him know, in confidence, that you thought R. was going to Poland ... He thinks R. may be all right, but that any of you seeking to go to Poland might end the journey in Moscow ...[13]

Marian Rejewski left for Poland in November 1946, carrying the secret story of Enigma code-breaking with him. As far as he was concerned, it would all stay secret forever.

● ● ●

There was a code of silence about Enigma code-breaking which bound all who had ever touched it. The induction ceremony at Bletchley Park was centred around a solemn ritual called 'signing the Official Secrets Act', where recruits signed a piece of paper printed with the relevant sections of the Act (which bound them to silence whether or not they signed), while enduring an alarming speech about what would happen if they ever spoke about their work. In America, women naval personnel hired to operate Bombes were given a similar introductory lecture which told them that they would be shot if they breathed a single word. The Polish code-breakers did not need the dramatics, but the code of silence was the same.

The silence continued long after the war was over. Nobody had released the players in the grand drama of Enigma from their bonds of secrecy, and anyhow, nobody was interested in encipherment machinery which, even during the war, had been superseded by newer, cleverer techniques.

Then one day, when researching a book on Polish inter-war intelligence operations against Germany, Colonel Władysław Kozaczuk came across an interesting document – to be exact, a copy of a document, for the original was in London – in the Military Archives in Warsaw. It was the report, dated 1940, by Major Ludwik Sadowski, setting out his findings on the intelligence failures of the 1939 Battle of Poland. The report discusses, in some detail, the attack on Enigma. Kozaczuk's book, *Bitwa o tajemnice* [*Battle for Secrets*], first published in 1967, included the following passage:

> Even though Germany-orientated intelligence was not given priority, work in that area was still bearing significant fruit during the few years leading up to the war. The breaking of the Enigma machine cipher by Polish cryptologists allowed for the reading of a number of dispatches, which the German staff thought of as being totally secure ... The teams of cryptanalysts working in the Cipher Bureau of the Second Department were very well qualified. Furthermore, the results of their work – in their own as well as others' opinions – 'significantly surpassed the results achieved by the cryptologists working not only in the French Staff, but even the English.'[14]

The story was out, but there was an Iron Curtain between Kozaczuk's Poland and the other countries which partnered in the breaking of Enigma. Then, in the same year as *Bitwa o tajemnice*, the French author Michel Garder published a book called *La Guerre secrète des services speciaux français 1939–1945*, which suggested that a German spy had given information to the French about a cipher machine. Garder's book contained (as did many early accounts of Enigma) errors, which provided a perfect excuse for others to step in and offer corrections. Whether the secret still needed to stay secret, more than twenty years after the war had ended, was another story altogether.

• • •

Few of those who knew the real story of Enigma survived to read Kozaczuk's or Garder's books.

Rex had given away the source of the Enigma secrets, and much more, to the Germans in early 1943. On 16 September that year, in a prison in Berlin, Hans-Thilo Schmidt ended his own life. 'Is it not written that "he who has betrayed his country will, sooner or later, be betrayed himself?"' commented Gustave Bertrand.

Rex was released by the Germans at the end of the war and then found himself being interrogated by his former colleagues of the French Service de Renseignements.[15] Rex being Rex, he attempted to escape by suborning a non-commissioned officer, using a razor to slice open the left shoulder of his overcoat from which spilled four gold $20 coins. It didn't work. Rex admitted what he had disclosed, but any decision about the consequences for him was irrelevant. He was already mortally ill and, on 3 October 1946, he died aged 75. Rex's colourful life had finally played out.

Biffy Dunderdale had had a colourful life too. His entry in the *Oxford Dictionary of National Biography* says that:

> After the war Dunderdale refused to have an office in MI6's head-quarters because the aura of Whitehall was intolerable to him; he was allowed to set up a small office nearby. There, with lovely oriental carpets, portraits of the queen and the Tsar, a whiff of incense, and a fine model of a Russian destroyer of 1912, he provided a home from home for many foreign visitors from pre-war days.

Dunderdale died in 1990, celebrated for his 'romantic' role in helping the Polish model Enigma machine reach London in 1939, though he always maintained that his other activities had been of far greater significance.

Marian Rejewski's life in post-war Poland was marked with personal tragedy. In 1947, his son Andrzej died suddenly of an undiagnosed illness and in the following year his father-in-law also died, leaving Marian responsible for supporting his mother-in-law as well as his own family (which included three unmarried sisters). He was also the focus of attention of the 'Public Safety Office' in Bydgoszcz, which wanted to get to the bottom of what being a 'contract worker' for the General Staff of the Polish Army might have entailed. The machinery of the People's Republic cranked around rustily and it took until 1956 before there was material in his file. During this time, Rejewski had reinvented himself as an accountant, dealing with financial reporting for the Kabel Polski company, until hounded out of his job as a result of the security service's concerns. Then he took a succession of invisible jobs in the finance departments of various cooperatives. By 1956, Rejewski had established a good track record of being wholly uninteresting as a case-study in political subversion, and political shifts in Communist Europe of that year created new priorities, making it irrelevant to pursue an accountant on the basis of not very much.[16]

Towards the end of his life, after the Kozaczuk book came out, Rejewski's remarkable role in the events of the 1930s came to be recognised. An informative memoir, written by Rejewski for the Polish Military Historical Institute in 1967, was published and Rejewski wrote several articles and gave interviews on his pre-war work. There was still a need to be discreet: Rejewski never made mention of what he had done at Felden after the attacks on German ciphers were discontinued. Marian Rejewski received the Officer's Cross of the Order of the Rebirth of Poland in 1978 and, in 1979, the Silver Cross for Services to the Country's Defence. He died in 1980 aged 74.

Henryk Zygalski stayed in Britain with Bertha. The RAF officer died in December 1947 and Zygalski became a British citizen in 1949. Meanwhile, an academic opportunity had opened up with the Polish University College. Originally started by the Polish government-in-exile in 1942, the college taught technical subjects to exiled Poles, in both Polish and English. Zygalski's Polish qualifications in mathematics cut no ice in Britain, so he had to re-qualify. A testimonial from Imperial College London, dated August 1951, says that 'he has also shown himself to be capable of originality in Mathematics', hardly a glowing commendation for a veteran already decorated for some of the most original and imaginative work on a problem of unprecedented difficulty. Henryk Zygalski was a big enough character, with a sense of humour to match, to rise above such pettiness. He became a respected teacher and enjoyed his music and a family life with Bertha, eventually moving out of the London area when the College, later Polytechnic, later still College of Advanced Technology, became the University of Surrey at Guildford. (Guildford happens to be Alan Turing's home town and there is now a very large statue in the University grounds which commemorates that other code-breaker, who had precisely nothing to do with the institution.) Henryk Zygalski's friendship with Marian Rejewski had buckled, but not broken in 1946, and they stayed in amicable touch until Henryk's death in 1978.[17]

Gwido Langer continued to pursue his financial claim in respect of the lost years in prison, leaving a bitter trail of correspondence with the now-powerless residue of the Polish General Staff, as well as several first-hand accounts of what he had been through. Aged 53, on 30 March 1948, Langer died of a heart attack at the Kirkland Hotel in Kinross, where he had stayed since arrival in Scotland.[18]

Maksymilian Ciężki, suffering from his lungs and an addiction to cigarettes, was demobilised from the Polish Resettlement Corps on 18 September 1948. He held a job with a cleaning company in London for a month in 1949 and in May of that year he moved to Cornwall. Without a job he was unable to satisfy the visa conditions for his wife Bolesława to come to Britain, so their separation which had been imposed by the war lengthened to over a decade. Ciężki's last two years were marked by various illnesses and surviving on a meagre level of state benefits. He died on 9 November 1951, also aged 53.[19]

Why, in April 1945, when the war in Europe was all but over, it was necessary to send a flight of bombers over Sachsenhausen to obliterate the Heinkel factory, is perhaps unclear. The bombs fell as much among the wooden huts in the residential compound as on the factory and a bomb fragment put an end to Antoni Palluth's career as code-breaker, spy and saboteur-engineer. He was 44.

Edward Fokczyński also died at Sachsenhausen, though of starvation. Of the three code-breakers imprisoned there, only Kazimierz Gaca survived. He was 50m away from Antoni Palluth when the fatal bomb dropped. Kazimierz Gaca and Sylwester Palluth, Antoni's cousin, both entered Bertrand's new intelligence service in 1947 and spent the rest of their lives in France. For Gaca, a relationship that had started as tomfoolery in terracotta jars in the warmth of the south of France became something more serious. Monique Isambert – Bertrand's chauffeur's daughter – was now grown up and could give expression to a sentiment she had been keeping secret since those days; Kazimierz and Monique were married in 1950. In due course, Kazimierz Gaca became enrolled in the Légion d'Honneur, outlived all the other members of Ekspozytura 300 and reached the age of 89, long enough to see the fall of communism in Poland.[20]

Gaca's boss, Gustave Bertrand, remains the most enigmatic character of this story. Having started as a private soldier, it was something of an achievement to finish his career as a general. He also has the distinction of being the first to bring into the open the full, detailed story of the breaking of Enigma, the role of Hans-Thilo Schmidt, the contribution of the Poles and the secret double-play with Vichy. These are all described in his book *Enigma, ou la plus grande énigme de la guerre*, pulbished in 1972. After Bertrand had revealed the existence of the X-Y-Z secret, a snowball began to roll, eventually forcing the British government to disclose more and more of its code-breaking operations and the existence of what is now widely believed to be a British national treasure, the operation at Bletchley Park. As to Bertrand himself, his book ends with a splendid recitation of his personal honours and awards: Grand Officier de la Légion d'Honneur; Médaille de la Résistance; Distinguished Service Order (GB); Officer of the Legion of Merit (US); Krzyż Walecznych [cross of valour] and bar (PL), Złoty Krzyż Zasługi [golden cross of merit] (PL), and, to his annoyance, absolutely nothing for the war of 1939–40.

APPENDIX

CYCLES

Marian Rejewski's breakthroughs were based on his understanding of 'cycles' which can appear when permutations are examined. He used his analysis of cycles which appeared from the study of Enigma 'indicators' to reveal the wiring of the machine's rotors. This summary explains how cycles can emerge from the doubly-enciphered indicator used by the German Wehrmacht up until the spring of 1940; how observation of cycles could help the Polish code-breakers identify the rotors and their start-positions and how their invention of a cyclometer speeded up the process. Cycles-of-one, known as 'females', and their exploitation through Zygalski's sheets, are also discussed here.

I The doubly-enciphered indicator

When German Enigma operators sent out their messages, they added a preamble to the text which helped the recipient to set up his machine correctly. Each day (until September 1938) the high command pre-ordained a ground setting to be used for the whole day's cipher traffic. This took the form of three letters, corresponding to the positions of the three rotors (also chosen for that day's traffic by the high command). So, the ground setting might be KGC. The ground setting was not, however, used for sending the message itself, only the 'indicator', which was data about how the message was being encrypted. The Enigma operator would need to choose his own starting-position for the three rotors, which would be used when it came to transmitting the actual message text. Let's say the operator chose QWE, being the first three letters on his Enigma keyboard: such a lack of imagination was surprisingly common. The operator would then set his machine to the ground setting and encipher the chosen indicator, twice over. QWE would thus come out as something like PLH JRW. The operator then transmitted PLH JRW, then set his machine's rotors to the new start position of Q, W and E, and then begin the encipherment of the real message. The recipient would receive a message beginning PLH JRW and, by first setting his machine to the known ground setting for the day, he would then discover that the main message could be deciphered if the rotors were re-set to Q, W and E.

When hundreds of Enigma messages were sent on a given day using the same ground setting, that meant that all the indicators being transmitted and intercepted were based on Enigma machines set up in identical ways. This gave Marian Rejewski something to work on. First, his training in permutation theory taught him to look out for patterns in the indicators. Take, for example, these actual sets of intercepted indicators:

bnh chl	ddb vdv	gpb zsv	khb xjv	pvj feg	vii pzk	ypc osq
cik bzt	fbr kle	ikg jkf	obu dlz	sjm spo	xyw gcp	zef yoc

Just looking at the first and fourth letters of these indicators you can see patterns coming out. Take the indicator beginning *ddb*: the fourth letter is *v*. In the indicator beginning *vii*, the fourth letter is *p*. In the indicator beginning *pvj*, the fourth letter is *f*. The process of trailing through the indicators can continue, but eventually you get *obu dlz*, which links *o* to *d*, which is the letter we started with. There is a cycle: d→v→p→f→k→x→g→z→y→o→d. Other trails are shorter: *s* leads only to itself, a cycle of one single letter; *b* leads to *c*, but *c* leads straight back to *b*. In fact, if you completed the analysis for the set of indicators you might find that, just looking at the first and fourth positions, a set of cycles can be found such as the following, where each cycle is shown between brackets:

(*dvpfkxgzyo*)(*eijmunqlht*)(*bc*)(*rw*)(*a*)(*s*)

But traffic on other days revealed different patterns of cycles, such as

$$(blfqveoum)(hjpswizrn)(axt)(cgy)(d)(k)$$

Rejewski noted that the number and length of the cycles he found differed according to the order of the rotors in the machine and their start position, though they always appeared in pairs, as in the above examples. Rejewski wrote:

> This structure is most characteristic, and although the representation of such a structure was different each day, one trait was always the same: in each line the cycles of the same length always appeared in pairs. In view of the role this structure played, I named it the *characteristic structure*, or simply the *characteristic* of a given day.[1]

Rejewski used this method to find the lengths of cycles referable to the first and fourth letters of the doubly-enciphered indicator, the second and fifth, and the third and sixth. Examples he gives of cycles are:

$$1 \ \& \ 4 = (dvpfkxgzyo)(eijmunglht)(bc)(rw)(a)(s)$$
$$2 \ \& \ 5 = (blfqveoum)(hjpswizrn)(axt)(cgy)(d)(k)$$
$$3 \ \& \ 6 = (abviktjgfcqny)(duzrehlxupsmo)$$

These show cycle-lengths of ten, two, one for positions 1 and 4; nine, three, one for positions 2 and 5; and thirteen for positions 3 and 6.

Exploiting the characteristic of each configuration would help the code-breakers unpick the wiring of the machine, and work out its daily settings.

II Using cycle characteristics to find the machine's settings

With a maximum cycle-length of thirteen, there are exactly 101 possible species of cycle which can be found for the twenty-six letters of the alphabet. Each configuration of rotors is associated with only one of these 101 species. So, if a particular day's Enigma message traffic is analysed and reveals a particular cycle, that cuts down the number of possible rotor combinations (with three rotors, about 105,000) by a factor of 100.

Eliminating combinations this way still looks like leaving a dauntingly large number to try, but in fact it made matters a lot easier. As well as testing for the characteristics of positions 1 and 4 in the indicator, tests could be done for the characteristics of positions 2 and 5, and of positions 3 and 6. Furthermore, some cycle-patterns occur more rarely than others. And then there was German operator laziness, which made it possible to guess in many cases that the start-position chosen was QWE, or something just as casual, like ABC. Using these methods, a catalogue of characteristics could be used to find the rotor choice and ground setting for the day. Marian Rejewski said that, with experience, they could get this information in as little as an hour.

But they still had to build their catalogue of characteristics.

III The cyclometer

To speed up the analysis of each of the 105,000 combinations and identify its characteristic, the Poles constructed the cyclometer.

The cyclometer has three essential parts. The first consists of two sets of Enigma rotors; one is 'offset' from the other by three spaces, thus corresponding to positions 1 and 4 (or 2 and 5, or 3 and 6) of the indicator. Each set of rotors is connected by a 26-wire cable to a central switchboard, which is the second component of the machine. By each switch is a light-bulb.

When the switch by a given letter (for example A) is thrown, current enters the cables along the A wire and the A bulb lights up. As the current enters the first bank of rotors, it will follow a circuit determined by the wiring of the rotors and the reflector, emerging somewhere (but, because it is an Enigma machine mock-up, it must emerge on some wire other than A: no letter can encipher as itself). Then the current is directed to the second set of rotors and the same thing happens.

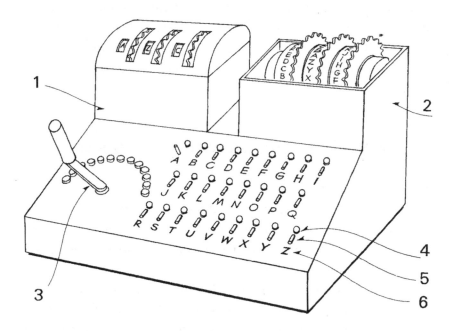

Cyclometer. 1) First bank of rotors (with cover). 2) Second bank of rotors (cover removed). 3) Rheostat. 4) Lamp. 5) Switch. 6) Letter. (Janina Sylwestrzak)

On each pass, current returns to the central switchboard, thereby light-ing up the bulb corresponding to the new live wire on which the current emerged from the rotors. It is quite possible that current emerges from the two different sets of rotors on different wires and when these wires are live that provides a new input for the rotors. Eventually, the current completes a circuit and no more wires are live: the circuit represents a pair of cycles and the number of bulbs lit up indicates the cycle-length (multiplied by two).

Having noted which bulbs were lit on the first test – making the A wire live – the A switch is put to the off position and a new letter, which did not light up in the first test, can be tested. In this way the whole alphabet can be quickly gone through and the characteristic of that rotor order and start-position determined.

The third and final component of the machine is the 'rheostat' or variable resistor. This is needed because the number of lit bulbs is not predictable in advance. Too many bulbs to light and not enough current will flow to get a good read-out. Too few, and the concentrated voltage applied to two bulbs could blow the bulbs. So the operator started with maximum resistance and gradually increased the current in each test.

IV Finding females with a cyclometer

Females indicate 'cycles of one'.

Taking the list of indicators reproduced above, two of them (*ddb vdv* and *ikg jkf*) have females. The same letter *d* appears in both the second and fifth positions in the first example; so does the letter *k* in the second. The cycle-length is one.

Using a cyclometer, if the circuitry in the second set of rotors sends the current round in such a way as to reverse the effect of the first set, only two bulbs will light up on the cyclometer: the one where the current went into the left bank of rotors and the one for where it went into the other. The two lit bulbs identify the pair of 'cycles of one' or females. Using the indicators in our example, the cyclometer (when set up with the right selection of rotors positioned in the correct orientation) will shine in only the *d* and *k* bulbs.

V Zygalski sheets

Each sheet corresponded to the (probably immobile) left-hand rotor and was ruled into an alphabetical grid, so that all combinations of the middle rotor (on the horizontal axis) and the fast right-hand rotor (on the vertical axis) were also represented by a square on the grid. Sets of sheets were thus needed for all combinations of the five rotors and, within each such set, for all twenty-six positions of the left-hand rotor. For three rotors, 156 sheets were needed (for five rotors, 1,560 sheets), each ruled and punched to show the positions of females.

If the code-breakers, using a cyclometer, had seen that a particular set-up of three rotors could generate a female – say, they had observed

Zygalski sheet. Henryk Zygalski's method for finding Enigma settings used stacks of punched cardboard sheets.

that rotor combination IV, II, III produced a female in positions 1 and 4 when the rotor-letters LMQ were showing through the windows of the machine – a hole would be punched in the sheet L from the IV-II-III set, at position MQ.

The basic idea in using Zygalski's sheets was to stack them on top of each other on a light-table, in order to find a single place where light penetrated through the entire stack. That would eliminate enough false possibilities to tell you how the German machine had been set up.

The sheets had to be stacked in a consistent way. This could be done using the starting-positions given by the Enigma operator in the preamble. Let us take two (post-1938) preambles such as *KGX YPC YRN* and *SID FET FHS*. These can be parsed: the first three letters are the ground setting, showing how the operator wanted the machine set up to decipher the indicator, and the next six are the repeated indicator. We can also see that there are females in positions 1 and 4 in both the indicators. To stack the sheets, it was necessary to align grid-square GX from the first message exactly over grid-square ID from the second. This alignment mimics the change of the middle rotor from G to I and the right-hand rotor from X to D, reflecting the way the two message recipients changed the ground setting to decipher the indicator.

Punching the holes was complicated by the stacking procedure. As the sheets would be offset when piled on top of each other, the alphabets had to be repeated both horizontally and vertically to ensure a good overlap. This necessitated the punching of each hole as many as four times.

The simplified description given above assumes that the ring settings, which allowed the core wiring of the Enigma rotors to be offset relative to the letters printed around the rim of the rotor, are always set to ZZZ. In practice this was not the case and Zygalski sheet procedure had to be adapted to accommodate, and find, the unknown ring settings.

NOTES

1. *Nulle Part*

1. Ciężki records, CAW I.481.C.4366, KN 25.07.1933.
2. Davies, *White Eagle Red Star*, p. 31.
3. Linda Colley, *Lewis Namier*, Weidenfeld & Nicolson (1989).
4. Kowalewski file in the David Kahn collection, CCH; original at the Piłsudski Institute of America.
5. Mieczysław Ścieżiński, *Radjotelegrafja Jako żródło wiadomościu o nieprzyjacielu (Polish Radio Interception and Decryptment in the Polish-Soviet War of 1929–20)* (1928), trans. Christopher Kasparek, CCH.
6. Jan Kowalewski, *Szyfry klucem zwyciestwa w 1920r.*, Zwiazek Lacznosciowcow 'Komunikat' (2001), pp. 13–18.

2. Enter the King

1. CAW I.481.C.4366
2. Jerzy Palluth interview with the author, January 2017; CAW 1769/89/3856
3. Piotr Michałowski, personal communication.
4. CAW Oddz.II S.G. I.303.4.2387.
5. CAW Oddz.II S.G. I.303.4.2387.
6. CAW Oddz.II S.G. I.303.4.2416.
7. CAW 1769/89/4072.
8. CAW AP 9449, AP 1769/89/2897.
9. JPI Kol 709/134/2.

10. Max Ronge, *Kriegs- und Industrie-Spionage*, Amalthea-Verlag (1930), p. 119.
11. Tomes, pp. 14–15.
12. SHD GR 7N 4235.
13. Tomes, p. 10.
14. Tomes, pp. 22, 151.
15. Énigme, p. 37, Tomes, pp. 21–24; Paillole NE, p. 43; Gilbert Bloch, *Enigma avant Ultra* (1988), Annexe 2.
16. Éric Maillard, *Rudolph Stallmann alias baron von König, Tentative de biographie* (undated).
17. *Straits Times*, 10 May 1913.
18. SHD GR 1K 545/949; Raymond Batkin, *The False Baron von König*, Christie Books (2015).
19. Énigme, pp. 35–36.
20. SHD GR 7 NN 3287.
21. Sebag-Montefiore, *Enigma*, p. 15f.
22. Paillole NE, p. 30f; SHD GR 1 K 545/987.

3. Mighty Pens

1. PISM Kol 242/55.
2. Paillole NE, p. 45.
3. Tomes, pp. 147–149.
4. TNA HW 25/6, HW 25/8, HW 25/9, HW 25/10, HW 25/13, HW 25/14.
5. Paillole NE, pp. 48–49.
6. Tomes, p. 151.
7. Énigme, p. 37.
8. Paillole NE, p. 53f.
9. Kozaczuk Enigma Appendix D, pp. 256–258.
10. Paillole NE, p. 103.
11. David Kahn, *Hitler's Spies*, Da Capo Press (2000), p. 178.
12. Henri Navarre, *Le Service de Renseignements 1871–1944*, PLON (1978), p. 55.
13. Paillole NE, pp. 85, 158–159.
14. Kozaczuk Enigma, pp. 26–27; CAW Oddz II S.G. I.303.4.189; Zdzisław J. Kapera, *How the reading of Enigma was nearly exposed in the spring of 1940* (2016).

4. The Scarlet Pimpernels

1. Tiltman Oral History, NSA Doc ID 4236153, CCH.
2. Tomes, p. 144.
3. Gilbert Bloch, *Enigma avant Ultra* (1988), Annexe 2.
4. CAW 1769/89/4265, Oddz. II S.G. I.303.4.558, Oddz II S.G. I.303.4.558.
5. Richard Holmes, introduction to Fitzgerald, *The Knox Brothers*.
6. Fitzgerald, *The Knox Brothers*, p. 188.
7. Fitzgerald, *The Knox Brothers*, p. 194.
8. TNA HW 43/78; HW 25/9.
9. CAW 1769/89/3856; Jerzy Palluth interview with the author, January 2017.
10. *Marian Rejewski*, EB8 p 43-44; TNA WO 315/28.
11. *Before Ultra*, EB6 p 21, 67; Sadowski Report, PISM Kol B.I.6; Ciężki deposition, PISM Kol B.I.6l.
12. SHD GR 7 NN 2701.
13. Mayer, p. 210.
14. Jackson & Maiolo, *Strategic Intelligence*, p. 450.
15. Hetherington, *Unvanquished*, p. 616.
16. TNA HW 25/12.
17. Bertrand Dossiers 186, 187, 192, 199 (all SHD DE 2016 ZB 25/3), Bertrand Dossier 211 (SHD DE 2016 ZB 25/4).
18. Tomes, p. 23.
19. TNA HW 65/9, HW 25/10, HW 43/78, HW 25/12.
20. Bertrand Dossier 261 (SHD DE 2016 ZB 25/5).
21. TNA HW 65/1.
22. Bertrand Dossier 262 (SHD DE 2016 ZB 25/5).
23. Tomes, p. 152; Énigme, p. 57.

5. How They Brought the Good News from Ghent to Aix

1. TNA HW 14/2; Brian Oakley, *The First Break into German Enigma at Bletchley Park*, Bletchley Park Trust Report No. 19 (2011), p. 19.
2. Kozaczuk Enigma Appendix D, p. 267; Tadeusz Lisicki, correspondence and other materials JPI Kol 709/100/53.
3. Langer Report JPI Kol 709/133/4.
4. Kozaczuk Enigma Appendix C, p. 242.

5. *Before Ultra*, EB6 pp. 19–22.
6. Supplement to Mayer, JPI Kol 709/100/53.
7. TNA HW 25/10.
8. TNA HW 65/3.
9. TNA HW 25/12; Bertrand Dossier 258 (SHD DE 2016 ZB 25/5).
10. Bertrand Dossier 265 (SHD DE 2016 ZB 25/5); TNA HW 25/12.
11. Bertrand Dossier 267 (SHD DE 2016 ZB 25/5).
12. Watt, *Bitter Glory*, p. 396.
13. Paillole NE, p. 167.
14. Paillole NE, p. 183.
15. Bertrand Dossier 268 (SHD DE 2016 ZB 25/5).
16. Kozaczuk Enigma Appendix B, p. 236.
17. Kozaczuk Wicher, Anhang D p. 319; Bertrand Dossier 268 (SHD DE 2016 ZB 25/5); TNA ADM 223/479.
18. Alastair Denniston, *How News was brought from Warsaw at the end of July 1939* in Robin Denniston, *Thirty Secret Years*, Polperro Heritage Press (2007).
19. TNA HW 25/12.
20. Bertrand Dossier 269 (SHD DE 2016 ZB 25/5).
21. TNA HW 25/12.
22. PISM Kol 398/5.
23. TNA HW 25/16.
24. TNA FO 366/1059, HW 3/82, HW 62/21/7.
25. Énigme, p. 61.
26. TNA HW 65/3.

6. Monstrous Pile

1. Colville, *The Fringes of Power*, 13 September 1939.
2. Mrs Różycka's diary kindly made available by Dr Z.J. Kapera.
3. Tomes, p. 151; Bertrand Dossier 260 (SHD DE 2016 ZB 25/5).
4. Ciężki deposition, PISM Kol B.I.6l.
5. Zygalski.
6. Jerzy Palluth interview with author, January 2017.
7. TNA HW 14/2.
8. Batey, *Dilly*, p. 90.
9. Zygalski; Langer Report JPI Kol 709/133/3, 133/4.
10. Jean Stengers, 'Enigma, the French, the Poles and the British

1931–1940', *Revue belge de philologie et d'histoire* (2004), vol 82, pp. 449–466, n. 30.

11. Kozaczuk Enigma, pp. 72–73.

12. Hanka Sowińska, *Życie szyfrem pisane*, Gazeta Pomorska, 7 January 2005.

13. Langer Report JPI Kol 709/133/4.

14. TNA HW 14/2.

15. TNA HW 65/2.

7. The Mirror Crack'd from Side to Side

1. Guy Liddell, *Diaries*, ed Nigel West, Routledge (2005), entry for 10 October 1939.

2. TNA HW 14/3.

3. Bertrand Dossier 277 (SHD DE 2016 ZB 25/5).

4. Sherborne School Archives.

5. Batey, *Dilly*, p. 94.

6. TNA HW 14/3.

7. Bertrand Dossier 278 (SHD DE 2016 ZB 25/5).

8. Kozaczuk Enigma, p. 97.

9. PISM Kol B.I.6; Zdisław J. Kapera, *How the reading of Enigma was nearly exposed in the spring of 1940* (2016) Siły Zbrojne Działania wywiadu w XX i XXI w, pp. 109–140.

10. Langer Report JPI Kol 709/133/4.

11. Énigme, p. 72.

12. HBI vol. 1, p. 108; Langer Report JPI Kol 709/133/4.

13. Rivet, 12 March 1940; TNA HW 5/1.

14. Wspomnienia p. 115f.

15. TNA HW 14/5; Kozaczuk Wicher, Anhang D p. 320.

16. Langer 1945T, p. 29.

17. Wspomnienia, pp. 115–116.

18. SHD GR 14 YD 755 (Dossier de Personnel); TNA HW 315/8.

19. Langer Report JPI Kol 709/133/4.

20. JPI Kol 709/133/1.

21. Tomes, p. 155; Bertrand Dossiers 272, 273 (SHD DE 2016 ZB 25/5).

22. Paillole NE, 195f.

23. Forcade, *Le renseignement*, p. 144.

24. Colville, *The Fringes of Power*, 9 November 1939, 7 January 1940.

25. HBI vol 1, p. 127.
26. HBI vol 1, p. 137.
27. Volume of material (Bletchley) February, March, April, May 1940: TNA HW 5/1; volume of material (Bruno): Énigme, p. 79.
28. First message JPI Kol 709/134/2; fourth message Bertrand Dossier 286 (SDH DE 2016 ZB 25/7); others from Langer papers JPI Kol 709/133/3.
29. Nigel West, *MI6*, Grafton Books (1985), p. 186.
30. Bertrand interview with David Kahn, David Kahn collection, CCH.
31. TNA HW 14/5.
32. Tiltman Oral History, NSA Doc ID 4236153, CCH.
33. Tomes, pp. 35–36.
34. Langer 1946M, p. 4.
35. TNA ADM 337/128/432; *Oxford Dictionary of National Biography*; TNA ADM 137/2296; Keith Jeffery, *MI6*, Bloomsbury (2011), p. 199; Jackson & Maiolo, *Strategic Intelligence*, p. 436.
36. TNA HW 14/5; the last sentence of the original for 28 June reads 'Vous pouvez compter sur moi pour securite votre travail'.
37. Batkin, *The False Baron*.
38. Paillole NE, p. 212.

8. Into Three Parts

1. TNA HW 14/5.
2. Brian Oakley, ed, *The Bletchley Park War Diaries*, Wynne Press (2006).
3. Bertrand Dossier 278 (SHD DE 2016 ZB 25/5).
4. JPI Kol 709/133/8.
5. Tomes, p. 40.
6. JPI Kol 709/133/1.
7. Wspomnienia, p. 117.
8. Zygalski.
9. Rivet, 17 August 1940.
10. NARA RG 242 microfilm T-501 Roll 122.
11. Rivet, 23 September 1940.
12. Énigme, p. 108, Tomes, p. 44.
13. Langer 1946M, p. 8.

14. JPI Kol 709/133/1.
15. Énigme, p. 120; Tomes, p. 45. Énigme has 7 French 'service' personnel, but presumably this figure excludes other residents such as David, Maurice and their families.
16. JPI Kol 709/133/3; 709/133/7.
17. PISM Kol 242/63.
18. JPI Kol 709/133/1.
19. PISM Kol 79/50, copy of declaration by Gustave Bertrand.
20. Langer 1946M, p. 26.
21. Rivet 9, 11 October 1940.
22. JPI Kol 709/133/8.
23. TNA HW 14/8.
24. TNA HW 14/12; Tomes, pp. 110–111.
25. TNA HW 14/9, Tomes, p. 40.
26. TNA HW 14/12.
27. JPI Kol 709/133/3.
28. Słowikowski, *In the Secret Service*, pp. 60–61.
29. Smith, *The Secrets*, p. 149.
30. TNA HW 25/1.
31. Wspomnienia, p. 118f.
32. Wspomnienia, p. 73f.
33. JPI Kol 709/133/3, telegrams 591f; Tomes, p. 49 (Langer's contemporary statistics preferred where there is a discrepancy).
34. Zygalski, Anna Zygalska-Cannon photographic archive.
35. Kozaczuk Wicher, Anhang D p 322.
36. PISM Kol 79/50, telegram of 19 January 1942; Tomes, p. 49.
37. Énigme, pp. 111–112.
38. Paillole NE, pp. 39, 277.
39. HBI vol 2, p. 18.
40. APHC vol 2, pp. 78, 299.
41. TNA HW 14/15.
42. TNA HW 14/16.
43. SHD GR 14 YD 755, Dossier d'archives.
44. Nigel West & Oleg Tsarev, *The Crown Jewels*, HarperCollins (1998), p. 307.

9. A Mystery Inside an Enigma

1. TNA HW 47/1; WO 208/5097; HW 14/7; HW 14/8.
2. TNA HW 14/15.
3. APHC vol 2, p. 387.
4. HBI vol 1, p. 452.
5. Colville, *The Fringes of Power*, 21 June 1941.
6. HBI vol 1, p. 199.
7. PISM Kol 242/55.
8. TNA HW 65/7 [*sic*].
9. Michałowski Report, PISM Kol 242/69.
10. PISM Kol 79/50 telegram 599.
11. TNA HW 65/7; SHD GR 7 NN 2502.
12. Bertrand Dossier 180 (SHD DE 2016 ZB 25/3).
13. Tomes, p. 95, Bertrand Dossier 179 (SHD DE 2016 ZB 25/3).
14. Langer 1945T, p. 28.
15. Langer 1946M, p. 22.
16. Winston S. Churchill, *The Second World War*, Cassell & Co (1950), 3.537.
17. JPI Kol 709/133/3 telegrams 373, 606.
18. Langer 1945T, p. 28.
19. Michałowski Report, PISM Kol 242/69.
20. www.wrecksite.eu, accessed 20 April 2018.
21. PISM Kol 79/50, statement of 'Materon'.
22. Słowikowski, *In the Secret Service*, pp. 109, 140.
23. Zygalski; PISM Kol 79/50; APHC vol 2, p. 267.
24. Kozaczuk Enigma, p. 127.
25. JPI Kol 709/134/1 reverse side of Safe-conduct.
26. TNA HW 65/7; JPI Kol 709/100/2, item 18.
27. TNA HW 14/24; HW 65/7; TNA HW 25/27.
28. TNA HW 65/7; Rivet, 22 July 1942; Kozaczuk Wicher Anhang D, p. 322.
29. Énigme, p. 123; *In the Shadow of the Pont du Gard*, EB7, p. 48.
30. Langer 1945T, p. 28.
31. Tomes p 49, p. 207.
32. Michałowski Report, PISM Kol 242/69.
33. Navarre, *Le Service de Renseignements*, p. 136.
34. Rivet, 29 August 1942.

35. Tomes, p. 41.
36. Paillole SS, p. 303f.
37. Langer 1946M, p. 36.
38. Énigme, p. 134.
39. TNA HW 25/12.
40. Bletchley Park collection, ISK series 41.
41. Paillole SS, p. 306f.
42. Bertrand Dossier 302 (SHD DE 2016 ZB 25/7), Énigme, p. 136.
43. Langer 1945T, pp. 2, 28.
44. Langer 1945T, p. 3, Énigme, p. 134f.

10. Hide and Seek

1. Langer 1946M, p. 139.
2. Énigme, p. 137.
3. Langer 1945T, p. 3.
4. Énigme, p. 137.
5. APHC vol 2, pp. 248, 295; PISM Kol 79/50, Bertrand declaration of 1973.
6. Langer 1946M, p. 33.
7. Rivet, 7 November 1942; Énigme, p. 138.
8. Gelb, *Desperate Venture*, p. 168.
9. Énigme, p. 146; Langer 1946M, p. 52; Langer 1945T, p. 4.
10. Langer 1945T, p. 5.
11. Langer 1945T, p. 6f.
12. Zygalski; Énigme, p. 141.
13. Rivet, 15 October 1942.
14. AAPA s8 (TICOM series) T-1686 box 2 file 3.
15. Langer 1945T, p 11.
16. Langer 1945T, p. 12; Wspomnienia, p. 84.
17. Langer 1945T, p. 12f.
18. SHD GR 7 NN 2053.
19. Jerzy Palluth interview with author, January 2017.
20. Langer 1946M, pp. 39, 81; Énigme, p. 142 [*sic*].
21. Zygalski; Wspomnienia, p. 84.
22. Latour-de-Carol: railway buffs like this place, because here the standard-gauge line from Toulouse and Ax terminates, as does the broad-gauge line from Spain and a third, narrow-gauge, line comes

along the mountains from the French side. The last-mentioned is the touristic line of the *'petit train jaune'* from Villefranche-de-Conflent, but getting a ticket is the devil of a job.

23. Paillole NE, pp. 39, 147f, 224, 228, 252.
24. SHD GR 7 NN 2775.
25. Paillole NE, pp. 245–246.
26. SHD GR 1 K 545/987; TNA HW 65/7.
27. SHD GR 1 K 545/949.
28. Énigme, p. 142.
29. Langer 1945T, p. 30.
30. Michałowski report PISM Kol 242/69. Michałowski's chronology differs from Langer's, in relation to Langer's party. Langer's/Zygalski's chronology has been preferred for Langer's party and for Rejewski and Zygalski, Michałowski's for his own party.
31. Going rate for evacuees: Michèle Cointet, *Secrets et Mystères de la France occupée*, Broché (2015).
32. Langer 1945T, p. 17f.
33. *Before* Ultra, EB 6, p. 77f.
34. Oskar Reile, *Der Deutsche Geheimdienst im II. Weltkrieg – Ostfront*, Weltbild (1990), p. 289.
35. NARA RG 457 HMS Entry P4 Box 35 and www.TICOMarchive.com, accessed 20 April 2018, TICOM Depositions of Mettig (I–78, I–127) and Buggisch (I–176).
36. Kozaczuk Wicher, pp. 205–206; Mauzoleum Walki i Męczeństwa w Warszawie.
37. NARA RG 457 HMS Entry A1 9032 Box 625 www.TICOMarchive.com, accessed 20 April 2018, TICOM depositions of Buggisch (I–92), Fenner (I–200), Hüttenhain (I–31).
38. NARA RG 242 Microfilm roll 445, 446, 447 (Fahndungsnachweise for 1 February 1943, 1 November 1943, 1 May 1944); Indre et Loire (Archives de Touraine) collection allemande 17 ZA 6.
39. SHD GR 1 K 545/958.

11. The Last Play

1. PISM Kol 242/69.
2. JPI Kol 709/133.
3. Langer 1945T, p. 20.

4. SHD GR 1K 545/958; Paillole NE, pp. 261, 277.
5. AAPA S8 (TICOM series) T-1717.
6. PISM Kol 242/69.
7. Wspomnienia, p. 86.
8. Eugenia Maresch, *The Radio-Intelligence Company in Britain*, LWTES, pp. 185–200.
9. PISM Kol 242/55.
10. Langer 1945T, p. 22.
11. Langer 1946M, p. 139.
12. Jean Delmas, article on Kléber in *Dictionnaire historique de la Résistance*, Robert Laffont (2006); Jeffery, *MI6*, p. 529.
13. Langer 1946M, Appendix; Langer 1945T, p. 24; Barbara Ciężka personal archival collection.
14. Énigme, p. 151f.
15. Rémy, *Mémoires d'un agent secret*.
16. SHD GR 7 NN 3264.
17. Jean-Pax Méfret, *Un flic chez les voyous*, Broché (2009).
18. Paillole SS, p. 145, Énigme, p. 82–83. Méfret has the man with the transmitter aged 62; Bertrand and Paillole say 70.
19. Zygalski; Maresch, *The Radio-Intelligence Company*.
20. PISM Kol 242/92; PISM Kol 242/55.
21. TNA HW 25/27; PISM Kol 242/92; TNA HW 14/90.
22. NARA RG 457 HMS Entry A1 9032 Box 625 and www. TICOMarchive.com, accessed 20 April 2018, TICOM depositions of Buggisch (I–92), Fenner (I–200).
23. Langer 1946M, p. 127.
24. Langer 1945T, p. 25.
25. Kozaczuk Enigma, p. 211.
26. Énigme, p. 213.
27. Navarre, *Le Service de Renseignements*, pp. 225–226.
28. Paillole NE, p. 337.
29. TNA HW 65/7.
30. SHD GR 1 K 545/1030.
31. SHD GR 28 P2/93; Bertrand Annexes 302, 303 (SHD DE 2016 ZB 25/7).
32. SHD GR 14 YD 753.
33. Kozaczuk Wicher, p. 209.
34. Jerzy Palluth interview with author, January 2017.
35. PISM Kol 242/92.

36. Translation by Eugenia Maresch, *The Radio-Intelligence Company in Britain*, LWTES p. 199.
37. PISM Kol A.XII.24/63.
38. JPI Kol 709/134/2; TNA HW 25/27.
39. PISM Kol 242/55.
40. PISM Kol A.XII.24/63; Kol 242/54; Kol 242/92.
41. Kol 242/55; Kol A.XII.24/64; APHC vol 1 chapter 40.
42. W.H. Edwards, *The Experimental Station at Abbassia*, in *The Enigma Symposium 1992*, p. 53.
43. Barbara Ciężka interview with author, February 2017.
44. Jerzy Palluth interview with author, January 2017.
45. Janina Sylwestrzak interview with author, January 2017.
46. TNA HW 14/128, HW 53/54; PISM Kol 242/93; NARA RG 457 Entry A1 9032 Box 808.
47. Jeffery, *MI6*, p. 717; NARA RG 226 Entry 210 Box 475 folder WN 17719; TNA KV 3/142.
48. TNA HS 4/319.
49. SHD GR 14 YD 755, Dossier d'archives.
50. PISM Kol 242/93, Kol 242/69.
51. Rejewski letter to Col T. Lisicki, PISM Kol 389/II/6.
52. Langer 1945T, p. 26.

Epilogue: Poles Apart

1. Colville, *The Fringes of Power*, 27 February 1945.
2. Halik Kochanski, *Eagle Unbowed*, Penguin (2013), p. 553.
3. PISM Kol 242/55.
4. PISM Kol 242/69; JPI Kol 709/133/8; Mayer, p. 215; Langer 1946M, p. 2.
5. PISM Kol A.XII.24/58; Kol 242/55.
6. *Kinross-shire Advertiser*, 17 January 1945, 3 January 1946, 18 May 1946, 15 June 1946.
7. *Before Ultra*, EB6, p. 49.
8. Barbara Ciężka interview with author, February 2017; Barbara Ciężka personal archival collection.
9. TNA WO 315/8.
10. TNA WO 315/30.
11. Bliss Lane, *I Saw Poland Betrayed*, p. 141.

12. Zygalski.

13. Anna Zygalska-Cannon personal archival collection.

14. Władysław Kozaczuk, *Bitwa o tajemnice*, Książka i Wiedza (1969), p. 190f.

15. Paillole NE, p. 282f.

16. Jerzy Lelwic, *Marian Rejewski – the man from Bydgoszcz who helped the allies win the war*, LWTES, pp. 45–66; Wojciech Polak, *Marian Rejewski in the sights of the Security Services*, LWTES pp. 75–88.

17. Michael Stephens, *The Silent Code-breaker* (2017); Anna Zygalska-Cannon personal archival collection.

18. Register of deaths 462/11; JPI Kol 709/133/8.

19. JPI Kol 709/134/1.

20. APHC vol 2, p. 678.

Appendix: Cycles

1. Marian Rejewski, 'How Polish Mathematicians Deciphered the Enigma', *Annals of the History of Computing*.

ABBREVIATIONS

Archival collections

AAPA: Auswärtiges Amt Politisches Archiv, Berlin, Germany.

CAW: Centralne Archiwum Wojskowe (Polish Military Archive), Rembertów, Poland.

CCH: Center for Cryptologic History library at the National Cryptologic Museum, Ft Meade, MD, USA.

JPI: Józef Piłsudski Institute, Ravenscourt Park, London.

NARA: National Archives and Records Administration, College Park, MD, USA.

PISM: Polish Institute and Sikorski Museum, South Kensington, London.

SHD: Service Historique de la Défense, Château de Vincennes, Vincennes, France.

TNA: The (UK) National Archives, Kew, London.

Other materials

APHC: Tessa Stirling et al, eds, *The Report of the Anglo-Polish Historical Committee*, Vallentine Mitchell (2005). I am indebted to the Embassy of the Republic of Poland for their kind donation of a copy of this priceless resource.

Bertrand Dossier: See under 'Tomes' *infra*.

EB: The series of Enigma Bulletins edited by Zdzisław Kapera, published by the Enigma Press.

HBI: Harry Hinsley et al, *British Intelligence in the Second World War*, HMSO (1979).

Énigme: Gustave Bertrand, *Énigme, ou la plus grande énigme de la guerre*, Plon (1973).

Kozaczuk Enigma: Władysław Kozaczuk, *Enigma*, trans Christopher Kasparek, Greenwood Press (1984).

Kozaczuk Wicher: Władysław Kozaczuk, *Geheimoperation Wicher*, Karl Müller Verlag (1989). This revised and extended version of Kozaczuk's original book in Polish (called *'Enigma'* in its English translation) is in German and contains a different set of appendices.

Langer 1945/1946: In July 1945, Gwido Langer wrote a long (150 pages in the manuscript version) account of his experiences at, and the evacuation of, Ekspozytura 300. It exists in two versions which are markedly different in places. '1945T' refers to the shorter, typewritten version in JPI Kol 709/133/5 and '1946M' to the photocopy manuscript version in PISM Kol 79/50, which is dated from Kinross, 1946 and sarcastically entitled 'Fond Memories'.

LWTES: (Various contributors) *Marian Rejewski: Living with the Engima Secret*, Bydgoszcz City Council (2005).

Mayer: Stefan Mayer, *The breaking up of the German ciphering machine 'Enigma' by cryptological section in 2nd Department of the General Staff of the Polish Armed Forces*, reproduced in LWTES (*supra*).

Tomes: Gustave Bertrand's long account (in five volumes or 'tomes') *Étude et Résultats de la Recherche du Renseignement par les Moyens Techniques (de 1930 à 1942)* (1949) is cote No. DE 2015 ZB 25/1 at the SHD. The Annexes to Bertrand's account are referred to as 'Bertrand Dossier' together with the relevant cote number.

Paillole NE: Paul Paillole, *Notre Espion chez Hitler*, Nouveau Monde (2011).

Paillole SS: Paul Paillole, *Fighting the Nazis* (published in French as *Services Secrets*), Enigma Books (2003).

Rivet: Louis Rivet, *Carnets du chef des Services Secrets*, ed Olivier Forcade and Sébastien Laurent, Nouveau Monde (2010).

Wspomnienia: Marian Rejewski's memoirs, published in a dual-language edition as *Memories of my work at the Cipher Bureau of the General Staff Second Department 1930–1945*, Adam Mickiewicz University Press (2011); page references are to the English version.

Zygalski: Henryk Zygalski wrote a chronology of his wartime experiences. Special thanks are due to Anna Zygalska-Cannon and Aleksander Markiewicz for access to their translation of Henryk Zygalski's war chronology and other papers in their archive.

SELECT BIBLIOGRAPHY

Anon, 'Le Réseau F2', *Revue Historique des Armées*, 8 (1952), pp. 81–116

Mavis Batey, *Dilly: The Man Who Broke Enigmas* (Dialogue, 2009)

Arthur Bliss Lane, *I Saw Poland Betrayed* (Bobs-Merrill, 1948)

Frank Carter, *The First Breaking of Enigma* (Bletchley Park Trust Report No. 2, 2008)

Frank Carter, *The Turing Bombe* (Bletchley Park Trust Report No. 4, 2008)

John Colville, *The Fringes of Power: Downing Street Diaries 1939–1955* (Hodder & Stoughton, 1985)

J.F. Clabby, *Brigadier John Tiltman, a giant among cryptanalysts* (NSA publication, 2007)

D. Cluseau, 'L'Arrestation par les Allemands du Personnel du 2e Bureau Français', *Revue d'Histoire de la Deuxième Guerre Mondiale*, 8 (1958), pp. 32–48

Norman Davies, 'Lloyd George and Poland, 1919–20', *Journal of Contemporary History*, 6 (1971), pp. 132–154

Norman Davies, *White Eagle Red Star* (Pimlico, 2003)

Penelope Fitzgerald, *The Knox Brothers* (Fourth Estate, 2013)

Krzysztof Gaj, *Szyfr Enigmy: Metody Złamania* (Wydawnictwa Komunikacji i Lacznosci, 1989)

Norman Gelb, *Desperate Venture* (Hodder & Stoughton, 1992)

Marcel Givierge, *Cours de Cryptographie* (Berger-Levrault, 1925)

Marek Grajek, *Maksymilian Ciężki: Architekt triumfu nad Enigmą* (Muzeum Zamek Górków, 2016)

Stephen Harper, *Capturing Enigma* (Sutton Publishing, 1999)

John Herivel, *Herivelismus and the German Military Enigma* (M&M Baldwin, 2008)

Peter Hetherington, *Unvanquished* (Pingora Press, Second edition: 2012)

Thaddeus Holt, *The Deceivers* (Phoenix, 2005)

Peter Jackson & Joseph Maiolo, 'Strategic Intelligence, Counter-Intelligence and Alliance Diplomacy in Anglo-French relations before the Second World War', *MGZ*, 65 (2006) pp. 417–461

Magdalena Jaroszewska & Julian Musielak, *Zdzisław Krygowski, Pionier Matematyki Poznańskiej* (PTPN, 2011)

David Kahn, *Seizing the Enigma* (Frontline Books, 2012)

Zdzislaw Kapera, *Before Ultra there was Gale* (EB6, 2002)

Zdzisław Kapera, *In the Shadow of the Pont du Gard* (EB7, 2011)

Zdzislaw Kapera, *Marian Rejewski: The Man Who Defeated Enigma* (EB8, 2013)

Zdzisław Kapera, *The Triumph of Zygalski's Sheets* (EB9, 2015)

Judith Márffy-Mantuano Hare Listowel (Countess of), *Crusader in the Secret War* (Christopher Johnson, 1952)

Jean Medrala, *Les Réseaux de Renseignements Franco-Polonais* (L'Harmattan, 2005)

Lascelle Meserve de Basily, 'The conference at Spa in 1920', *Russian Review*, 32 (1973), pp. 72–76

Grzegorz Nowik, *Zanim złamano 'Enigmę'* (Rytm, 2004)

Marian Rejewski, 'How Polish Mathematicians Deciphered the Enigma', *Annals of the History of Computing*, 3 (1981), pp. 213–232

Colonel Rémy, *Mémoires d'un agent secret* (Raoul Solar, 1950)

Hugh Sebag-Montefiore, *Enigma: The Battle for the Code* (Weidenfeld & Nicolson, 2000)

Michael Smith, *The Secrets of Station X* (Biteback Publishing, 2011)

Mieczysław Słowikowski, *In the Secret Service* (Windrush Press, 1988)

Dermot Turing, *Demystifying the Bombe* (Bletchley Park/Pitkin Publishing, 2014)

Dermot Turing, *Prof: Alan Turing decoded* (The History Press, 2015)

Piotr Wandycz, *France and her Eastern Allies 1919–1925* (University of Minnesota Press, 1962)

Richard Watt, *Bitter Glory: Poland and its Fate 1918–1939* (Simon & Schuster, 1979)

Charles Webster, *The Foreign Policy of Castlereagh 1812–1815* (G. Bell & Sons, 1950)

H.O. Yardley, *The American Black Chamber* (Naval Institute Press, 2004)

Tomasz Ziarski-Kernberg, *The Polish Community in Scotland* (Caldra House, 2000)

INDEX

Note: page numbers in *italics* are illustrations.